Riveting! I read the whole book in one day. I only wish it had been available to me during the dark and dreary time when I fought depression.

JOHN MARSHALL
PASTOR, SECOND BAPTIST CHURCH
SPRINGFIELD, MISSOURI

Finding Hope Again is good medicine for body, soul and spirit. It speaks to physical, psychological and spiritual causes and cures for depression. Far from pat answers and simplistic solutions, this book speaks to the whole person.

CHUCK MYLANDER
ADJUNCT PROFESSOR, C. P. HAGGARD SCHOOL OF THEOLOGY
AZUSA PACIFIC UNIVERSITY

Far from advocating a simplistic name-it-and-claim-it or cast-it-out treatment for depression, Neil Anderson and Hal Baumchen present a realistic, yet hope-filled approach to understanding and dealing with this most pervasive of human problems. In our do-away-with-pain-at-all-costs society, it is so important to be reminded that, in God's hands, the crucible of depression may contain the refining fire that forges a priceless maturity in Christ.

DANIEL J. RUMBERGER, PSY.D.
PSYCHOLOGIST, INTERNATIONAL CENTER FOR BIBLICAL COUNSELING
SIOUX CITY, IOWA

Neil Anderson and Hal Baumchen have captured the biblical answer to the plague of human depression. This delightful book comes with a bring-back-the-joy guarantee. It's a must-read for every generation!

STAN TOLER
PASTOR AND AUTHOR
OKLAHOMA CITY, OKLAHOMA

overcoming depression

FINDING HOPE AGAIN

AGAIN

NEIL T. ANDERSON & HAL BAUMCHEN

Regal

A Division of Gospel Light
Ventura, California, U.S.A.

Published by Regal Books
A Division of Gospel Light
Ventura, California, U.S.A.
Printed in U.S.A.

Regal Books is a ministry of Gospel Light, an evangelical Christian publisher dedicated to serving the local church. We believe God's vision for Gospel Light is to provide church leaders with biblical, user-friendly materials that will help them evangelize, disciple and minister to children, youth and families.

It is our prayer that this Regal book will help you discover biblical truth for your own life and help you meet the needs of others. May God richly bless you.

For a free catalog of resources from Regal Books and Gospel Light please call your Christian supplier, or contact us at 1-800-4-GOSPEL *or at* www.gospellight.com.

Cover Design by Kevin Keller
Interior Design by Robert Williams
Edited by Ron Durham and Virginia Woodard
Cover Photo © Wilhelm Scholz/Photonica

Library of Congress Cataloging-in-Publication Data
Anderson, Neil T., 1942–
    Finding Hope Again / Neil T. Anderson and Hal Baumchen.
    p.   cm. – (Includes bibliographical references.)
    ISBN 0-8307-2356-0 (hardcover)
    1. Depression, Mental—Religious aspects—Christianity.
    2. Depressed persons—Religious life.   I. Baumchen, Hal, 1956- .
    II. Title.   III. Series.
    BV4910.34.A53   1999   98-48428
    248.8'625—dc21   CIP

01 02 03 04 05 06 07 08 09 10 11 12 13 14 15 / 04 03 02 01 00 99

Rights for publishing this book in other languages are contracted by Gospel Literature International (GLINT). GLINT also provides technical help for the adaptation, translation and publishing of Bible study resources and books in scores of languages worldwide. For further information, write to GLINT at P.O. Box 4060, Ontario, CA 91761-1003, U.S.A. You may also send e-mail to Glintint@aol.com, or visit their web site at www.glint.org.

CONTENTS

FOREWORD

Freedom. Release. Relief. These are all too familiar words of request and pleading from countless patients suffering from the agonizing symptoms of depression. "Will it ever end?" "What did I do wrong?" "What can I do to make it go away?"

As mental health professionals, we daily see the pain and anguish of this most common of all emotional illnesses. Depression is the "common cold" of mental health problems. At least 80 percent of people presenting to our office will be dealing with some kind of affective or mood disorder ranging from mild situational and stress-related "Adjustment Disorder with depressed mood," through more persistent and long-standing "Dysthymic Disorder," to severe and life threatening "Major Depression."

Depression with suicidal attempt or plan is by far the leading diagnosis on admission to any psychiatric facility. The lifetime prevalence of depression is 20 percent. That is, one in five people will suffer a significant bout of depression sometime during his or her lifetime. This demonstrates the importance of both a thorough understanding and a comprehensive treatment for this all-so-frequent malady painfully suffered by so many human beings.

In this exciting new book, Dr. Hal Baumchen collaborates with Dr. Neil Anderson of Freedom in Christ Ministries to provide us a clear, comprehensive look at this increasingly prevalent condition. Theirs is a holistic approach, balancing physical, psychological, and spiritual causes for depression in an honest, insightful way. It's a good road map. Their expertise lies especially in providing insight into the spiritual roots or inroads (routes) for depressions, an area usually neglected in secular books on this subject.

We have been privileged to work with Dr. Anderson and the Freedom in Christ staff on a number of occasions and have personally seen the results. We have been truly amazed and grateful at the healing experienced by many persons from persistent depression as they were counseled in God's truths and led through the Steps to Freedom in Christ. Bondages lifted; oppressions were released; and hopeless, helpless, discouraged, depressive symptoms vanished.

God's miraculous power in the name of Jesus was clearly manifested, and countless men, women and children have been set free! We believe every person can benefit from the truths of these spiritual insights.

To their credit, the authors fairly balance the possible spiritual causes with a clear acceptance of and information about the biological and psychological causes. This is encouraging, because in our experience some Christians have difficulty giving themselves permission to accept biological intervention even when a chemical imbalance is clearly indicated (as in approximately 10 percent of cases). We agree with the authors that medication is another gift from God when used appropriately.

In most cases of depression, more than one cause is at work. God's created "handiwork" is not only beloved, but also complicated! In this excellent book, the authors are able to provide direction for appropriate therapeutic intervention. It may be medication, counseling or prayer, either individually or in combination. The goal is to relieve the agonizing pain of depression and to return the afflicted "back home" to a stable, positive, balanced mood with confident realistic thinking and an unfettered receptive spirit.

Dr. Anderson's telling of his own story lends an appealing vulnerability, a compassionate tenderness and a personal credibility to this work. Our heavenly Father is a healing God. Whatever the intervention, He is the Healer. You'll find Him reaching out to you with compassion and hope through the pages of this sensitive work. We encourage you to read this enlightening book and highly recommend it so that you too may experience freedom from the bondages of depression and embrace the "joy of the Lord."

STEPHEN KING, M.D.
JUDITH KING, M.S.W., A.C.S.W.

ACKNOWLEDGMENTS

Writing a book takes a lifetime of living, listening, learning and growing. First and foremost, we want to thank our heavenly Father for calling us into ministry and gracing us with His presence. Without Him, we are nothing. Second, our lives have been shaped by our families, teachers, friends and colleagues in ministry. We couldn't have written this book without them. Especially, we want to thank our wives, Joanne and Jane, for their patience, support, constructive criticism and encouragement. You have contributed to our joy.

We want to thank Dr. Timothy Warner, Dr. Stephen and Judith King, Dr. Terry and Julie Zuehlke, Dr. George Hurst and Dr. Lyle Torguson for their medical, theological and psychological critiques and advice. We are indebted to all those who have shared their stories with us. Our lives have been enriched because the Lord brought us together in their times of need. We are all on one rung of a giant recovery ladder, reaching down to the person below us. Because we have been loved and comforted, we have the capacity to love and comfort others.

We thank Bill Greig and Kyle Duncan for their patience and support of this project. It has been a blessing to work with you and all the fine staff at Gospel Light who make books like this possible. May the Lord use it to His honor and glory.

NEIL ANDERSON
HAL BAUMCHEN

INTRODUCTION

My (Neil's) wife, Joanne, informed me that Mary was in the hospital again. This was the third time she had been admitted for clinical depression. At the hospital, Joanne had an opportunity to pray for Mary and discuss her situation. She had dutifully followed her doctor's orders and tried every scientific remedy known—to no avail. Somewhat apologetically, Joanne suggested, "Why don't you go see Neil?"

"Him!" Mary responded incredulously. "What good would it do to see him? He's always up!"

Well, isn't that the sort of person you *should* see for depression? If you weren't well physically, would you seek out the most sickly, emaciated and wasted doctor in town and ask him what his health secret is? Surely, if you are down, you would want to see or at least learn from someone who is "always up." That kind of person must be doing or believing something that is enabling him to live above his circumstances.

From Mary's perspective, however, I don't think that is the primary issue. I suspect that she was thinking: *How could someone who is "always up" understand what I am going through? Do you really know what it's like to get up every morning with no sense of hope, and not enough energy to climb out of bed? Negative thoughts pepper my mind, and I'm emotionally drained all the time. I may have a few good moments, but they never last. "Think positive thoughts," you say! I can't even muster up enough energy to think at all. The slightest little irritation sets off another round of despair. One more bad report and I'll be ready to cash it in. I can't take it anymore. I don't have the strength or the will to fight. I just want to curl up in a ball and die. That seems to be the only way out, and everyone else would be better off if I did.*

Such are the negative, repeated, oppressive thoughts of the melancholic. It is bad enough to suffer from such a malady, but the stares, rejection or pious platitudes of those who don't understand add insult to injury. There was a time when my natural bent would be to "jolly" such a person up. Then I read in the Bible, "He who blesses his friend with a loud voice early in the morning, it will be reckoned a curse to him" (Prov. 27:14). In some situations, a little comic relief can be a shaft of light in a dark world; but it usually doesn't last or resolve the state in which depressed people find themselves.

If depressed persons don't believe that a joyful mortal can relate to their circumstances or understand what they are going through, then how could they expect God to understand? After all, if He doesn't like the circumstances, He can create new ones. God doesn't have to deal with our finite limitations; He is eternal and infinite. He has no impure thoughts, nor does He struggle with insurmountable odds.

JESUS CAN RELATE

All this is wonderfully true of our heavenly Father, but remember Jesus. He humbled Himself and took on the form of a man (see Phil. 2:6-8). He voluntarily surrendered the independent use of His divine attributes. All the political and religious forces were united against Him. In the end, He was all alone. Even His chosen disciples deserted Him. Peter denied that he even knew Him. In the garden of Gethsemane, He was grieved and distressed to the point of death—the Man of sorrows, acquainted with grief. Finally, He faced the indignities of a mock trial and was found guilty of trumped-up charges. They crucified the most innocent Man who ever lived. According to Hebrews 4:14-16, we can go to God because of Jesus:

> Since then we have a great high priest who has passed through the heavens, Jesus the Son of God, let us hold fast our confession. For we do not have a high priest who cannot sympathize with our weaknesses, but one who has been tempted in all things as we are, yet without sin. Let us therefore draw near with confidence to the throne of grace, that we may receive mercy and may find grace to help in time of need.

Jesus not only made it possible for us to go to God because He died for our sins and gave us eternal life, but also because He, by His own experience, can relate to our weaknesses. He knows from personal experience how we feel.

Have you ever felt rejected and unloved? So has He. Have you ever had people you counted on let you down? So has He. Do you face overwhelming temptation? He was tempted in *all* ways. Do you have to live with the consequences of someone else's sins? He took upon Himself the sins of *all* mankind, then faced what you and I will never have to face as the Father turned His back on Him.

Yet, in the end, God did not abandon His Son. And we can say with confidence that He will never leave us nor forsake us (see Heb. 13:5). In spite of all that Christ endured, He never lost hope or faith in our heavenly Father. The resources that sustained God's Son are now ours because we belong to Him. He is the God of all hope.

THE CRY FOR MERCY AND THE NEED FOR GRACE

We have the assurance that if we go to God, we will receive mercy and find grace to help in time of need. He will not give us what we deserve (which demonstrates His mercy); instead, He will give us what we need (which demonstrates His grace), even though we don't deserve it.

People often turn to the Church in time of need. Yet they don't always find mercy there. In too many cases, they receive more mercy and less judgment in a secular treatment center or a local bar. However, those places don't have the eternal grace of God to help in time of need. The Church has the grace to help in time of need, but we won't have the opportunity to share it unless we first show mercy.

The cry of the depressed is, "Have mercy upon me. I don't need to be scolded, judged, advised or rejected. I need to be understood, accepted, affirmed and loved." If that doesn't come first, then all the biblical answers we have to give them will fall upon deaf ears.

HIDING IN THE SHADOWS

Determining the causes and cures of depression presents a challenge because the symptoms reveal that the whole person is affected—body, soul and spirit. We know that many people are physically sick for psychosomatic reasons.[1] We also know that many people who suffer from emotional problems can establish a physical cause. Humanly speaking, people often find themselves hoping that a physical cause and cure can be found for depression, because there is less social stigma associated with physical illness than mental illness. Somehow we feel absolved of responsibility if a physical cause can be established. Our self-image is left intact. We believe others will be more sympathetic if they know it isn't our fault.

With that kind of thinking, people are afraid to share their real problems. Tremendous needs go unmet when people feel free to share only their physical problems, but not their emotional or spiritual ones. Generally speaking, the Christian community doesn't respond appropriately to those who are struggling emotionally. On the other hand, if someone breaks her leg, we flock to the hospital, pray for her and sign her cast. Meals are brought over to her house. She is treated almost like a hero, because people understand physical illness, and they can sympathize.

But watch what happens when a prayer request is given for someone who is depressed. A gloom hangs over the room, and a polite prayer is offered. "Dear Lord, help Mary get over her depression. Amen." We don't know how to respond to emotional problems. There is no cast to sign, and everyone is silently thinking (or the depressed believe that others are thinking): *Why doesn't she just snap out of it? I wonder what skeletons she has in her closet. If she would just pray and read her Bible more, she wouldn't be in such a state. No sincere Christian should be depressed. There must be some sin in her life.* These critical thoughts are not helpful to the depressed person, and often aren't even true. Contributing to the person's guilt and shame does not help mental functioning. We must learn to reflect the love and hope of God, who is close to the brokenhearted.

Is there a physical cause and therefore a potential physical cure for some forms of depression? Yes, and we will examine those possibilities. Christians are no more immune to endogenous (from within the body, or physical in its origin) depression than any other person. Therefore it is wrong to jump to the conclusion that it is a sin for a Christian to be depressed.

We have a far greater hope for cure, however, if the cause of our depression is *not* endogenous, but reactive—a response to something outside the body. This is because changing brain chemistry is far less certain and less precise than changing what we believe or how we think about external circumstances or events. However, it is usually easier to get people to take a pill with the hope of changing brain chemistry than it is to get them to change what they believe and how they think.

People who are depressed because of the way they think and believe are often shunned or judged. But what about those whose thinking makes them arrogant, prideful and self-sufficient? The depressed person would find a more kindred spirit with the biblical prophets, who thundered against such arrogance, than they find in many Christian groups.

SEEKING A HOLISTIC ANSWER

In one sense, it doesn't make any difference whether the precipitating cause for depression is physical, mental or spiritual. Depression affects the whole person, and a complete cure requires a holistic answer. No human problem that manifests itself in one dimension of reality can be isolated from the rest of reality. Like any other sickness of the body and soul, depression is a whole-life problem that requires a whole-life answer.

Depression is related to our physical health, to what we believe, how we perceive ourselves, our relationship with God, our relationship with others, the circumstances of life and, finally, to Satan, the god of this world. You cannot successfully treat depression without taking into account all related factors. We have a whole God, who is the Creator of all reality, and He relates to us as whole people.

WE ARE IN THIS TOGETHER

It is no shame to feel depressed, because it is an inevitable part of our maturing process. Approximately 18 million people in the United States (about 10 percent of all adults) will suffer from depression in any given year, according to the National Institute of Health. Only a third of those people will seek treatment for their depression. In too may cases, pride prevents us from seeking the help we need, and the consequences are often predictable and tragic. As the Bible says, pride comes before a fall, and God is opposed to the proud.

It is more honest to admit that we need help than to pretend we can live the Christian life in isolation. Our drive to be self-sufficient destroys our dependency on Christ. Only those who are secure in Christ readily admit to their need for one another, and they don't hesitate to ask for help when it becomes necessary. We absolutely need God, and we necessarily need each other. It is the essence of love to meet each other's needs.

David was said to have a heart for God, yet his numerous bouts of depression are recorded throughout the psalms. Martin Luther battled depression most of his life. Abraham Lincoln said, "I am now the most miserable man living. If what I feel were equally distributed to the whole human family, there would not be one cheerful face on the earth."[2] Friends of Lincoln said, "He was a sad looking man; his melancholy dript from him as he walked,"[3] and "He was so overcome with mental depression that he never dare(d) carry a knife in his pocket."[4]

Sir Winston Churchill, prime minister of England during World War II, referred to his recurrent depression as "the Black Dog." A biographer notes, "He had an enemy worthy of the word [black dog], an unambiguous tyrant whose destruction occupied him fully and invigorated him totally year in and year out."[5]

Let's face it: living in this fallen world can be quite depressing. But there are positive benefits to acknowledging all our struggles. Positive Christian growth can come from times of loss and feelings of helplessness or hopelessness. The richest treasures are often discovered in the deepest holes. What we need is the assurance that can only come from a God of all hope. As someone once said, "We can live about 40 days without food, about three days without water, and about eight minutes without air—but only one second without hope."

TRUTH RESTORES HOPE

If you have ever struggled with depression, we wrote this book to help you establish your hope in God and enable you to live according to the truth of God's Word. We want to extend to you the mercy and grace of God. Depression, despair and hopelessness may have crept into your life and tainted your view of reality. Truth restores hope. We want to help you see the reality of the world we live in through the grid of Scripture. Wisdom is seeing life from God's perspective.

As I (Neil) will describe later, my wife, Joanne, and I lived through a horrible period when she was so deeply depressed that it almost destroyed us. We will also share stories about other people finding freedom from depression, some of whom were almost destroyed by the severity of their depression. Their names have been changed except for some who wanted to share openly their testimonies of finding freedom in Christ.

For the sake of smooth reading, we usually use "I" and "we" without distinguishing whether we are writing in Neil's or Hal's "voice." In this book we hope to accomplish the following:

1. Describe the symptoms and signs of depression, to facilitate a proper diagnosis;

2. Explain medical terminology, brain chemistry and neurological functions to show how depression can have an organic impact on our bodies;

3. Show how thinking and believing affect the way we respond to the world about us;

4. Establish the spiritual connection between depression and mental health;

5. Reveal the Father nature of God, and how He relates to us;

6. Explain the gospel and emphasize its message of who we are in Christ and what it means to be a child of God;

7. Uncover the truth from Scripture that replaces our sense of hopelessness and helplessness;

8. Show how to survive the inevitable losses of life, and remind you of the way any crisis can be a stepping-stone to greater maturity;

9. Show how suffering is an essential part of sanctification;

10. Provide a step-by-step process for overcoming depression.

Listen to how Jesus prays in His "high priestly prayer": "But now I come to Thee; and these things I speak in the world, that they may have My joy made full in themselves" (John 17:13). Paul says, "Not that we lord it over your faith, but are workers with you for your joy; for in your faith you are standing firm" (2 Cor. 1:24). God wants you to experience the joy of the Lord. It is a fruit of the Spirit (see Gal. 5:22,23), not the fruit of circumstances. We are workers with you for your joy. However, the Christian walk is not about trying to be happy; that would be trite, misguided and self-serving.

We are called to be mission-minded overcomers in Christ. We are not called to live lives that are continuously beaten down, defeated or in bondage. To see yourself as rejected, unwanted and useless is to be deceived. To see the circumstances of life as hopeless is to take your eyes off Jesus, the Author and Finisher of your faith. To think you are unloved, unappreciated and unworthy is to believe a lie, because you are a child of the King who has rescued you from the domain of darkness, and transferred you to the kingdom of His beloved Son (see Col. 1:13). God's love for you is unconditional because God *is* love. It is His nature to love you.

Our prayer is that you will sense our compassion and understanding derived from years of helping people who have lost their hope. It is imperfect; but God's love and compassion are perfect, and He is your hope. We wanted to be hard hitting enough to break down the mental strongholds of hopelessness and helplessness, yet tender enough to bind up the brokenhearted. We believe the personal presence of Christ in your life, and the truth of His Word, are ultimately the answer. Our desire is to make that truth relevant to your struggles, and practical enough to inspire immediate action.

Now may the God of hope fill you with all joy and peace in believing, that you may abound in hope by the power of the Holy Spirit (Rom. 15:13).

Neil and Hal

Notes

1. It is a well-established fact that people are physically sick from mental, emotional and spiritual causes. The minimum estimate is 50 percent, and you will hear as high as 75 percent. At least 25 percent of the "healings" in the Gospels are actually deliverances from evil spirits.
2. In a letter to a friend, William Henry Herdon, cited in Michael Burlingame, *The Inner World of Abraham Lincoln* (Urbana, Ill.: University of Illinois Press, 1994), p. 100.
3. Ibid., p. 93.
4. Ibid., p. 97.
5. Anthony Storr, "Churchill's Black Dog," *Kafka's Mice and Other Phenomena of the Human Mind* (New York: Grove Press, 1987), p. 5.

CHAPTER ONE

THE AGONY OF DEPRESSION

*Thus I hated all the fruit of my labor for which
I had labored under the sun, for I must leave it to the
man who will come after me. And who knows whether
he will be a wise man or a fool?...Therefore I completely
despaired of all the fruit of my labor for which
I had labored under the sun.*

ECCLESIASTES 2:18-20

*The signs of approaching melancholy are...anguish
and distress, dejections, silence, animosity...sometimes a
desire to live and at other times a longing for death,
suspicions on the part of the patient that a plot
is being hatched against him.*

CAELIUS AURELIANUS, FIFTH CENTURY A.D.

A pastor and his wife began their session in tears. Their son had been killed in an auto accident nine days earlier. They had been through hard times before, and were intimately acquainted with sorrow and grief. They reminisced about their son as we talked and prayed together. Being in ministry, they knew of God's grace and comfort. As a pastor, he had helped many others work through their crises; but now he was despondent and unable to sleep. The loss was overwhelming to him.

Another man we'll call Steven had been unemployed for almost 20 weeks following a minor accident with his semi-truck. No one had been injured, but his company had suspended him from driving and he quit out of embarrassment and shame. He had been unable to explore new employment possibilities, and made up stories for my sake about the "activities" he used to occupy his time. He was passive, helpless, scared and resistant to change. Hopelessness was a constant theme in his outlook on life. He dreaded talking about the future.

A woman in her 30s was so deeply troubled that she physically shook during our meeting. A single parent of a nine-year-old child, she worked in a nursing home and was going to school at night. Although she had long ago left her parents, she talked of the ongoing strain and tension in their relationship. She reflected on her spiritual life, and the terrible condition of her soul. With trembling voice and frightened eyes she said she had committed the unpardonable sin. The "voices" in her mind harassed her at every turn. They called her "slut" and "nasty," and told her that Jesus would never talk to her again after what she had done. She was extremely agitated and anxious.

A SAD EPIDEMIC

These stories of extreme loss, hopelessness and spiritual defeat seem so different and unrelated, yet each person could be diagnosed as depressed. Depression is an ache in the soul that crushes your spirit. It wraps itself so tightly around you that you can't believe it will ever leave; but it can and it does! Depression is treatable. You do not have to live like this, at least not for long.

About 10 million people in the United States are presently suffering from depression. It can creep into the lives of all people regardless of age, sex, social or economic status. Twice as many women than men struggle with depression. Among college students, 25 percent struggle with some form of depression, and 33 percent of college dropouts will suffer serious depression before leaving school.

Depression is so prevalent it has been called the "common cold" of psychological disorders.

The number of doctor visits in which patients received prescriptions for mental problems rose from 32.7 million to 45.6 million in the decade from 1985 to 1994. Visits to the doctor that resulted in a diagnosis of depression almost doubled during the same 10-year period, from 11 million to more than 20.4 million.[1] This is an incredible increase, especially in light of the fact that many who struggle with depression do not seek medical help.

Depression is a complex, yet common, physical, emotional and spiritual struggle. It is so prevalent that it has been called the "common cold" of psychological disorders. Many people will have at least one serious bout of depression in their lifetimes, and all will experience some symptoms of depression due to poor physical health, negative circumstances, or their spiritual condition.

Too many Christians live in denial about their own depression, thinking that if they were spiritually mature then they would never have to struggle like the rest of us. Consequently, they don't reach out to others, or seek the help they need. It is actually shameful in some "Christian" communities to be sad or depressed. "You must be living in sin" is the subtle, deceptive assumption. Such erroneous or simplistic thinking causes depressed people to clam up and hide their true feelings instead of believing the truth and walking in the light.

DEFINING DEPRESSION

Depression is a disturbance or disorder of one's mood or emotional state. It is characterized by persistent sadness, heaviness, darkness or feelings of emptiness. The emotional state of depression is usually accompanied by thoughts of hopelessness and sometimes suicide. Those who are depressed believe that life is bad and that the prognosis for improvement is nil. Their thoughts are colored by negative and pessimistic views of themselves, their future and the circumstances surrounding them.

It is critically important to realize that sadness or other factors in the *emotional state* of depression are not the cause, but the symptom. Treating the symptom would only bring temporary relief at best. Any treatment for depression must focus on the cause, not the effect. The goal is to cure the disease, not the resulting pain. As we shall see later, the cause could be physical, mental or spiritual. We think it is important to understand the symptoms of depression in order to better understand the cause. A proper diagnosis is necessary before appropriate treatment can be considered.

PHYSICAL SYMPTOMS OF DEPRESSION

ENERGY LEVEL

"I just don't feel like doing anything" is the dirge song of the depressed. Loss of energy, excessive fatigue and unrelenting tiredness are the characteristics of melancholics. They live as though their internal transmission has only one gear—low—and they would prefer shifting into neutral. A recurring vignette in the old television program "Hee Haw" captured the image of depression. A bunch of hillbillies were flaked out in front of an old cabin, clutching their moonshine, with a droopy bloodhound by their side. Every night they sang the theme song of the depressed:

> Gloom, despair and agony on me;
> Deep, dark depression, excessive misery;
> If it weren't for bad luck,
> I'd have no luck at all;
> Gloom, despair and agony on me!

Ordinary body movements and actions are reduced to slow motion. Walking, talking, cleaning the house, getting ready for work or doing a project can take considerably longer than usual. The person suffering from depression often feels that time is moving at a snail's pace. Usual activities become monumental or seemingly insurmountable tasks. Complaints of fatigue are common. Lowered energy levels and lowered interest in activities affect job performance. The person can often see that his or her performance is sliding, but can't seem to pull out of it.

Approximately 10 percent of the melancholy seriously struggle with endogenous depression, which, as explained earlier, originates within the body and is characterized by physical symptoms. Many of these people simply do not function on a daily basis. They don't get dressed, and either stay in bed or lie around the house.

SLEEP DISTURBANCE

Having trouble sleeping is one of the most common symptoms of depression. Although some people feel like sleeping all the time, it is actually more common to hear about insomnia. "Initial insomnia" (or "sleep onset insomnia") is the difficulty of falling asleep. Depression is more commonly associated with "terminal insomnia," in which the person falls asleep out of sheer fatigue, but then wakes up and can't get back to sleep. Although insomnia is only a symptom of depression, it contributes to the downward spiral of those who can't seem to pull out of it. Inadequate sleep leaves the sufferer with less energy for tomorrow.

Psalm 77 is a call for help by Asaph, who is so depressed that he cannot sleep. He writes, "When I remember God, then I am disturbed; when I sigh, then my spirit grows faint. Thou hast held my eyelids open; I am so troubled that I cannot speak" (vv. 3,4). This sufferer also questions God's mercy and compassion (see vv. 7-9). His hope is gone because what he believes about God is not true; and the result is sleeplessness, despair about God's seeming absence and not enough energy to even speak. That is depression.

ACTIVITY LEVEL

Depression is accompanied by decreased involvement in activities, which is related to a lack of interest in things and commitment to follow through. Sufferers don't have the physical or emotional energy to sustain ordinary levels of activity, so their performance is often hindered. They have lost interest in activities that they formerly found to be meaningful and even pleasurable.

Many find it difficult to pray because God seems like a distant figure. Perhaps they enjoyed playing the piano or some other instrument, but no longer find it relaxing or satisfying. Why bother? is the question that screams for an answer! Tragically, the needs for self-expression and to be involved with others go unmet, and this only contributes to their depression.

LACK OF SEX DRIVE

In depression, there is often a decrease in sexual interest or drive. Accompanying this loss is a wish for isolation, feelings of worthlessness, criticism of one's personal appearance, loss of spontaneity, and apathy. The emotional state of depression usually creates problems in relationships, and this obviously further curtails the desire to be intimate.

SOMATIC COMPLAINTS

When depression strikes, many people report physical aches and pains such as headache, stomachache and lower back pain, any or all of which can be quite severe. Depression headaches are especially common. Unlike migraine headaches, they are usually dull, and feel like a band around the head with the pain radiating down the neck. Our knowledge of aches and pains associated with depression is certainly not new, for David laments: "I am bowed down and brought very low; all day long I go about mourning. My back is filled with searing pain; there is no health in my body" (Ps. 38:6,7, *NIV*).

LOSS OF APPETITE

Depression is often accompanied by a decrease in appetite. Indigestion, constipation or diarrhea commonly contribute to weight loss during depression. Those who struggle with anorexia and deny themselves adequate nourishment are usually depressed as well. On the other hand, 20 percent of depressed people experience an increase of appetite and craving for food.

MENTAL AND EMOTIONAL SYMPTOMS

The most dominant symptoms of depression are emotional. Some other mental problems also indicate severe to mild depression, but keep in mind that what a normal person thinks or believes is also a potential cause for depression. The following are the most common emotional symptoms and resultant mental states of those who are depressed.

SADNESS

Depression is most commonly characterized by a deep sadness. The "blues" seem to creep up slowly, and bring with them a spirit of heaviness. Crying and brooding or just "being in a funk" are common in depressed people. Some can hardly control the steady stream of tears. The sadness they experience is the antithesis of joy, which is a fruit of the Spirit (see Gal. 5:22,23). Proverbs 15:13 aptly says, "A joyful heart makes a cheerful face, but when the heart is sad, the spirit is broken."

DESPAIR

Despair is the absence of hope. Despair sees no light at the end of the tunnel, no hope at the end of the day and no answers for the endless round of questions that plague the mind of the depressed. Three times the psalmist cries out, "Why are you in despair, O my soul? And why have you become disturbed within me? Hope in God, for I shall again praise Him for the help of His presence" (Ps. 42:5; see also 42:11 and 43:5).

Hope, despair's opposite, is the present assurance of some future good; and the psalmist knew where his hope lay. Jeremy Taylor said, "It is impossible for a man to despair who remembers that his helper is omnipotent." The problem is, depression seems to impede the normal process of memory.

IRRITABILITY AND LOW FRUSTRATION TOLERANCE

Depressed people have very little emotional reserve. Small things tick them off, and they are easily frustrated. They have a low tolerance level for the pressures of life, and can be frequently heard saying, "I can't deal with that right now," or "I just can't take it any longer." One lady I was counseling said what others feel also: "How can I plan for tomorrow when survival for the day is at the top of my list?"

ISOLATION AND WITHDRAWAL

As Henry David Thoreau said, "The mass of men lead lives of quiet desperation." John Gray observed that typically, males in such a state retreat to caves, while women climb into holes.[2] Men tend to isolate themselves more readily, but spend less time in their caves than women do in their holes. Most men are generally less image-conscious and less introspective than women. Many will go away and lick their wounds, then come back as though nothing has happened.

It is hard for some men to reveal their souls. The tendency is to cover their pain with work or vices. Consequently, they are more likely to become workaholics or alcoholics.

It is common to see people who suffer with depression pulling away from other people. They feel embarrassed to be with people when they feel so low. They don't want to be a wet blanket in the group and drag others down by their depression. Although some may think that isolation is a viable short-term solution, avoiding people often adds to the downward spiral of depression.

NEGATIVE THOUGHT PATTERNS

Generally speaking, depressed people have trouble thinking and concentrating. Their minds won't stay focused. Constant distractions rob them of any mental peace. As water seeks the lowest ground, depression seeps in and drowns out optimism. It seems easier to see a problem, think the worst, predict failure, find fault and focus on weakness.

First, people who are prone to depression have difficulty believing positive and good things about themselves. Feelings of worthlessness become the breeding ground for thoughts of self-destruction (see "Thoughts of Suicide" below). Their struggle with guilt prompts them to become irrational, unreasonable and even delusional. Second, they cannot think positively about the future. They can't stop worrying about tomorrow. They dread it, instead of looking forward to it. Third, the circumstances in which they find themselves are interpreted as negative. This is the well-known depression triad that cognitive therapists see repeatedly in their practices.

THOUGHTS OF SUICIDE

Sadness, isolation, loss of energy, strained relationships and physical problems contaminate one's perspective of self and the future. As helplessness and hopelessness stir in the mind, many begin to think of suicide as a way of escape. Others just wish they were dead, or that God would take them home!

In short, depressed people become self-absorbed. Mental exhaustion causes them to take the easy path, which is to think negatively about self, and makes thinking of others extremely difficult. They will avoid hearing any more bad news or taking on any more responsibility. They feel overwhelmed. It is a syndrome filled with misery, shame, sadness and guilt.

TWO DEPRESSED PEOPLE

It is not enough for Christians to merely be aware of the general symptoms of depression. If we want to reach out to those who struggle with depression, we must view them as people, not bundles of symptoms. Describing specific people who exhibit symptoms like the preceding can also help you see yourself in a more objective light.

MATT, A FORMER GO-GETTER

Notice how many of these characteristics became evident in Matt, a 46-year-old man who had a good job in a manufacturing firm. He and his wife, Linda, had raised two children in their nice suburban home. Their younger child was graduating from high school and the older one was in college.

Matt had been a real go-getter; but now he began to feel restless at work and his performance began to drop off. He hated going in to work, and he became irritable and feisty with his coworkers. Finally, his supervisor had to speak to him about his performance and his relationship with fellow workers. Matt just didn't see the problem in the same way. He felt picked on and condemned by his coworkers and his boss. He hated his job, his life and himself. Then one day, out of frustration and disgust with himself, Matt quit his job!

He felt even worse after quitting his job. He had been satisfied with his profession, which had given him a sense of worth and, of course, an income. Now he felt tormented in his mind and wasn't sleeping well. He lost his appetite and didn't want to visit anyone. He even quit studying his Bible, and stopped attending church—activities he had found meaningful and enjoyable. His marriage deteriorated, and relationships were strained with his children. Frequent fights about money and Matt's lack of interest in finding a job made living at home a source of constant irritation. He had no mental peace. His mind was flooded with negative thoughts about himself and life in general.

Matt was experiencing almost every sign of depression; and, as is typical, his problems were affecting every other person in his family. Because there was so much conflict at home, he and his wife sought counseling for their marriage. Their marriage problems, however, couldn't be resolved until Matt dealt with his personal issues.

Fortunately, through counseling, deep repentance and faith in God, Matt was able to overcome his depression by winning the battle in his mind.

KING DAVID

In Matt's case, sin was an issue in addition to many unresolved conflicts. His situation was similar to David's depression, described in Psalm 38:3-18:

> Because of your wrath there is no health in my body; my bones have no soundness because of my sin. My guilt has overwhelmed me like a burden too heavy to bear. My wounds fester and are loathsome because of my sinful folly. I am bowed down and brought very low; all day long I go about mourning. My back is filled with searing pain; there is no health in my body. I am feeble and utterly crushed; I groan in anguish of heart. All my longings lie open before you, O Lord; my sighing is not hidden from you. My heart pounds, my strength fails me; even the light has gone from my eyes. My

friends and companions avoid me because of my wounds; my neighbors stay far away. Those who seek my life set their traps, those who would harm me talk of my ruin; all day long they plot deception. I am like a deaf man, who cannot hear, like a mute, who cannot open his mouth; I have become like a man who does not hear, whose mouth can offer no reply. I wait for you, O Lord; you will answer, O Lord my God. For I said, "Do not let them gloat or exalt themselves over me when my foot slips." For I am about to fall, and my pain is ever with me. I confess my iniquity; I am troubled by my sin *(NIV)*.

David is depressed, even though he was a man Scripture says had a whole heart for God. David would have identified with most of Matt's symptoms. He describes in graphic detail his physical, spiritual and emotional pain. He even feels that he is near death. David knows that his only hope is God, as he cries out at the end of the psalm, "Come quickly to help me, O Lord my Savior" (v. 22).

DEPRESSION DIAGNOSIS

Are you depressed, or do you know someone who may be? Try taking the following questionnaire, which can serve as a rough evaluation for depression and help determine whether the condition is mild or severe.

Circle the number that best describes you or the person you are evaluating. For instance, on line 1, circle number 1 if you are exhausted all the time and 5 if you are normally a high-energy person. Circle 3 if you are generally neutral, having neither high nor low energy. If you are applying this inventory to yourself, you will get a more accurate picture of your general condition if you take it when you are not reacting to a crisis. Some mild depressions are a reaction to temporary setbacks or depressing circumstances that may last for a few hours or days. It is best to wait a few hours or days after such episodes before taking the inventory because they can momentarily skew the results.

1. Low energy	1	2	3	4	5	High energy
2. Difficulty sleeping or sleep all the time	1	2	3	4	5	Uninterrupted sleeping patterns
3. No desire to be involved in activities	1	2	3	4	5	Very involved in activities
4. No desire for sex	1	2	3	4	5	Healthy sex drive
5. Aches and pains	1	2	3	4	5	Feel great
6. Loss of appetite	1	2	3	4	5	Enjoy eating
7. Sad	1	2	3	4	5	Joyful
8. Despairing and hopeless	1	2	3	4	5	Hopeful and confident
9. Irritable (low frustration tolerance)	1	2	3	4	5	Pleasant (high frustration tolerance)
10. Withdrawn	1	2	3	4	5	Involved
11. Mental anguish	1	2	3	4	5	Peace of mind
12. Low sense of self-worth	1	2	3	4	5	High sense of self-worth
13. Pessimistic (about the future)	1	2	3	4	5	Optimistic (about the future)

14. Negative   1   2   3   4   5   Positive (Perceive
     (Perceive most   most circumstances
     circumstances as   as positive and
     negative or even   as opportunities
     harmful)   for growth)

15. Self-destructive   1   2   3   4   5   Self-preserving
     ("I and others would   ("Glad I'm here.")
     be better off if I
     weren't here.")

If you most often circled numbers 3 through 5, you are not struggling with depression. Most of the fluctuations on the right side of the scale can be explained by general health, differing temperaments, and growing levels of maturity. A person of average health and maturity, having an introspective or generally pessimistic temperament, would likely circle many 3s, and not be depressed. A person of good health and maturity with an optimistic and outgoing personality would likely circle 4s and 5s.

Temperament and personality can affect many of the individual items on the inventory. You can get a rough determination of your level of depression if you added up all the circled numbers and compared them with the following ratings:

45 – 75   Likely not depressed
35 – 44   Mildly depressed
25 – 34   Depressed
15 – 24   Severely depressed

SEVERITY OF DEPRESSION

Degrees of depression lie on a continuum from mild to severe. Everyone experiences mild depression from the normal ups and downs of life. These mood fluctuations are generally related to health issues, mental attitudes and the external pressures of living in a fallen world. In our experience, those who scored between 30 and 45 can manage their own recovery—and hopefully the contents of this book will help them do just that.

Those who score lower should seek the help of a godly pastor or Christ-centered counselor; or, if the cause is found to be "endogenous," as explained in the next chapter, a medical doctor.

Secure people in Christ have no problem admitting to their weaknesses. They are emotionally honest, as Jesus was when He wept over the city of Jerusalem and at the grave of Lazarus.

Those who score low on the inventory need the objectivity of someone else to help them resolve their conflicts.

Please keep in mind that it is not a sign of failure or weakness to seek the help of others. We are supposed to "Bear one another's burdens, and thus fulfill the law of Christ" (Gal. 6:2). Every person absolutely needs God, and we necessarily need each other. Usually it is a sign of pride and immaturity not to admit a need.

Have you ever noticed that few people struggle with seeing a medical doctor if they are sick, or seeing a lawyer when they need legal advice? But for some reason we resist seeking help for emotional and spiritual problems. In our observation, secure people in Christ have no problem admitting their weaknesses. They are emotionally honest, as Jesus was when He wept over the city of Jerusalem and at the grave of Lazarus. He willingly admitted His need for emotional support when He cried out in the garden of Gethsemane, "My soul is deeply grieved to the point of death; remain here and keep watch" (Mark 14:34). That is emotional honesty.

EMOTIONAL PAIN AS A WARNING SIGNAL

What are our emotions? I like to think that our emotions are to our souls what our ability to feel is to our bodies. Suppose I had the power to remove the sensation of pain, and offered it to you as a gift. Would you receive it? It sounds tempting, but if you could not feel pain your body would be a hopeless mass of scars within weeks. The ability to feel pain is your protection from the harmful elements of the world you live in. Depression is a pain in the soul signaling that something is wrong.

Think of emotional pain as an indicator light on the control panel of your car. When that light comes on you have three possible responses.

SUPPRESSION: IGNORING THE WARNING

You can ignore your warning signal by putting a piece of duct tape over it. You may even be able to convince yourself for a while that the light is not on. That is called "suppression"; and in the long run it is very unhealthy for you. It is also dishonest when the cover-up is intended to convince others that everything is okay.

INDISCRIMINATE EXPRESSION: BREAKING THE SIGNAL

Another option is to take a small hammer and break the light. Applied to our emotions, this is called "indiscriminate expression." It may be physically healthier for *you* to wear your emotions on your sleeves, but if you express them without discrimination it isn't healthy for others.

Scripture has a lot to say about being slow to speak and slow to anger (see Jas. 1:19). Be cautious about getting something off your chest at random, or letting your feelings be known to all. Such displays will never bring the desired result. In suppression, the hurting person pulls away. In indiscriminate expression, others pull away.

ACKNOWLEDGMENT: DISCOVERING THE CAUSE

The third option when your car's warning signal comes on is to look under the hood and seek to discover the cause. That is "acknowledgment." In other words, be honest about how you feel for the purpose of resolving conflicts and living in harmony with God and His creation. This book is an attempt to "look under the hood" to discover the causes and cures of depression.

Now it is time to examine the relationship between depression and the ways the "instrument panel" of your body may send a warning.

Notes

1. *The Denver Post*, 18 February 1998, no. 195, p. 106.
2. John Gray, *Men Are from Mars, Women Are from Venus* (New York: HarperCollins Publishers, 1992), pp. 30-35.

CHAPTER TWO

THE AGONY OF THE BODY

The endless cycle of idea and action,

Endless invention, endless experiment,

Brings knowledge of motion, but not of stillness;

Knowledge of speech, but not of silence;

Knowledge of words, and ignorance of the Word.

All our knowledge brings us nearer to our ignorance,

All our ignorance brings us nearer to death,

But nearness to death no nearer to GOD.

Where is the Life we have lost in living?

Where is the wisdom we have lost in knowledge?

Where is the knowledge we have lost in information?

The cycles of Heaven in twenty centuries,

Bring us farther from GOD and nearer to the Dust.

T. S. ELIOT

I urge you therefore, brethren, by the mercies of God, to present your bodies a living and holy sacrifice, acceptable to God, which is your spiritual service of worship.

ROMANS 12:1

We are living in an incredible age. I remember hearing in 1980 that knowledge was doubling every five years. Now, at the end of the twentieth century, given the advancement of microcircuitry, simplification of software and the explosion of information available on the internet, knowledge is doubling every two-and-a-half years.

Scientists and medical doctors know far more about brain chemistry and how our neurological systems function than ever before. Then why has the number of people seeking treatment for depression nearly doubled in the last 10 years? Is there a neurological explanation for depression? Has our hope shifted from God to science? Professing ourselves to be wise, have we become fools? "For the foolishness of God is wiser than man's wisdom, and the weakness of God is stronger than man's strength" (1 Cor. 1:25, *NIV*). Or are we asked to make a false either/or choice, when it should be both/and—utilizing both the wisdom of God and all the discoveries He has enabled humans to make?

NO "WORLDS IN COLLISION"

We don't believe that science and revelation are on a collision course. God is the Creator of all things, and He established the fixed order of the universe. "The heavens are telling of the glory of God; and their expanse is declaring the work of His hands" (Ps. 19:1). God is the author of science. We are a part of the Creation, not the Creator. The fact that God has revealed Himself in creation is usually referred to as "general revelation."

We can only make scientific discoveries through empirical research. How we interpret the data we observe from general revelation must be analyzed through the grid of "special revelation," which is God's Word. A 50-year-old science book would read more like a comic book today. Who can predict what scientists will be saying 50 years from now about our present understanding of scientific discoveries?

Our confidence must be in God, but this does not set us on a collision course with medical science. Advances in research neither disable nor diminish the power of God, nor do they collide with the revelation of His Word. We thank God for every advancement in medicine that will help alleviate human suffering.

INNER AND OUTER ASPECTS

God created us in His image to be spiritually alive as well as physically alive. He formed Adam from the dust of the earth and breathed into him life. This union of divine breath and earthly dust constitutes the unique nature of humankind created in the image of God. We have an outer person and an inner person, a material part and an immaterial part.

Since we are both physical as well as spiritual beings, we need both the Church as well as the hospital, in proper balance.

God created the Church to minister to the soul and the spirit through the proper functioning of each member's gifts, talents and intelligence. Based on general revelation, humankind developed medical models to cure the physical body. Because we are both physical as well as spiritual beings, we need both the Church as well as the hospital, in proper balance.

The material or physical part of humans relates to the external world through five senses. We can taste, smell, hear, feel and see. The inner person relates to God through the soul and spirit. Unlike the animal kingdom, which operates out of divine instinct, we have the capacity to think, feel and choose. Because we are "fearfully and wonderfully made" (Ps. 139:14), it would only make sense that God would create the outer person to correlate with the inner person. Please refer to the following diagram:

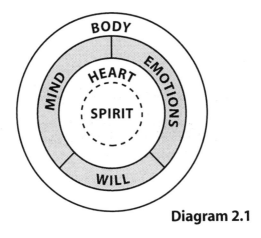

Diagram 2.1

THE MIND-BRAIN CORRELATION

The correlation between the mind and the brain is obvious, but there is a fundamental difference between the two. The brain came from the dust of this earth, and will return to dust when we die physically. At that moment we will be absent from our bodies and present with the Lord (see 2 Cor. 5:6-9), but we will not be mindless.

Today, we have a wonderful analogy to illustrate the working relationship between the brain and the mind. Between our ears is a very sophisticated computer operation. Like every computer system, it comprises two distinct components, the hardware and the software. The hardware (the computer itself) is obviously the brain in this analogy.

The brain functions much like a digital computer having millions of switching transistors that code all the information in a binary numbering system of 0s and 1s. The miniaturization of circuitry has made it possible to store and compile an incredible amount of information in a computer the size of a notebook. However, humankind has not even come close to making a computer as sophisticated as the one that is now making it possible for you to read and comprehend this book. A computer is mechanical, but our brains are living organisms composed of approximately 100 billion neurons. Each neuron is a living organism that in and of itself is a microcomputer.

A brief but basic anatomy lesson should be shared at this point because we will be referring to its components as we discuss possible causes and cures for endogenous depression. Every neuron is composed of a brain cell, an axon and many dendrites (inputs to the brain cell), as shown in the following illustration:

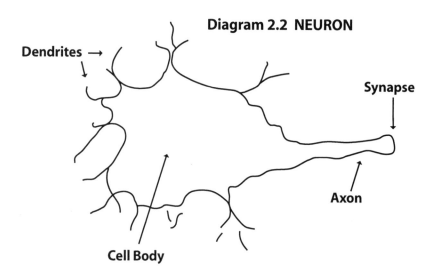

Diagram 2.2 NEURON

Each brain cell has many inputs (*dendrites*) and only one output through the axon that channels neurotransmitters to other dendrites. The *axon* has a covering known as the *myelin sheath* for insulation because the cell sends electrochemical messages along the axon. Every neuron is connected to tens of thousands of other neurons. Given that there are 100 billion neurons, the potential number of combinations is mind-boggling.

A junction between the axon of one neuron and the dendrites of another is called a *synapse*. Through its dendrites, every brain cell receives information, which it processes, integrates and sends on to other neurons.

In the axon exist many *mitochondria* that produce *neurotransmitters*. When a signal from the cell reaches the axon it releases neurotransmitters across the synapse to other dendrites. There are numerous types of neurotransmitters. The best known, and possibly the most important for our discussion of depression, are norepinephrine, dopamine, serotonin and acetylcholine.

BIPOLAR DEPRESSION

Endogenous depression is categorized as either bipolar or unipolar. A bipolar or manic-depressive illness has two poles: highs (called manic moods) and lows (depressed moods). The manic symptoms include the following: increased energy, unrealistic and grandiose beliefs in one's own power and ability, racing ideas and thoughts, poor judgment, increased talking or social activity, extreme euphoria, impulsivity, irritability and distractibility, obnoxious, insensitive or irritating behavior, and abuse of alcohol or drugs. Paranoid, delusional and psychotic thinking is also possible in the manic phase.

Current estimates indicate that about .5 to 1 percent of the adult population suffers from manic depression. That means between 1 and 2 million Americans have had or will have this affliction.[1] Bipolar illness is equally common in men and women. It is typically a recurrent or episodic disorder: a 1973 study examined nearly 400 patients who had an episode of manic-depressive illness, and only two failed to have a recurrence.[2]

Kay Jamison, one of the foremost experts on this illness, struggled with manic depression herself. She wrote a fascinating book called *Touched With Fire*[3] that revealed the relationship between art and madness (mania). Some of the most creative people in the world have struggled with this illness. Included in the list compiled by the author are, among writers, Hans Christian Andersen, John Bunyan, Samuel Clemens, Ralph Waldo Emerson, William Faulkner, Ernest Hemingway, Herman Melville, Robert Louis Stevenson, Tennessee Williams and Virginia Woolf; composers, George Frideric Handel,

Robert Schumann, Peter Tchaikovsky, Irving Berlin, Noel Coward, Stephen Foster and Cole Porter; and artists, Vincent van Gogh and Michelangelo.

Faulkner, Hemingway, Williams, Woolf, Schumann, Berlin and van Gogh all spent time in an asylum or psychiatric hospital. Hemingway, Woolf and van Gogh committed suicide.

In her autobiography, *An Unquiet Mind*,[4] Jamison shares her struggle with this illness and describes her incredible accomplishments during periods of mania. Treating her illness with lithium brought her great relief, but also decreased her creativity and productivity. She also said that taking medicine was not enough. She needed the objectivity of someone else to help her get through the depressive cycle. Like many who struggle with bipolar depression, her lows were so awful that suicide often seemed to be the only way out.

Leo Tolstoy shared what others are undoubtedly thinking during the low moments of depression:

> The thought of suicide came to me as naturally then as the thought of improving life had come to me before. This thought was such a temptation that I had to use cunning against myself in order not to go through with it too hastily. I did not want to be in a hurry only because I wanted to use all my strength to untangle my thoughts. If I could not get them untangled, I told myself, I could always go ahead with it. And there I was, a fortunate man, carrying a rope from my room, where I was alone every night as I undressed, so that I would not hang myself from the beam between the closets. And I quit going hunting with a gun, so that I would not be too easily tempted to rid myself of life. I myself did not know what I wanted. I was afraid of life. I struggled to get rid of it, and yet I hoped for something from it.
>
> And this was happening to me at a time when, from all indications, I should have been considered a completely

happy man; this was when I was not yet fifty years old. I had a good, loving, and beloved wife, fine children, and a large estate that was growing and expanding without any effort on my part. More than ever before I was respected by friends and acquaintances, praised by strangers, and I could claim a certain renown without really deluding myself.[5]

Endogenous depression may have nothing to do with external circumstances, as in the case of Tolstoy. This is an internal or physical struggle due to a chemical imbalance in the brain or possibly a battle for the mind, as shall be examined in later chapters.

The transmission of a message through the brain cells requires a certain balance of sodium (positive) and chloride (negative) ions. In bipolar illnesses, the balance and polarity of positive and negative ions is abnormal. In depression, the sodium ions increase about 50 percent, and along with the mania they increase as much as 200 percent. (Compare the way electricity flows through copper better than it does through iron, due to the chemical makeup of each substance.)

The drug of choice for treating bipolar depression is lithium carbonate, which is an inert salt. This reduces the number of sodium and chloride ions that allow the transmission to proceed more normally through the cell and into other neurons.

UNIPOLAR DEPRESSION

Episodes of serious depression without corresponding "highs" often indicate "unipolar" depression. Depression of this type affects nearly 10 percent of the American population and appears to be growing. Two major studies in the late 1970s revealed a tenfold increase in depression over the course of this century! As noted earlier, the diagnosis of depression has nearly doubled since the mid-1980s. This tremendous increase in depression has experts everywhere proclaiming that an epidemic of "the blues" is upon us.

MEDICAL TREATMENT

The focus on curing unipolar depression medically has been on the production, preservation and transmission of neurotransmitters. Some of the earlier antidepressant drugs were the monoamine oxidase inhibitors (MAOIs). The purpose of these drugs was to block the action of monoamine oxidase, which is an enzyme that destroys certain neurotransmitters.

Tricyclic antidepressants were the next group of prescription drugs to arrive on the scene. Their purpose was to keep the neurotransmitters in productive service longer. Presently, more focus has been given to stimulating the production of mood-altering neurotransmitters such as serotonin. The overall purpose of antidepressant medication is to get the brain functioning normally again so the mind can think clearly and start the process of recovering physical energy, sex drive, sleep and involvement in activities that make life meaningful.

The advent of antidepressant medications in the mid-1950s has given medical doctors a better understanding of brain chemistry and neurophysiology.

There is a major difference between antidepressants and antipsychotic or antianxiety (tranquilizers) medications. The latter two are sedatives (downers). They don't cure anything. They slow down the mind to inhibit distracting thoughts (or voices), or allow the person to relax in order to get some rest from a mind that won't shut off.

Antidepressant medications can actually cure a neurological condition. Even if they are not necessary, little harm will come by taking them. All of the modern antidepressants have few side effects and are not habit forming.

Serotonin is only one of many neurotransmitters in the brain, but it is the one most commonly linked to mood, and has been the one most studied.

Serotonin, or the lack of it, has been implicated not only in depression, uncontrollable appetite and obsessive-compulsive disorder but also in autism, bulimia, social phobias, premenstrual syndrome, anxiety and panic, migraines, schizophrenia and even extreme violence.[6]

Certain antidepressant medications enhance the availability of serotonin. Because there are no clinically available tests for serotonin, serotonin boosters are often used to help make a diagnosis. If the person's condition improves after taking it from four to six weeks, the doctor would conclude that they have a serotonin deficiency (i.e., a chemical imbalance). If the serotonin level is normal, no change is observed.

These are not "happy pills," and they do not alter moods by themselves; they only work if they are needed. Compared to most other drugs, they are relatively safe. Overdosing on pain relievers such as acetaminophen and ibuprofen would be more dangerous than taking too much of a serotonin booster.

Serotonin-boosting medications currently make up 65 percent of a primary-care doctor's prescriptions for depression. Choosing a serotonin medication that is right for you requires the assistance of your physician. Serotonin boosters, if needed at all, are like a key that unlocks the gate regulating neurotransmitters in your brain. Because everyone has a different lock, you may need to try different keys until you find the one that fits—knowing that each key has only a 70 percent chance of working on the first try.

A host of antidepressant medications are available. All are about equally effective, but work for any one individual only about 70 percent of the time. If the first one doesn't bring the desired effect, a second one may be tried. There is no way your doctor can accurately measure your brain chemistry and its production of neurotransmitters and select with any great precision the right medication to match. It is somewhat of an educated guessing game.

Following is a brief description of modern medications most frequently prescribed for depression in the last 10 years.

SELECTIVE SEROTONIN REUPTAKE INHIBITORS (SSRIs)

SSRIs are popular and easy to use. Usually the dose you start on is the dose you stay on. They work well for all the serotonin deficiency conditions listed previously. As a class, the SSRIs can cause sexual dysfunction and, in some cases, weight gain. Some studies show that SSRIs can cause disruption of sleep. Some physicians find it best to start this medication at half the dosage for the first week to allow the body to adjust.

1. *Prozac.* Among antidepressants that affect serotonin, Prozac has been around the longest. This drug tends to be more activating, and would work well with people who are lethargic. Prozac can cause sleep disturbance in some people.
2. *Zoloft.* In addition to increasing serotonin levels, this medication, when taken in higher doses, can also boost a neurotransmitter called dopamine. This can be helpful in people who have attention deficit disorder. Zoloft can cause intestinal side effects in some people.
3. *Paxil.* This medication has a calming effect on most people, but can be sedating to some. Paxil appears to work especially well on muscle conditions such as stress headaches, irritable bowel syndrome and fibromyalgia.
4. *Luvox.* In the United States, Luvox has been mostly used for obsessive-compulsive disorder, but can also be used for the other serotonin deficiency conditions. It may have more drug interactions than the others.

NON-SSRI ANTIDEPRESSANTS

1. *Effexor.* This is an interesting medication that can boost serotonin levels at low doses, noradrenergic levels at medium doses and dopamine levels at high doses. This makes Effexor a good choice in the treatment of attention

deficit disorder, muscle conditions and lethargic patients. It has a far lower incidence of sexual dysfunction than the SSRIs. Some people experience sleep disturbance on Effexor. When you want to discontinue this medication, you must be weaned off gradually to avoid side effects.

2. *Serzone.* This medication boosts serotonin in a more natural way. Serzone has no dopamine effect and tends to be calming. It is a good choice when some anxiety is present, and may work more quickly than others. This has been one of the few drugs that have been shown to normalize sleep. Serzone has no effect on sex drive or weight gain. Like Effexor, this medication has to be started at low doses and increased slowly over a period of three to four weeks to allow the body to adapt.

3. *Remeron.* This is one of the newest and most complete medications for depression. It stimulates the release of serotonin and norepinephrine. Sedation and weight gain are the main side effects.

4. *Wellbutrin.* This medication works by boosting dopamine levels, and is useful for attention deficit disorder or addiction problems. Wellbutrin has been recently marketed for smoking cessation under the name Zyban. Like Serzone, this medication has no effect on sex drive or weight gain. It can cause sleep disturbance in some people.

5. *Ritalin.* This medication is well known for its use in attention deficit disorder. It works by substituting for dopamine. Ritalin and similar drugs work very quickly and are considered mood altering. They also have a high habituation potential. This drug should be used only in special situations because so many other medications are safer and, in most cases, more effective.

Your physician will let you know if you should avoid any other medications when taking a serotonin booster. Alcohol should always be avoided by anyone taking these or similar medications. If an antidepressant medication works for you, it is best to stay on it for a period of 9 to 12 months to achieve maximum benefit.[7]

Depression is inseparably a condition that affects body, soul and spirit.

HELP FROM A COMBINED APPROACH

The temptation among many people is to believe that depression is purely a physical disorder requiring medical attention. That would be incomplete. Depression is inseparably a condition that affects body, soul and spirit combined. If all three components were implicated in the initiation of depression, then all three areas would be avenues of intervention as well. Physical assessment or a medical exam is often warranted when depression is moderate or severe.

Marcia struggled with extreme tiredness and felt incapable of doing even routine things around the house. She couldn't eat and wasn't sleeping more than a few hours a night. Later, she wrote this letter describing her condition:

> When I am in my depression, I feel like there is no hope. I see no way out. I sit in my chair or on the couch and I can't do much of anything. When I am depressed everything seems so overwhelming. It is even hard for me to eat. My mind and body are weak. I feel this is the way it's going to be forever. I want to wake up in the morning for once and not dread the day, knowing it will be filled with fear and hopelessness. No, I want to wake up and feel joy.
>
> The only thing I could do is to cry out to God. In those times when things felt the darkest, that's when God would speak to me. He always seemed to bring scripture to me.

Marcia discovered through Christian counseling that truth could indeed set her free, but she was also helped by seeing a doctor who examined her physically. An antidepressant medication was prescribed to help her concentrate better, thus enabling her to mentally process issues in her life that needed to be resolved.

Some people mistakenly think that science has found a way to measure brain chemistry with great precision, and can then prescribe the exact medication that will cure all types of depression. That is not the case, and the vast majority of psychiatrists and doctors who can legally prescribe medications have no readily available means of measuring brain chemistry. The general procedure is to get a good reading of the symptoms, and then prescribe a drug that has proven to be helpful for others who had similar symptoms. A *Time* magazine article commented on the present level of understanding about serotonin:

> Despite years of study and impressive breakthroughs, researchers are only beginning to understand the chemical's complex role in the functioning of the body and brain—and how doctors can make adjustments when serotonin levels go out of balance. So far, the tools used to manipulate serotonin in the human brain are more like pharmacological machetes than they are like scalpels—crudely effective but capable of doing plenty of collateral damage. Says Barry Jacobs, a neuroscientist at Princeton University: "We just don't know enough about how the brain works."[8]

Even though doctors readily admit to a low degree of precision, medication is still accepted as a primary way of treating depression. Prozac has been prescribed for more than 17 million Americans, and 580,000 children are currently on the drug—which now comes in peppermint flavor.

ELECTROCONVULSIVE THERAPY (ECT)

Electroconvulsive therapy, or shock treatment as it is commonly called, is used to treat severe cases of endogenous depression that are not responsive to medication. It is one of the most misunderstood of medical treatments for mental illness. Primarily because of perceived abuses in the past, it is widely distrusted by the public.

ECT administers a small electrical shock to the brain to induce a convulsion. Muscle relaxants and a short anesthetic are administered so the seizures are not felt by the patients. They usually experience mild amnesia, but very little pain. The one occasional side effect is short-term memory loss. Nobody knows why, but ECT seems to stimulate the production of neurotransmitters. In some cases, it is more effective than antidepressants, works much faster and has fewer side effects. Still, most psychiatrists see ECT as very useful, but a much later treatment option.

TOWARD A COMPLETE SOLUTION

If you have read only this far, you could easily conclude that depression can be cured simply by taking the right medications. That kind of thinking would be unfortunate, and very inaccurate. We have helped many resolve their conflicts and find their freedom in Christ without medication, but we have seen few if any find total resolution of personal and interpersonal conflicts by using medications only.

Only truth can set us free. Medications cannot change your circumstances, or cause you to resolve personal and spiritual conflicts, but they can fix the computer so the proper program can run. Similarly, it is hard to pray and read our Bibles when we have the flu.

Dr. David Antonuccio, a psychologist, and his colleagues at the University of Nevada School of Medicine in Reno found in their research that "despite the conventional wisdom, the data suggest that there is no stronger medicine than psychotherapy in the treatment of depression, even if severe."[9]

Consumer Reports recently reached similar conclusions. After 4,000 of its subscribers responded to the largest-ever survey on the use of therapy and/or drugs to treat depression, researchers at the Consumers Union determined that "psychotherapy alone worked as well as psychotherapy combined with medication, like Prozac and Xanax. Most people who took the drugs did feel they were helpful, but many reported side effects."[10]

Of course, conclusions drawn from surveys filled out by the general population can easily be skewed. Take, for example, the critical question of *causation*. Which came first in the cases reported—external negative circumstances, poor mental evaluation of life, lack of faith in God or chemical imbalance?

A depressed mood will likely *accompany* biochemistry changes in the body, but to say that changed biochemistry *caused* depression is as incomplete as saying a dead battery caused the car not to start. We would have to ask, What caused the battery to fail? Are there other possible reasons the car wouldn't start? Was it out of gas? A faulty alternator or a broken belt? Were the lights left on? Is the battery old and worn out? You can jump-start the car by using booster cables, which would work if you had just left the lights on. A good mechanic would consider many possible causes to ensure that the car would continue to run.

The fact that antidepressant medications help depressed people feel better is not even arguable. They do. On the other hand, taking medications every time you have a symptom of depression is like getting a jump start every time your car won't start. The car is designed to function as a whole unit; and so are we. After having been on an antidepressant medication for almost three weeks, one woman declared, "I didn't know the promises in the Bible were true for me until now." That is, a proper use of medication enabled her to assume a responsible course of action. Martin Seligman, a noted researcher on depression, reflected on its causes:

> I have spent the last twenty years trying to learn what causes depression. Here is what I think. Bipolar depression (manic-depression) is an illness of the body, biological in

origin and containable by drugs. Some unipolar depressions, too, are partly biological, particularly the fiercest ones. Some unipolar depression is inherited. If one of two identical twins is depressed, the other is somewhat more likely to be depressed than if they'd been fraternal twins. This kind of unipolar depression can often be contained with drugs, although not nearly as successfully as bipolar depression can be, and its symptoms can often be relieved by Electroconvulsive therapy.

But inherited unipolar depressions are in the minority. This raises the question of where the great number of depressions making up the epidemic in this country come from. I ask myself if human beings have undergone physical changes over the century that have made them more vulnerable to depression. Probably not. It is very doubtful that our brain chemistry or our genes have changed radically over the last two generations. So a tenfold increase in depression is not likely to be explained on biological grounds.

I suspect that the epidemic depression so familiar to all of us is best viewed as psychological. My guess is that most depression starts with problems in living and with specific ways of thinking about these problems.[11]

We generally agree with Seligman, but we disagree that all severe unipolar and bipolar depressions are only illnesses of the body. It certainly can be the primary problem, and physical and chemical imbalances should definitely be considered in severe cases. But we have found that many severe depressions have a definite spiritual component that is totally overlooked in the secular world, and often in our churches. We will discuss that possibility in following chapters, but to illustrate this point listen to the following testimony:

I am writing in regards to your seminar in Minnesota. The day it was to start, I was to be admitted to a hospital for the fifth time for manic depression. I have been dealing with this for almost two years. We had gone to several doctors and tried about every drug they could think of. I also had shock treatments. I attempted suicide twice. Unable to work any longer, I spent most of my days downstairs wishing I were dead or planning my next attempt. Also, it was a good place to protect myself from people and the world around me. I had a history of self-abuse. I have spent 30 odd years in jail or prisons. I was a drug addict and an alcoholic. I have been in drug and alcohol treatment 28 times.

I became a Christian several years ago but always lived a defeated life. Now I was going back to the hospital to try new medications or more shock treatments. My wife and friends convinced me your seminar would be of more value. The hospital was concerned because they believed I needed medical help. As the four days of the conference progressed my head started to clear up! The word of God was ministering to me, even though I was confused and in pain. I told one of your staff that I was in my 11th hour. He set up an appointment for me.

The session lasted seven hours. They didn't leave one stone uncovered. The session was going great until I came to bitterness and unforgiveness. The three things that motivated my life were low self-esteem, anger, and bitterness which were the result of being molested by a priest and suffering from many years of physical and verbal abuse in my childhood. I can honestly say I forgave them and God moved right in, lifting my depression. My eyes were now open to God's truth. I felt lighter than ever before.

I did go to the hospital, but after two days they said I didn't need to be there. My doctors said I was a different person. They had never seen a person change so fast. They said, "Whatever you are doing, don't stop." I have been growing in the Lord daily. There is so much before Christ and after Christ that I could go on forever.

Secular counselors seldom if ever see that kind of resolution. Too many people continue in their depression because professionals they have consulted have considered only one possible cause and therefore only one possible cure.

ONE-SIDED PERSPECTIVES

One Christian said, "My problem is neurological and my psychiatrist says I shouldn't let anyone tell me differently." She did admit that she hasn't yet found the right combination of drugs, but she had all the hope in the world that they eventually would.

In the same church, another Christian said, "Taking drugs shows only a lack of faith." Of course he had never experienced depression!

How could two people in the same church draw such diverse opinions? We have observed the following four perspectives in our churches that do not reflect a balanced Christian approach to helping those who are depressed:

1. "Taking medications is not trusting God."
2. "Depression is a physical illness that can only be resolved simply by taking medications."
3. "Depression is a spiritual attack and deliverance from demons is the only answer."
4. "Depression is the guilt we feel which is the result of unconfessed sin."

Such views are incomplete, inadequate and therefore less than helpful for those who suffer from depression. We believe that God relates to us as whole people (body, soul and spirit), people who live in a physical as well as a spiritual world.

FOCUSING ON THE "SOFTWARE"

We close this chapter by looking again at our computer analogy. If our brain represents the hardware, then our mind represents the software. The tendency of our Western world is to assume that mental or emotional problems are primarily caused by faulty hardware. There is no question that organic brain syndrome, Alzheimer's disease or lesser organic problems such as chemical and/or hormonal imbalances can impede our ability to function. The best program won't work if the computer is turned off or in disrepair.

It would be a tragedy for a godly pastor or Christ-centered counselor to try helping a person who is physically sick without suggesting some medical attention. On the other hand, for a doctor to think that he or she can cure the whole person with medication is equally tragic. Taking a pill to cure the body is commendable, but taking a pill to cure the soul is deplorable. Fortunately, most doctors know that the medical model can take you only so far. Many in the medical profession acknowledge that a majority of their patients are suffering for emotional and spiritual reasons.

Our perspective, however, is that in dealing with mental or emotional disorders the hardware is not the primary problem. We believe it is the software—the mental, emotional and spiritual components of the whole person.

Other than submitting our bodies to God as a living sacrifice and taking care of ourselves physically, we can't do a whole lot to change the hardware; but we can totally change the software. How we think and what we choose to believe can actually change our biochemistry. In the next chapter, we will explore how this software, the mind, functions in relation to the rest of the body and the external world in which we live.

Notes

1. David Burns, M.D., *The Feeling Good Handbook* (New York: Plime, 1989), p. 59.
2. Demitri and Janice Papolos, *Overcoming Depression* (New York: Harper Perennial, 1992), p. 7.
3. Kay Redfield Jamison, *Touched with Fire* (New York: Free Press Paperbacks,

division of Simon and Schuster, Inc., 1993).

4. Jamison, *An Unquiet Mind* (New York: Vintage Books, 1995).

5. Leo Tolstoy, *Confessions* (New York: W. W. Norton, 1983), pp. 28, 29.

6. Michael Lemonick, "The Mood Molecule," *Time*, no. 29 (September 1997): 75.

7. Medical information compiled in conjunction with Lyle Torguson, M.D., and Steven King, M.D.

8. *Time*, loc. cit., p. 76.

9. Mitch and Susan Golant, *What to Do When Someone You Love Is Depressed* (New York: Villard Books, 1996), p. 10.

10. Ibid., p. 11.

11. Martin Seligman, *Learned Optimism* (New York: Pocket Books, 1990), pp. 65, 66.

THE AGONY OF
THE SOUL

And by a strange alchemy of brain
His pleasure always turn'd to pain
His naiveté to wild desire
His wit to love—His wine to fire
And so, being young and dipt in folly
I fell in love with melancholy.

EDGAR ALLAN POE

Have your heart right with Christ, and He will visit you
often, and so turn weekdays into Sundays, meals into
sacraments, homes into temples, and earth into heaven.

CHARLES HADDON SPURGEON

For as he thinks within himself, so he is.

PROVERBS 23:7

Jim walked into my office physically shaking and totally defeated. For the past six months, he had been hospitalized in a Veterans Administration (VA) hospital for severe depression. He was nearing retirement from a good civil service job, and the government was generously holding his position open for his return. The grace period was soon coming to an end, however, and the knowledge of that only contributed to his depression.

Jim would have good retirement benefits if he completed his career in the next two years, and his present financial status was well above average. Six months earlier he had made a substantial financial investment in a housing project that went broke. At the time, he wasn't sure if he would lose some or all of his investment, but there was little doubt in his own mind that hearing the bad news is what precipitated his depression.

I asked Jim if he could recall any dominant thoughts that entered his mind at that time. He said, "I was sitting alone in my study considering what to do when the thought came to me, *You're going down.*" And he believed it—even though it was untrue. As we mentioned, his financial picture was far better than most.

I asked him if he would like to resolve these issues, and he agreed to go through the Steps to Freedom in Christ[1] (see appendix A). We dealt with many issues and renounced the lie that he was "going down." Three hours later Jim was sitting calmly before me with peace of mind and a sense of hope for the first time in months.

How does one explain such an abrupt change? And can it last? To answer such questions, we need to explain further how our body (material or outer self), soul and spirit (immaterial or inner self) function in relationship with the external world and our Creator.

In the preceding chapter, we pointed out the correlation between the brain and the mind. The brain records input from the external world through our five senses. It enables us to taste, smell, see, hear and feel. Every external input is recorded in the brain and processed by the mind. The mind is the compiler, interpreter and programmer in our computer analogy (i.e., the software). One cannot operate without the other.

HOW OUR COMPUTER GOT PROGRAMMED

Before we came to Christ, we were spiritually dead in our trespasses and sins (see Eph. 2:1). In other words, we were born physically alive, but were spiritually dead. We had neither the presence of God in our lives nor the knowledge of His ways. Consequently, we all learned to live our lives independent of God. From our earliest days, our minds were programmed from the external world. That is why the heart of an unregenerate person is deceitful and desperately sick (see Jer. 17:9).

Our worldview and attitudes about life are assimilated from the environment in which we are raised. This occurs first through prevailing experiences in settings such as our home, the neighborhood we played in, the friends we had and the church we attended—or didn't attend. Second, we assimilate attitudes from traumatic experiences such as the death of a family member, our parents' divorce, and emotional, sexual or physical abuse. These lasting impressions are burned into our minds over time through repetition, or by the intensity of powerful experiences, both good and bad.

We also live our lives according to what we have chosen to believe about ourselves and the world around us. We aren't always aware that we are continuously gathering information that forms, alters or intensifies our beliefs. Many cruise through life having a carefree attitude, and are unaware of how they are being influenced by the world they live in.

These external sources of information vary greatly from one culture to another. There is no value-neutral culture. All of us have some safe and healthy inputs from our surroundings, but contaminated and unhealthy external stimuli also affect our worldview and our perception of ourselves. Our belief system is always changing as we process positive and negative information and experiences.

Unfortunately, not every piece of information we receive comes clearly marked as productive or unproductive, good or evil, true or false!

THE NECESSITY OF REPROGRAMMING OUR MINDS

Without the gospel, we would all be nothing more than a product of our past. But Ezekiel prophesied that God would put a new heart and a new spirit within us (see Ezek. 36:26). That actually happened when we were born again. We became a new creation in Christ (see 2 Cor. 5:17), and we now have the mind of Christ (see 1 Cor. 2:16) in the very center of our being (inner self).

Then why don't we always think differently and feel better? Because everything that has been previously programmed into our computers from the external world is still there, and subject to recall. Nobody pushed the "clear" button, because there isn't one. Because the computer that is our mind has no delete button, it needs to be reprogrammed. The lies of this world must be replaced by the truth of God's Word. That is why Paul wrote, "And do not be conformed to this world, but be transformed by the renewing of your mind, that you may prove what the will of God is, that which is good and acceptable and perfect" (Rom. 12:2).

Before we came to Christ, we were all conformed to this world—and we will continue to be if we allow ourselves to be influenced by it. In Christ, however, although messages from this world are still being received by our brains and interpreted by our minds, we now have a totally new internal input, "Which is Christ in you, the hope of glory" (Col. 1:27). The Spirit of truth will lead us into all truth, and that truth will set us free (see John 8:32).

THE WHOLE PICTURE

Now let's see how the rest of the outer self correlates with the inner self. The brain and the spinal cord make up the central nervous system, which splits off into a peripheral nervous system, as shown in the following diagram.

The peripheral nervous system has two channels—the *autonomic* and the *somatic* nervous system. The somatic nervous system regulates our muscular and skeletal movements such as speech, gestures, etc.—functions over which we have volitional control. This channel obviously correlates to our will. Except for functions of our autonomic nervous systems, as discussed in the following material, we normally do nothing without first *thinking* it. The thought-response sequence is so rapid that we are hardly aware of the sequence, but it is always there. Of course, involuntary muscular movements can occur when the system breaks down, as is the case with

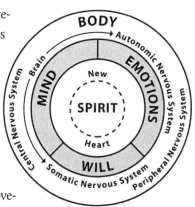

Diagram 3.1

Parkinson's disease (shaking palsy), a progressive degeneration of nerve cells in one part of the brain that controls muscle movements.

The autonomic nervous system regulates our internal organs. We do not have direct volitional control over our glands. We don't consciously say to our hearts, "beat, beat, beat," or to our adrenal glands, "adren, adren, adren," or to our thyroid, "thy, thy, thy." All these organs function automatically.

The autonomic nervous system correlates to our emotions. In a general sense, we don't have direct volitional control over feelings. We cannot will ourselves to feel good or like somebody we hate. We can, however, exert indirect control of our emotions by what we *think* and *believe*.

Just as our glands are regulated by our central nervous system, so our emotions are primarily a product of our thoughts. The circumstances of life do not determine how we feel. Negative external events do not cause depression. Between the external stimulus and the emotional response is the brain (receiver) and the mind (interpreter). So how we feel is primarily determined by *how we interpret life events* (i.e., what we choose to think and believe), and secondarily by *how we choose to behave*. We can become depressed by interpreting circumstances with something less than a biblical worldview, or failing to believe what God has said.

We can become depressed by interpreting circumstances with something less than a biblical worldview, or failing to believe what God has said.

WHEN STRESS BECOMES DISTRESS

Let's apply this to the problem of stress. When external pressures put demands on our physical system, our adrenal glands respond by secreting cortisone-like hormones into our physical bodies. This means that our bodies automatically respond to external pressures—as in the natural "fight" or "flight" responses. If the pressures persist too long, our adrenal glands can't keep up, and stress becomes *dis*tress. The result can be physical illness, or we may become irritated about things that, in less stressful times, wouldn't bother us physically or emotionally.

Why, then, do two people respond differently to the same stressful situation? Some actually seize the opportunity and thrive under the pressure, while others fall apart. What makes the difference? Does one have superior adrenal glands? We don't think so. Although we may differ considerably in our physical conditions, the major difference lies in the "software." It isn't just the superior glands or external factors such as deadlines, schedules, trauma and temptations that determine the degree of stress. The major difference is how we mentally interpret the external world and process the data our brain is receiving.

The mind can choose to respond by trusting God with the assurance of victory, or to see ourselves as the helpless victims of circumstances. The Israelites saw Goliath in reference to themselves, and stressed out. David saw the same giant in reference to God, and triumphed in the same situation that left the others in defeat. Faith in God (i.e., what we believe) greatly affects how we interpret and respond to the pressures of this world.

THE SPIRIT CAN AFFECT THE FLESH

It is critically important to understand that the adrenal glands do not initiate the release of adrenaline. They are the responders, not the initiators. The hormone is released into the bloodstream after the brain has recorded the external inputs and the mind has interpreted them. The brain itself can only function according to how it has been programmed.

God obviously created us with some natural programming for survival, such as the sucking instinct in a newborn baby and other necessary bodily functions that sustain life. This would be similar to how the animal kingdom operates through divine instincts. Applying the same logic, a natural or normal production of neuro-transmitters also allows the brain to function, or else no physical life could be sustained in infancy. In other words, we are preprogrammed from birth to physically exist. There is a natural will to live, to seek food, clothing, shelter and safety.

Could the programming of our minds, or how we choose to think, affect how the brain operates? If the secretion of adrenaline from our adrenal glands is triggered by how we think or perceive reality, could serotonin or other neurotransmitters be affected by how we think and what we choose to believe?

Does the presence of the "Wonderful Counselor" transform the outer self or the inner self? In other words, what physically changed in our lives at the moment we were born again? Nothing changed that was observable to the naked eye. In a similar fashion, we might ask what physical changes you observed in your computer when you slipped in a new program. Even though the same number of hardware components existed in the computer, the screen began to show a different output. The electronic flow through the computer changed.

Would we begin to live differently if a new program were loaded into the "computer" that is our brain? We should have the potential to do so because our eyes have been opened to the truth, and the power of the Holy Spirit enables us to live by faith. The flow of neurotransmitters would certainly change, even though the number of brain cells would remain the same.

The presence of God in our lives will slowly affect even our physical being. According to the words of Paul, "He who raised Christ Jesus from the dead will also give life to your mortal bodies through His Spirit who indwells you" (Rom. 8:11). This is evident when we walk by the Spirit because "the fruit of the Spirit is love [the character of God], joy [the antithesis of depression], peace [the antithesis of anxiety], patience [the antithesis of anger], kindness, goodness, faithfulness, gentleness, self-control" (Gal. 5:22,23). The connection between the initiating cause, which is the Spirit of truth working in our lives, and the end result, which is self-control, is the *mind*. The mind directs the brain, which in turn regulates all our glands and muscular movements.

God never bypasses the mind. He makes possible the renewing of our minds by His very presence in our lives.

BIBLICAL FAITH LEADS TO WHOLENESS

Jesus asked the blind men, "'Do you believe that I am able to do this [to heal them]?' They said to Him, 'Yes, Lord.' Then He touched their eyes, saying, 'Be it done to you according to your faith'" (Matt. 9:28,29). The external power of Jesus was made effective by the blind men's choice to believe. In other words, the Lord chose to bring about a physical healing through the channel of their belief.

Is this not true in every other way God works in our lives? We are saved by faith (see Eph. 2:8), sanctified by faith (see Gal. 3:3-5) and we walk or live by faith (see 2 Cor. 5:7). God never bypasses the mind. He makes possible the renewing of our minds by His very presence in our lives. We respond in faith by choosing to believe the truth, live by the power of the Holy Spirit and not carry out the desires of the flesh (see Gal. 5:16).

Jesus is "the way [how we ought to live], and the truth [what we ought to believe], and the life [our spiritual union with God]" (John 14:6). Even the operation of spiritual gifts incorporates the use of our minds. Paul concludes, "I shall pray with the spirit and I shall pray with the mind also; I shall sing with the spirit and I shall sing with the mind also" (1 Cor. 14:15).

TRUTH AND THE BIOLOGICAL SYSTEM

If truth sets us free and faith transforms our lives, how is our neurological system affected? Scientific studies shed light on the relationship between "learned helplessness" and neurochemical changes in the body. In one experiment, rats were "taught" helplessness by the use of shock. Scientists were able to measure neurological changes indicating depression at various beta receptor sites. The researchers commented on these secular studies as follows:

Dr. Henn and his colleagues induced depression in another group of rats, but treated them without medication. They made a behavioral intervention and "taught" the rats how to escape the shock. Actually, a medical student working in the lab knit the rats little sweaters with long sleeves over their front paws. Strings were attached to the sleeves and the researchers could pull the rats' paws up, marionette-like, and train them to push the lever that would stop the shock. With the rats no longer helpless, their symptoms of depression abated, and the beta receptor sites returned to their previous state. Dr. Henn and others have concluded from these studies that, just as neurochemistry affects behavior, changes in behavior affect neurochemistry.

Complementary findings have been found in the treatment of human depression. A brief psychotherapeutic treatment called cognitive therapy focuses on the thought processes of a depressed person, in particular the hopeless and helpless thinking, and by changing the negative thought patterns, has proved to be as effective as the antidepressant imipramine in treating the depression.[2]

Research strongly suggests a link between brain chemistry and hope. Your body is affected when you think you are helpless, hopeless and out of control. Symptoms of depression such as sadness, despair, lethargy, loss of appetite and sleep problems increase. Once hope is restored, depression leaves.

This has tremendous implications both for those who are struggling with depression and those who are ministering to them. God established faith as the means by which we relate to Him and live our lives. Because *He* doesn't bypass our minds, then neither should we as we try to help others live whole and productive lives. If the way we perceive reality and choose to believe has an effect on our physiology and biochemistry, then treatment for depression should not be limited to medications.

THEN WHAT ABOUT MEDICATIONS?

If God works through our faith, should a Christian ever take medications for emotional problems? Perhaps an analogy will help sort out an answer to that question. Suppose you are suffering regularly from acid indigestion because of your eating habits. Should you take medication to relieve the heartburn? I'm sure most people would, and there is nothing wrong with getting temporary relief; but the long-term answer is to change your eating habits. Your body is telling you something: "Stop feeding me this junk." You are (physically) what you eat, drink and breathe. There is also the possibility that you have a serious stomach illness such as an ulcer or cancer, or you could have a heart problem.

Taking medication to relieve pain is advisable, but the wise person will seek to know the original cause of the condition. In the vast majority of cases, a change in lifestyle will be necessary if you want to live a healthy life. Good health is a product of a balanced routine of rest, exercise and diet.

No matter how well you learn to take care of your physical body, it is still destined to deteriorate over the course of your natural life. But our hope doesn't lie in the preservation of our mortal bodies. Our hope lies in proven character (see Rom. 5:4), and the final resurrection when we will receive resurrected, immortal bodies. "Therefore we do not lose heart, but though our outer man is decaying, yet our inner man is being renewed day by day" (2 Cor. 4:16).

If negative thinking has affected a depressed person's neurochemistry, then taking antidepressants may be advisable to alleviate the depressed mood; but it is not the long-term solution in the vast majority of cases. The danger is to establish one's hope in medication for the cure of depression instead of establishing our hope in God and learning to live a balanced life according to what He says is true. However, we must also be open to the possibility that there really could be an organic brain problem such as encephalitis, some other viral infection or chemical imbalance that comes from a decaying body living in a fallen world.

There is also the possibility that some will have to live with the physical consequences of being depressed for long periods of time. Long-term depression may do lasting damage to their neurological systems. Certain medications may be necessary for the rest of their lives. That would be similar to the alcoholic who has done irreparable damage to his liver. The Lord may heal such a person in response to prayer, but Scripture gives no absolute assurance of that happening. There would be little incentive for us not to sin or believe incorrectly if all consequences were removed.

In the Western world, we have been programmed by our culture to search for every natural explanation first, and if none is found, then "there is nothing left to do but pray." But the Bible doesn't quite put it like that. In the context of explaining how faith in God is the answer for anxiety, Jesus concluded, "But seek first His kingdom and His righteousness; and all these things shall be added to you. Therefore do not be anxious for tomorrow; for tomorrow will care for itself" (Matt. 6:33,34). When we struggle with emotional problems, go to God *first*, as He instructed us to do!

COGNITIVE THERAPY

Recall from the last chapter that physical pain is necessary for our self-preservation. In a similar fashion, the presence of emotional pain stimulates the process of renewing our minds and the development of our character. Let's look at what the Bible calls the "inner man" to gain a better understanding of how our thinking affects our emotions.

We mentioned earlier that we have very little direct control of our emotions. But we can have indirect control over them by changing how we think, and we can choose what we believe. Many secular therapists such as Albert Ellis and Aaron Beck have been saying much the same thing for years in their work as "cognitive therapists." They maintain that our emotions are essentially a product of our thoughts. They believe that the primary source of depression is the way people perceive themselves, their circumstances and the future—which is often referred to as "the depression triad." Several Christian counselors, such as William Backus who wrote *Telling Yourself the Truth*, and David Stoop who wrote *Self Talk*, say essentially the same thing.

The basic procedure of cognitive therapy is probably the most accepted approach in Christian counseling at the present time. According to this approach, helping others or yourself to maintain or regain mental health would follow this sequence:

1. People are taught to recognize and monitor their negative thoughts or distortion of reality. Thoughts or beliefs are identified as ineffective or dysfunctional, leading to improper responses to life.
2. Then they are helped to see the connection between these negative thoughts, the emotions they create and the subsequent behavior that follows.
3. Next they must examine the evidence for and against such distorted thinking or perceptions of reality. This is decision time. Are they going to continue thinking what they are thinking, believing what they are believing, and therefore doing what they are doing, or are they going to change?
4. If they have concluded that what they have believed is not true, and their perception of reality wasn't right, then they must substitute old ways of thinking and respond with new ways.
5. Finally they are helped to identify and change the inappropriate assumptions that predisposed them to distort their experiences.

All this is about as close to the concept of Christian repentance as you can get. We would add one crucial element to this list. If you have distorted, false and negative beliefs about God, yourself and the world, you disagree with what God said about Himself, yourself and the world you live in. This "disagreement" is missing the mark—which is sin. "Whatever is not from faith is sin" (Rom. 14:23).

Christians confess sin and repent of it when they become aware of it. Confession is agreeing with God that what they have believed is not true. The word "repentance" in the original Greek language of the New Testament literally means a change of mind. That must happen for all of us if we are going to live a liberated Christian life. Repentance is turning from false beliefs and destructive behaviors. True repentance involves substituting Christian beliefs based on God's Word for the old false beliefs that were based on what the world says is true.

RENEGADE THOUGHTS

Returning to the story of Jim at the beginning of this chapter: He was depressed because he believed a renegade thought—a lie about himself and his financial condition. The thought he entertained in his mind was, *You're going down!* He chose to believe that lie and continued to believe that he was going down even though it wasn't true. Then he started to think he was a failure. Of course, that was another lie. The failed financial investment and the possible loss of money did not cause Jim's depression. His perception of the experience, and the lies he believed about himself, caused the depression.

Renegade thoughts are wandering, fugitive patterns of thinking that are defiant, independent and in opposition to the nature, character and Word of God. To entertain renegade thoughts leads only to confusion, mental anguish and despair.

Perhaps you have renegade thoughts such as, *You're no good; God doesn't love you; You're going to fail; You're a failure; You're stupid* (or ugly, unlovable, arrogant, sinful, going to lose, going down, ad nauseam). If the negative messages we receive from this world aren't enough, add to them the devil's attacks because he relentlessly accuses the brethren day and night (see Rev. 12:10).

As I sat and listened to Jim's story, it didn't make sense to me that he was feeling depressed because of his financial situation. It was far better than mine at the time. I was probably thinking, *Get real! You are far better off than I am, and there is no good reason for you to be depressed.*

Of course, telling people they shouldn't feel a certain way is not only less than helpful, but it is also condemning. It is better and more accurate to suggest that they may not be interpreting the data correctly or seeing the situation from the right perspective. If what people believe does not conform to truth, then what they feel does not conform to reality. The vast majority of people around the world would have far more reason to be depressed about their finances than Jim did. But he couldn't change how he felt until he revised his beliefs. To make things worse, the VA hospital had medicated him to the point of numbness; but they never made the connection between his inaccurate (renegade) thoughts and what he was feeling.

We are continually making evaluations and judgments that affect our actions and our feelings, based on past experiences. We think, *The mail carrier should have been here by now: I'll go and get the mail.* The thought about the mail carrier is a judgment call based on previous behavior and the reliability of the mail carrier.

When such a thought pops into your mind, you make a decision to go get the mail or wait until later. If you believe the mail carrier has not come, you are less likely to go check the mail. If you are anxiously waiting for an important piece of mail, you may get angry if he shows up late. But the fact that he was late didn't make you angry. You became angry because you believed he should have been there sooner, and the plans you made based on his timely arrival were dashed when he came late. You wouldn't have become angry if you had told yourself, "I have no right to expect him to arrive at a time that is convenient for me, therefore I will patiently (a fruit of the Spirit) wait until he comes."

TAKING EVERY THOUGHT CAPTIVE

The most damaging thoughts we entertain are lies about ourselves and God. That is the subject of the next two chapters, but we should note here that the apostle Paul makes a critical connection between thoughts we have toward God and the potential spiritual battle going on for our minds.

> For though we live in the world, we do not wage war as the world does. The weapons we fight with are not the weapons of the world. On the contrary, they have divine power to demolish strongholds. We demolish arguments and every pretension that sets itself up against the knowledge of God, and we take captive every thought to make it obedient to Christ (2 Cor. 10:3-5, *NIV*).

Computer programmers coined the term "GIGO," which means garbage in, garbage out. If we put garbage into our minds we will probably live a life that looks and smells a little bit like garbage. Jesus said, "The good man out of the good treasure of his heart brings forth what is good; and the evil man out of the evil treasure brings forth what is evil; for his mouth speaks from that which fills his heart" (Luke 6:45).

We have to be very careful what we put into our minds; hence the urgency of taking every thought captive and making it obedient to Christ. It doesn't make any difference whether the renegade thought originated from the television set, the radio, a book, a speaker, from your own memory bank or from deceiving spirits. Even if it is an original thought of our own, we must take *every* thought captive to the obedience of Christ.

If what you are thinking is not true according to God's Word, then don't pay attention to it. Instead, do what the apostle Paul says to do:

If we put garbage into our minds we will probably live a life that looks and smells a little bit like garbage.

Finally, brethren, whatever is true, whatever is honorable, whatever is right, whatever is pure, whatever is lovely, whatever is of good repute, if there is any excellence and if anything worthy of praise, let your mind dwell on these things (Phil. 4:8).

You don't get rid of negative thoughts by trying not to think of them. You overcome them by choosing the truth and continuing to choose it until the negative thoughts are drowned out or completely replaced by the truth. If you want to experience the freedom that Christ purchased for you and the peace of mind that passes all understanding, then choose to think only those thoughts that perfectly align with the Word of God.

DETECTING VIRUSES

Computer owners have all been warned about the potential for their computers contracting a "virus." A virus can cause severe damage to existing programs already loaded into the computer. Computer viruses are often not accidental, but intentional. They may come from store-wrapped software that gets contaminated by disgruntled employees. In addition, some devious people have purposefully created programs that are designed to introduce a killer virus into any system that accesses them. Therefore, most computer systems have programs that scan for viruses. Similarly, we need to have the capability to stand against the deceiver.

It is not always easy to detect a virus in our own belief system, because the major strategy of the enemy is deception. Every Christian is subject to tempting, accusing and deceiving thoughts. That is why we are to put on the armor of God. That is why we are to stand against the fiery darts Satan aims at our minds by taking up the shield of faith.

The most devious of Satan's schemes is deception. If you were tempted or accused, you would know it. But when you are deceived you don't know it. That is why Jesus prays for those who would follow Him, "I do not ask Thee to take them out of the world, but to keep them from the evil one....Sanctify them in the truth; Thy word is truth" (John 17:15,17).

From the very beginning Eve was deceived, and she believed a lie. So Paul writes, "But I am afraid, lest as the serpent deceived Eve by his craftiness, your minds should be led astray from the simplicity and purity of devotion to Christ" (2 Cor. 11:3). Commenting about the later days of the church age, Paul also wrote, "But the Spirit explicitly says that in later times some will fall away from the faith, paying attention to deceitful spirits and doctrines of demons" (1 Tim. 4:1).

We have seen evidence of this around the world—people struggle with their thoughts, have difficulty concentrating and even hear "voices." These voices or negative thoughts are usually self-condemning, suicidal, delusional and phobic. They result in feelings of guilt, hopelessness, sadness and deep despair.

These symptoms are what therapists typically associate with severely depressed people, both bipolar and unipolar. Of course, it's depressing to think those kind of thoughts! If a depressed person shared those symptoms with a secular therapist or doctor he would assume that a chemical imbalance is the cause and would likely place the client on some kind of antipsychotic medication and/or antidepressant. The consensus of opinion in the secular world is that severe depression needs to be treated with medication and milder depression requires therapy.

Again, we have to be careful that we don't rule out that possibility all together; but serious questions need to be asked. How can a chemical change a personality? How can our neurotransmitters randomly fire in such a way as to produce a thought that one is opposed to thinking? That is hard to believe. It should be much easier for the Christian to believe that those negative thoughts were patterns of the flesh learned from living in a fallen world, or the fiery darts from Satan that Scripture has clearly warned us about. A therapist with a secular worldview would not even consider such a possibility.

In our experience, the symptoms described reveal a battle for the mind more times than not. Instead of medication, or in addition to medication if they are already under a physician's care, we help these people resolve their personal and spiritual conflicts by submitting to God and resisting the devil (see Jas. 4:7). The intervention we use is the Steps to Freedom in Christ (see appendix A).

The apostle Paul spoke of "the peace of God, which surpasses all comprehension," that is able to "guard your hearts and your minds in Christ Jesus" (Phil. 4:7). Potentially, every born-again Christian should be able to experience that peace. Although most Christians apparently are not experiencing that freedom in Christ, we believe that they could, and that God desires it for all His children.

PROOF THAT IT WORKS

At a "Living Free in Christ" conference conducted by the Freedom in Christ Ministry, Judy King, a Christ-centered therapist, handed out a survey to those who desired a personal counseling session after the conference. The conference covers the material in Neil's first two books, *Victory over the Darkness* and *The Bondage Breaker*, and concludes by taking the group through the "Steps." The intention is to give people every opportunity to resolve their personal and spiritual conflicts. They learn who they are in Christ, what it means to be a child of God, how to relate to one another in love and forgiveness, how to walk by faith; and finally they are taught their position, authority and protection in Christ.

In our experience, 85 percent of those who come to the conference find resolution to their conflicts as a result of going through the "Steps" on their own. Judy gave these questionnaires to those who couldn't get through the process on their own because of a lack of time, or because their problems were too intense to deal with them in a room full of people.

After the conference, they had one counseling session with a layperson using the "Steps," and usually one or more prayer partners were also present. Keep in mind that it didn't matter what their presenting problem was. Some of them could have been depressed, but others may not have been.

Three months later these same people were given the questionnaire again. The group as a whole showed:

48 percent improvement in depression
46 percent improvement in anxiety
70 percent improvement in tormenting thoughts/voices
46 percent improvement in uncontrolled habits
55 percent improvement in inner conflict/distress.

Most of the lay counselors had very little training other than what the conference provided, which makes the results that much more remarkable. We believe that Jesus is the wonderful Counselor, and that only He can grant "repentance leading to the knowledge of the truth" (2 Tim. 2:25). Medication, therapy, diet and exercise can be helpful, but only God can remove the guilt and heal the brokenhearted. These lay-Christian encouragers only facilitated a process that is made possible by the presence of Christ.

It is important to keep in mind that the "Steps" don't set you free. Christ sets you free, through your response to Him in repentance and faith.

This process of helping people to repent and affirm the truth is certainly not new. But it is often overlooked in helping people who are struggling, which is probably why we have an epidemic of the blues upon us.

REPLACING LIES WITH LAUGHTER

You cannot experience the fruit of the Spirit if you are believing a lie, dabbling in the occult, holding on to your bitterness, sinking in pride, living in rebellion or sinning. Depression is riddled with contaminated thinking and erroneous beliefs built upon contradictions and lies. "The Lord detests lying lips, but he delights in men who are truthful" (Prov. 12:22, *NIV*). Those issues must be resolved in order to experience the peace of God that guards your heart and your mind.

To illustrate this, let us close with the following testimony a friend of our ministry shared in a newsletter:

> A year ago, Simon fell captive to severe depression. The doctors did what they could, but without much effect. From time to time I had the opportunity to speak with him about the love of Christ, but he wasn't very responsive. Last fall we began to meet more frequently, but I always came away frustrated. Nothing seemed to change, and our conversations ran in circles around the same morbid themes. However, God used these times to show me that I was relying too much on my own efforts and not nearly enough on His power to effect change. In desperation, I was driven to seek God in a more profound way through prayer. God worked on Simon's distorted view of truth, while He worked to cut through the pride that was in my own heart. Just before Christmas, Simon made a commitment to follow Christ as Lord and Savior. His depression, however, was only mildly improved.
>
> Simon had a history of occult and New Age involvement, and it became evident that there was demonic oppression in his life. For this reason, I lent him *The Bondage Breaker.* At the end of the book the believer is invited to walk through the seven "Steps to Freedom in Christ." I told Simon that I would help him work through these steps when I returned from a trip. During our time away, I called Simon to see how he was doing. The voice that spoke to me was changed. Simon had not waited for me to take him through the seven steps. He had done it himself the previous evening. The old thoughts which had constantly

filled his mind were gone. I heard him laughing for the first time. Praise the Lord.

Notes

1. The "Steps to Freedom in Christ" is a tool developed by Neil Anderson that helps people resolve their personal and spiritual conflicts. This discipleship model for setting people free is explained in his book *Helping Others Find Freedom in Christ* (Ventura, Calif.: Regal Books, 1995).
2. Demitri and Janice Papolos, *Overcoming Depression* (New York: Harper Perennial, 1992), pp. 88, 89.

CHAPTER FOUR

UNDERSTANDING YOUR HEAVENLY FATHER

Dearest,

I feel certain I am going mad again. I feel we can't go through another of those terrible times. And I shan't recover this time. I begin to hear voices, and I can't concentrate. So I am doing what seems the best thing to do. You have given me the greatest possible happiness. You have been in every way all that anyone could be. I don't think two people could have been happier till this terrible disease came. I can't fight any longer.

A FINAL LETTER FROM VIRGINIA WOOLF
TO HER HUSBAND[1]

He brought light out of darkness, not out of lesser light;
He can bring your summer out of winter, though you have no spring; though in the ways of fortune, or understanding, or conscience, you have been benighted until now, wintered and frozen, clouded and eclipsed, damped and benumbed, smothered and stupefied till now, now God comes to you, not as in the dawning of the day, not as in the bud of the spring, but as the sun at noon.

JOHN DONNE

An attractive, talented 18-year-old young lady made an appointment with me to deal with a multitude of problems. She was the daughter of a pastor and had grown up in the Church. She had made a decision for Christ and was committed to follow Him.

Her presenting problem was a serious eating disorder. Reluctantly she revealed her tormented secret life, which was riddled with starvation, manipulation, depression and thoughts of suicide. She was obsessed with her appearance and held a general disdain for herself. Realizing this, I shared with her how Christ saw her. I reminded her that she was a loved, chosen daughter of the King. I told her she was a new creation in Christ and a personal friend of Jesus. Tears streaming down her face, she summarized her basic problem by saying, "I wish I could believe that!"

Believing is not a matter of wishing. It is a matter of knowing and choosing. It is not something you feel like doing; it is something you choose to do based on what you have come to believe is true.

Faith is the operating principle of life. Everybody lives by faith. You drive your car by faith, believing that your car will run, that the road is safe, that the traffic signs are right, that the lights at the intersection are performing up to standard and that other people will basically obey the traffic laws. If you didn't believe that, you would probably never get into a car again, or you would at least have serious apprehensions about it.

You eat by faith, believing that the canned food and packaged meat is safe. By eating the product you are showing great faith in the rancher and food processor. Your confidence is bolstered by the law, which is enforced by the Food and Drug Administration and by your county health department.

THREE PRINCIPLES OF FAITH

FAITH IN WHAT OR WHOM?

The first principle we need to know about faith is that it is dependent upon its object. The primary issue isn't how much you believe;

it is *what* or *whom* you believe in that counts. The only difference between non-Christian faith and Christian faith is the object of our faith. Christian faith is not wishful thinking; it is based on truth revealed to us by God. The person and nature of God and His word is the only valid object of our faith.

The writer of the book of Hebrews lists in chapter 11 several biblical heroes who believed God. They had great faith because they believed in a great God. Then the writer says, "Remember those who led you, who spoke the word of God to you; and considering the result of their conduct, *imitate their faith*" (Heb. 13:7, emphasis added). He didn't say that we should imitate what these heroes *did*, but that we should imitate their faith—because what they believed is what determined their conduct. The next verse reveals the object of their faith. "Jesus Christ is the same yesterday and today, yes and forever" (v. 8).

The fact that God is immutable (i.e., He cannot change) is what makes Him the only reliable object for our faith. Nor can His Word change. "The grass withers, the flower fades, but the word of our God stands forever" (Isa. 40:8). The fact that God and His Word never change is what gives us stability in a changing world. God is always faithful, and His Word is always true. Because God is faithful, we can live with the confidence that His promises are also true: "For as many as may be the promises of God, in Him they are yes" (2 Cor. 1:20). Herein lies the basis for our hope, according to Hebrews 6:16-19:

> For men swear by one greater than themselves, and with them an oath given as confirmation is an end of every dispute. In the same way God, desiring even more to show to the heirs of the promise the unchangeableness of His purpose, interposed with an oath, in order that by two unchangeable things, in which it is impossible for God to lie, we may have strong encouragement, we who have fled for refuge in laying hold of the hope set before us. This

hope we have as an anchor of the soul, a hope both sure and steadfast.

HOW FAITH IS INCREASED

The second principle of faith is that it cannot be "pumped up." Many express the sentiment, "If only I could believe." They *can* believe. Belief is a choice. If I can believe, can't anybody else?

How much faith we have depends on how well we know the object of our faith. If you know seven promises from the Word of God, the best you can have is a seven-promise faith. If you know 7,000 promises from God's Word, you can potentially have a 7,000-promise faith. That is why "faith comes from hearing, and hearing by the word of Christ" (Rom. 10:17).

Any attempt to step out on faith beyond that which you know to be true is presumption, not faith. If your faith is weak, then seek the counsel you need to make sure that what you are believing is indeed true. The consequences of doing otherwise are predictable. "Through presumption comes nothing but strife, but with those who receive counsel is wisdom" (Prov. 13:10). Remember: faith is dependent upon its object, and we are called by God to walk by faith according to what He says is true.

If I wanted to take away your hope, all I would have to do is distort your concept of God and of who you are as His child. Ask Christians who have been depressed for any length of time about their concept of God and what they believe about themselves. You will hear people questioning God or their salvation, or believing things about themselves and God that are not true. Visit a psychiatric ward in a hospital and you will find some of the most religious people you have ever met. But what they believe about themselves and God is totally distorted.

To illustrate this second principle of faith, look at Psalm 13:

How long, O Lord? Will you forget me forever? How long will you hide your face from me? How long must I wrestle with my thoughts and every day have sorrow in my heart? How long will my enemy triumph over me? Look on me and answer, O Lord my God. Give light to my eyes, or I will sleep in death; my enemy will say, "I have overcome him," and my foes will rejoice when I fall. But I trust in your unfailing love; my heart rejoices in your salvation. I will sing to the Lord, for he has been good to me (vv. 1-6, *NIV*).

This psalm portrays King David with many of the classic symptoms of depression, including hopelessness, negative self-talk, thoughts of death and sadness. Even though he believes in God, David is depressed because what he believes about God is not true. How can an omnipresent and omniscient God forget David for even one minute, much less forever?

"Wrestling with my thoughts" is nothing more than talking to himself, which is not the answer. So David asks God to enlighten his eyes, and by the end of the psalm his reason has returned. He remembers that he has trusted in God's unfailing love, then expresses hope that his heart shall again rejoice. Finally he exercises his will by singing to the Lord.

FAITH DETERMINES OUR WALK

If we really believe the truth, it will affect our walk and our talk. This is the third principle of faith. If there were five frogs on a log and three decided to jump off, how many were left on the log? The answer is five—we only said that three *decided* to jump off. They may have come to this decision because they thought it was the right thing to do, but it is only wishful thinking or good intentions until they actually hop off the log.

"But someone may well say, 'You have faith, and I have works; show me your faith without the works, and I will show you my faith by my works'" (Jas. 2:18). James is not contradicting the glorious truth that we are saved by faith and by faith alone. He is saying that the way we live our lives reveals what we believe. People will not always live according to what they profess, but they will always live according to what they believe. The road to hell is paved with good intentions, and the apparent profession of faith by some is just wishful thinking.

Much the same can be said about hope. Hearing somebody say, "Oh, I hope so," probably means, "Wouldn't it be nice if that were really true!" That is not biblical hope. Hope is the present *assurance* of some future good based on the Word of God.

> Now faith is the assurance of things hoped for, the conviction of things not seen. And without faith it is impossible to please Him, for he who comes to God must believe that He is, and that He is a rewarder of those who seek Him (Heb. 11:1,6).

If you want to experience the blessings of God, hop off the log! "If you know these things, you are blessed if you do them" (John 13:17).

In your Bible, the English words "faith," "trust" and "belief" all derive from the same word (*pistis*) in the original Greek language. Believing something is not just giving mental assent or credence to something. Scriptural belief is a demonstrated reliance in the object of faith.

It is also important to understand that believing something does not make it true. Christianity teaches, "The word of God is true, therefore I believe it and I will live accordingly by faith." Believing does not make it true, and not believing doesn't make it false. Truth is truth whether we believe it or not. According to Paul, if we renew our minds according to the truth of God's Word, we prove that the will of God is good, acceptable and perfect, and other people would see it as they observe how we live our lives (see Rom. 12:2).

The present New Age philosophy is distorting this basic premise. New Age teaches, "If you believe hard enough, it will become true." That is false. It would also have us believe that we can create reality with our minds. To do that we would have to be God; and that is exactly what they are saying. That is the same lie the devil tried to get Eve to believe in the Garden of Eden. We are created in God's image, but we are not God. We don't create reality with our mind; we respond to reality by faith according to what God says is true. God has not given us the right to determine what is true or false. He has given us the privilege to respond by faith to what He has said is true.

Suppose you just bought a new computer, but you didn't bother to look at the manufacturer's handbook explaining how it should work. So you attempt to use it the way you think it should work; but it won't work. That computer was designed to work only one way. Any attempt to use it any other way will fail.

Similarly, the wise man said, "There is a way which seems right to a man, but its end is the way of death" (Prov. 14:12). God created us in His image, and told us what the truth is and how we are to live by faith. Jesus said, "I am the way, and the truth, and the life" (John 14:6). Try another way and you will be lost. Believe something other than the truth as revealed by God and you will never become the person God created you to be, nor experience the freedom of forgiveness He purchased for you on the cross. If you try to "get a life," other than the life of Christ, you will remain dead in your trespasses and sins.

Like every other perception of reality, much of what we have come to believe about God was assimilated from the environment in which we were raised. If we were fortunate enough to have been raised in a loving Christian home where the Word of God was honored, then our perceptions of God could be fairly accurate.

DISTORTION AND DAMAGE

While the preceding statement is a general rule, some legalistic churches and homes that know little of the grace of God can give children a very distorted concept of their heavenly Father.

Jim would be an example of that. This 35-year-old man who came for counseling stared quietly at the carpet as he gathered his thoughts. Slowly he began to unravel the twisted story of his life, as one would unravel the intertwined fibers of the carpet on which his gaze was fixed.

Jim was the firstborn son in a family of five children. His mother was a gentle woman, kind and compassionate. She loved all her children. In Jim's mind, she had only one fault. She was too weak and passive to stand up to his father.

Jim's father wasn't physically abusive, but he was critical and judgmental. He complained about Jim's behavior and found fault with his every move. When Jim played basketball, he would only hear of the missed shot, or blundered pass or lack of hustle. If Jim cleaned the garage, his father would point out the poorly aligned garden tools piled in the corner. The focus was always on Jim's shortcomings.

In spite of his fine performances on the basketball court, in his marriage and on the job, Jim always felt inadequate. He thought, *I could have done better and I should have done more.* Feeling like a failure, he longed for attention and the approval of others, but there was never enough to overcome the message he heard again and again as he was growing up. When praise came, Jim had trouble receiving it because he really didn't believe it. His perfect heavenly Father was too much like his perfectionist earthly father. God was a distant Judge who disapproved of Jim because he wasn't perfect. Jim didn't like himself, and he battled periodically with depression.

If what you believe does not conform to truth, then what you feel does not conform to reality.

Jim's concept of God and himself was distorted because of his external circumstances. Just telling people like Jim the truth about God and who they are in Christ is often not enough. Kindly spoken words of truth by a godly pastor or a Christ-centered counselor may not by themselves overcome years of programming by the world. The nature of God will never change, but such people's perception of Him has been changed by being filtered through the grid of living in a fallen world.

Note the following diagram. We have seen good students of the Bible point to the left side of the diagram when asked which side reveals the true nature of God. But when asked how they feel about God in their personal experience, they point to the right side! Somehow, during their experience of growing up they entertained thoughts about God that were not true.

Diagram 4.1

Truth about God is filtered through the grid of:		
Loving and caring Good and merciful Steadfast and reliable Unconditional grace Present and available Giver of good gifts Nurturing and affirming Accepting Just, fair and impartial	1. Ignorance 2. False prophets and teachers 3. Blasphemous thoughts 4. Unhealthy interpersonal relationships during early developmental years 5. Role model of authority figures—especially parents	Hateful and unconcerned Mean and unforgiving Unpredictable and untrustworthy Conditional approval Absent when needed Takes away, "killjoy" Critical and unpleasable Rejecting Unjust, unfair, partial

Remember: *If what you believe does not conform to truth, then what you feel does not conform to reality.* Consequently, there are people sitting in every church in America who intellectually know that God loves them, but they don't feel loved, and they don't feel saved. It would be safe to say that everyone has conjured some thoughts against the knowledge of God. But we have divinely powerful spiritual weapons to tear down those strongholds (see 2 Cor. 10:3-5).

LOVING AND KNOWING GOD

Matthew records the time an unnamed Pharisee asked Jesus the question, "Teacher, which is the great commandment in the Law?"

(Matt. 22:36). Today we are more inclined to ask, "God, what is the secret for living a successful and victorious life?" But for either question, Christ's answer would be the same today as it was then:

> "You shall love the Lord your God with all your heart, and with all your soul, and with all your mind." This is the great and foremost commandment. The second is like it, "You shall love your neighbor as yourself." On these two commandments depend the whole Law and the Prophets" (Matt. 22:37-40).

The whole purpose for having the Bible is to govern our relationship with God and humankind. We are commanded to love God more for our sake than His. He doesn't need our love, but we need to love Him.

The commandment to love God is not a commandment to feel good about Him. How we feel is the product of what we choose to believe. However, a joyful countenance would certainly follow if we really knew Him because to know God is to love Him.

We need to know that God is love, and that He is beautiful beyond comprehension.

We also need to know that God is omnipresent. No matter where we go, God is there.

We need to know that He is omniscient. He knows the thoughts and intentions of our hearts.

We need to know that God is omnipotent. Consequently, we can do all things through Christ who strengthens us (see Phil. 4:13).

God is faithful and true. God is light, and in Him is no darkness at all. He is holy and just.

OVERCOMING BARRIERS TO KNOWING GOD

FROM DISTANCE TO INTIMACY

We can intellectually know all about our heavenly Father and not really know Him at all. In the same way, we can know all about

Abraham Lincoln. He was the sixteenth president of the United States of America. He knew a lot of Scripture, and quoted it frequently. John Wilkes Booth shot President Lincoln in April 1865. We know these and many more facts about Abraham Lincoln; but we have never met him, nor do we know him personally.

Paul knew all about God from an Old Testament perspective. He was taught by the best. He was a Hebrew of Hebrews, a Pharisee who kept the law and was found blameless until Christ struck him down on the Damascus road. Reflecting on his past self-righteousness, Paul wrote:

> But whatever things were gain to me, those things I have counted as loss for the sake of Christ. More than that, I count all things to be loss in view of the surpassing value of knowing Christ Jesus my Lord, for whom I have suffered the loss of all things, and count them but rubbish in order that I may gain Christ (Phil. 3:7,8).

Paul no longer just knew *about* God. Now he *knew* Him. He realized that he was a child of the King, and that he was in a love relationship with his heavenly Father.

FROM REBELLION TO OBEDIENCE

All born-again children of God have established a relationship with their heavenly Father, but many are not living in harmony with Him. Let us explain. When we were born physically, we had a relationship with our earthly fathers. Could we do anything that would change the fact that we were related? What if we ran away? Would we still be related to our fathers? What if they kicked us out of the house? Nothing would change the fact that we are blood related. It is a biological fact.

But could we do some things that would cause us to no longer live in harmony with our earthly fathers? Sure—and we probably discovered almost every way by the time we were five years old.

Although living in harmony with our fathers has nothing to do with our blood relationship, it has everything to do with trusting and obeying.

This was true even of Jesus, "Although He was a Son, He learned obedience from the things which He suffered" (Heb. 5:8). We also learned to trust and obey our earthly fathers, or chances are the relationship we had with them was not very personal, and we really didn't know them very well other than as taskmasters or absentee parents.

Now that we are children of God, is there anything we can do that would change the fact that we are related to our heavenly Father? The answer is the same, and for the same reason. We are blood related.

> You were not redeemed with perishable things like silver or gold from your futile way of life inherited from your fore-fathers, but with precious blood, as of a lamb unblemished and spotless, the blood of Christ. for you have been born again not of seed which is perishable but imperishable, that is, through the living and abiding word of God (1 Pet. 1:18,19,23).

Scripture also says that nothing can separate us from the love of God (see Rom. 8:35), and no one can snatch us out of the Father's hand (see John 10:28). Our eternal life is not dependent on our ability to hold on to Him in our strength; it is primarily dependent upon His ability to hold on to us. The Lord said, "I will never desert you, nor will I ever forsake you" (Heb. 13:5). Not only that, but "You were sealed in Him with the Holy Spirit of promise, who is given as a pledge of our inheritance" (Eph. 1:13,14).

FROM DEFEAT TO VICTORY
Although theologians disagree on the question of eternal security, there is no dispute about the fact that living out of harmony with

God damages the quality of our life in Christ. We can be related to our heavenly Father as His children, but our relationship with Him will not be very personal or intimate if we don't learn to trust and obey Him, and our knowledge of Him will be very shallow. Although our destiny may not be at stake, our daily victory is.

If two people are going to get personal and close, they must resolve any conflicts that are going on between them. You may desire to know your neighbor better, but you won't be able to if you have offended each other. You would have to first forgive and seek forgiveness before you would have any chance of drawing closer.

The same holds true in our relationship with God. You will not be able to relate personally to God and get to know Him better until you get right with Him. Even your ability to read the Bible and understand truth will be hampered until you have resolved personal and spiritual conflicts that affect your relationship with God and people. Remember, the great commandment is to love the Lord your God with your total being, and your neighbor as yourself.

Paul also teaches that these conflicts must be resolved before we can understand God's Word. "I gave you milk to drink, not solid food; for *you were not yet able to receive it*. Indeed, even now you are not yet able, for you are still fleshly. For since there is jealousy and strife among you, are you not fleshly, and are you not walking like mere men?" (1 Cor. 3:2,3, emphasis added). We have observed this happening around the world. Christians try to read their Bibles, but it doesn't make any sense. They try to pray, but it is like talking to the wall. They hear a message at church, but it goes in one ear and out the other.

A missionary was seeing her psychiatrist, psychologist and pastor once a week just to hold her life together. The next step would be hospitalization. I talked with her one Friday afternoon, and two and a half months later, I received this letter.

> I've been wanting to write to you for some time, but I've waited this long to confirm to myself that this is truly "for

reals" (as my four-year-old daughter says). I'd like to share an entry from my journal which I wrote two days after our meeting.

"Since Friday afternoon I have felt like a different person. The fits of rage and anger are gone. My spirit is so calm and full of joy. I wake up singing praise to God in my heart.

"That edge of tension and irritation is gone. I feel so free. The Bible has been really exciting and stimulating and more understandable than ever before. There was nothing 'dramatic' that happened during the session on Friday, yet I know in the deepest part of my being that something has changed. I am no longer bound by accusations, doubts, and thoughts of suicide or murder, or other harm that comes straight from hell into my head. There is a serenity in my mind and spirit, a clarity of consciousness that is profound.

"I've been set free!

"I'm excited and expectant about my future now. I know that I'll be growing spiritually again, and will be developing in other ways as well. I look forward happily to the discovery of the person God has created and redeemed me to be, as well as the transformation of my marriage.

"It is so wonderful to have joy after so long a darkness."

It's been two and a half months since I wrote that, and I'm firmly convinced of the significant benefits of finding freedom in Christ. I've been in therapy for several months, and while I was making progress, there is no comparison with the steps I'm able to make now. My ability to "process" things has increased many-fold. Not only is my spirit more serene, my head is actually clearer! It's easier to make connections and integrate things now. It seems like everything is easier to understand now.

My relationship with God has changed significantly. For eight years I felt that He was distant from me. Shortly before I met you, I was desperately crying out to Him to set me free—to release me from this bondage I was in. I wanted so badly to meet with Him again, to know His presence was with me again. I needed to know Him as friend, as companion, not as the distant authority figure He had become in my mind and experience. Since that day two and a half months ago, I have seen my trust in Him grow; I've seen my ability to be honest with Him increase greatly. I really have been experiencing that spiritual growth I'd anticipated in my journal. It's great!

This good woman had all the symptoms of severe depression and was being treated accordingly. Her thoughts went from scrambled to clear. She could now mentally process issues that she was unable to process before. Her feelings toward God went from the right side of diagram 4.1, showing the false attributes of God, to the left side, which are the true attributes of God.

Her perception of God not only changed, but it was also God Himself who granted the repentance and brought the change. It is not enough to know the Word of God; we need the life of Christ to change. I had the privilege of encouraging her as she worked through the Steps to Freedom in Christ.

The discipleship counseling process that helped resolve this missionary's relationship with God can help you resolve the issues that are critical between yourself and God. Let's examine these issues.

COUNTERFEIT VS. REAL

In making a public profession of faith, early Christians would stand, face the west and say, "I renounce you, Satan, and all your works and all your ways." This was the first step in repentance. The Catholic Church and most other liturgical churches still require that statement to be said at confirmation.

In addition to that generic statement, individual Christians would specifically renounce every counterfeit religious experience they had, every false vow or pledge they had made and every false teacher or doctrine they had believed. We encourage every person we counsel to do this as well.

To renounce means to give up a claim or a right. To renounce means that you are making a definite decision to let go of your past commitments, pledges, vows, pacts and beliefs that are not Christian. "He who conceals his sins does not prosper, but whoever confesses and renounces them finds mercy" (Prov. 28:13, *NIV*).

Some people commit themselves to Christ and choose to believe the Word of God, but they hold on to past commitments and still believe what they always have believed. That would make salvation a process of "addition" instead of transformation. Such people just add something to what they already had.

Every believer must decisively let go of the past, which is the first step in genuine repentance. If we totally embrace the truth, then we are also defining what is not true. Our new life in Christ was made possible because of His crucifixion and resurrection. Our sins are forgiven, but nobody pushed the "clear" button. Now that we have the mind of Christ (see 1 Cor. 2:16), we must renew our minds to the truth of God's Word.

The apostle Paul reveals the close link between renouncing and not losing heart (i.e., not being depressed or discouraged):

> Therefore, since we have this ministry, as we received mercy, we do not lose heart, but we have renounced the things hidden because of shame, not walking in craftiness or adulterating the word of God, but by the manifestation of truth commending ourselves to every man's conscience in the sight of God (2 Cor. 4:1,2).

Paul is contrasting the truth of divine revelation with that of false teachers and prophets. Knowing God's holiness and His call for church purity, Paul exhorts us to renounce every immoral practice, every distortion of truth and any deceitfulness of the heart.

God does not take lightly false guidance and false teachers. In Bible times such teachers were to be stoned to death, and there were serious consequences for those who consulted them. "As for the person who turns to mediums and to spiritists, to play the harlot after them, I will also set My face against that person and will cut him off from among his people" (Lev. 20:6). Similar warnings about false teachers and false prophets are found in the New Testament. That is why it is necessary to renounce any and all involvement with false guidance, false teachers, false prophets and every cult and occult practice. We don't want to be cut off by God; we want to be connected to Him.

DECEPTION VS. TRUTH

The ultimate battle is between the kingdom of light and the kingdom of darkness, between the Christ and the anti-Christ, between good and evil, between the father of lies and the Spirit of truth. Therefore, an important step in being set free from depression is the process of sorting out lies and choosing the truth.

We are admonished to speak the truth in love (see Eph. 4:15,25), and to walk in the light (see 1 John 1:7). Many who struggle with depression believe lies, walk in darkness and avoid intimate contact with others. In order to overcome depression, and live free in Christ, we must choose the truth by winning the battle for our minds. This requires an uncompromising commitment to God's Word, regardless of how one feels.

The first step in recovery is to admit that we have a problem, then find at least one person with whom we can be totally honest. The worst thing we can do is to isolate ourselves and sit alone with our troubled thoughts.

The Greek word for "be anxious" is *merimnao*, which may have been derived from two words—*merizo*, which means "divide," and *nous*, which means "mind." An anxious person is double minded, and James says that a double-minded person is unstable in all his ways (see 1:8). Jesus said, "No one can serve two masters; for either he will hate the one and love the other, or he will hold to one and despise the other....For this reason I say to you, do not be anxious for your life" (Matt. 6:24,25). There can be no mental peace or emotional health if one is double minded.

BITTERNESS VS. FORGIVENESS

We have never met a depressed person who isn't struggling with bitterness. Depressed people carry the emotional scars and bear the pain of wounds others have inflicted upon them. They have never known how to let go of the past and forgive from the heart. Some have chosen not to. They hang on to their anger as a means of protecting themselves from being hurt again—but they are only hurting themselves.

Forgiveness is the key to overcoming bitterness. Forgiveness is to set a captive free, then to discover you were the captive. We cannot be liberated from our past or be emotionally free in the present without forgiving from the heart. The future threat of torture that Christ promised to the unforgiving (see Matt. 18:34) turns out to be a present reality.

But God is not out to get us; He is out to restore us. He knows that if we hang on to our bitterness, we will only hurt ourselves and others (see Heb. 12:15). As Paul said, "Let all bitterness and wrath and anger and clamor and slander be put away from you, along with all malice. And be kind to one another, tender-hearted, forgiving each other, just as God in Christ also has forgiven you" (Eph. 4:31,32).

We forgive others for our sake, and for the sake of our relationship with God. What is to be gained in forgiving others is freedom. We are also warned by Paul that we need to forgive others so that Satan doesn't take advantage of us (see 2 Cor. 2:10,11). This critical issue must be resolved in order to find freedom from depression. Trying to overcome depression while holding on to our bitterness is like expecting physical well-being while simultaneously eating both health foods and poison.

REBELLION VS. SUBMISSION

We live in a rebellious age. Many seem to think it is their right to criticize and sit in judgment of those who are in authority over them. When sown, the seeds of rebellion reap anarchy and spiritual defeat. If you have a rebellion problem, you may have the worst problem in the world. Scripture instructs us to submit to and pray for those who are in authority over us. Honoring your mother and father is the first of the Ten Commandments that is accompanied by a promise (see Eph. 6:1,2). The New Testament clearly calls for submission to authorities:

> Let every person be in subjection to the governing authorities. For there is no authority except from God, and those which exist are established by God. Therefore he who resists authority has opposed the ordinance of God; and they who have opposed will receive condemnation upon themselves. For rulers are not a cause of fear for good behavior, but for evil. Do you want to have no fear of authority? Do what is good, and you will have praise from the same (Rom. 13:1-3).

There are times when we must obey God rather than humans (see Acts 5:29). When a human authority requires you to do something that is forbidden by God, and restricts you from doing what God has called you to do, then you must obey God rather than a human. The same principle applies when people try to exercise control over you when it exceeds the scope of their authority. A policeman can write a ticket for you for breaking the traffic laws, but he cannot tell you what to believe or prevent you from going to church. It is also legitimate and necessary to set up scriptural boundaries to protect yourself from abuse by tyrants. Such occasions, however, are rare.

Living under a repressive political regime, critical boss or abusive parents can be depressing if we let it. But oppressors do not determine who we are unless we let them. It takes a great act of faith to trust God to work through authority figures who are less than perfect, but that is what He is asking us to do. This is critically important for a right relationship with God, and such a relationship is essential for complete recovery from depression.

God created Adam and Eve to live dependent upon Him. All temptation is an attempt to get us to live our lives independent of God.

PRIDE VS. HUMILITY

Depressed people are usually filled with shame and guilt, whether it is real or imagined. Pride often keeps them locked in a pattern of false thinking that robs them of the help they need. *I should be able to work this out myself!* they commonly think. That is tragic thinking because we were never intended to live this life alone. God created Adam and Eve to live dependent upon Him. All temptation is an attempt to get us to live our lives independent of God.

Pride is an independent spirit that wants to exalt self. "God is opposed to the proud, but gives grace to the humble" (Jas. 4:6). Pride says, "I can do this, I can get out of this myself." Oh, no we can't! Such arrogant thinking sets us up for a fall because "Pride goes before destruction, and a haughty spirit before stumbling" (Prov. 16:18). We absolutely need God and we necessarily need each other. Paul says, "We are the true circumcision, who worship in the Spirit of God and glory in Christ Jesus and *put no confidence in the flesh*" (Phil. 3:3, emphasis added).

Shame and self-deprecation are not humility; humility is confidence properly placed. That is why we put no confidence in our flesh; our confidence is in God. Self-sufficiency robs us of our sufficiency in Christ because only in Christ can we do all things through Him who strengthens us (see Phil. 4:13). God intended for His children to live victoriously by having great confidence in Christ, and in His ability to make us able. "Not that we are adequate in ourselves to consider anything as coming from ourselves, but our adequacy is from God, who also made us adequate as servants of a new covenant, not of the letter, but of the Spirit; for the letter kills, but the Spirit gives life" (2 Cor. 3:5,6).

BONDAGE VS. FREEDOM

It has been estimated that 25 percent of those who struggle with severe depression are chemically addicted. This addiction may be to prescription drugs, alcohol or street drugs. Drowning your sorrows in drugs and alcohol only adds to the downward spiral of depression.

On the other hand, the fear of becoming addicted to prescription drugs has kept many from taking antidepressants, which would often help them. That is unfortunate because the possibility of becoming addicted to antidepressants when properly administered is virtually nil.

Others think that taking even legitimate drugs to relieve depression would indicate that they don't want to depend on God. That is a false dichotomy and faulty reasoning. It does not take into account that many of our needs are met in Christ as we live interdependently upon one another. Would you deny yourself food because you don't want to be dependent upon it for daily existence? Are you not trusting God if you take medicine that would heal a sick body?

There is also a strong correlation between depression and sexual bondage. Many women who struggle with depression have been sexually abused, and many depressed men are sexually addicted. Addictive behavior is degrading and spiritually defeating for those who are supposed to be alive in Christ and dead to sin (see Rom. 6:11). The sin-and-confess, sin-and-confess cycle only adds to feelings of defeat and depression.

We believe that Christ is the only answer for those in bondage to sin, and that the truth of God's Word will set them free. If you are struggling with a chemical addiction or sexual bondage, we encourage you to see two of Neil's books, *Freedom from Addiction* and *A Way of Escape*.

Habitual sin will keep us in bondage, which is very depressing to those who want to live free in Christ. Paul wrote,

> The night is almost gone, and the day is at hand. Let us therefore lay aside the deeds of darkness and put on the armor of light. Let us behave properly as in the day, not in carousing and drunkenness, not in sexual promiscuity and sensuality, not in strife and jealousy. But put on the Lord Jesus Christ, and make no provision for the flesh in regard to its lusts (Rom. 13:12-14).

Repentance and faith in God are the only answers for breaking the bondage to the sin that so easily entangles us. You can be free from such bondage because every believer is alive in Christ and dead to sin (see Rom. 6:11).

ACQUIESCENCE VS. RENUNCIATION

The last step in helping others find freedom in Christ is to renounce the sins of *our past* and our ancestors, actively take our place in Christ and resist the devil.

The Ten Commandments reveal that the iniquities of fathers can be visited upon the third and fourth generation. This is evident in our society in the well-known cycles of abuse. Jesus said:

"Woe to you, scribes and Pharisees, hypocrites! For you build the tombs of the prophets and adorn the monuments of the righteous, and say, 'If we had been living in the days of our fathers, we would not have been partners with them in shedding the blood of the prophets.' Consequently you bear witness against yourselves, that you are sons of those who murdered the prophets" (Matt. 23:29-31).

In other words, "Like father, like son." We are not *guilty* of our fathers' sins, but because they sinned we will have to live with the consequences of their sin. And we are doomed to continue to live in the way we were taught by them unless we repent. "A pupil is not above his teacher; but everyone, after he has been fully trained, will be like his teacher" (Luke 6:40). The primary teachers in the first five years of our lives were our parents, and much of our personality and temperament was established in those early and formative years of our lives.

When God's Old Covenant believers repented, they confessed their sins and the sins of their fathers (see Lev. 26:39,40; Neh. 1:5; 9:2; Jer. 14:20; Dan. 9:10,11). We have the same responsibility today, "knowing that you were not redeemed with perishable things like silver or gold from your futile way of life *inherited from your forefathers*, but with precious blood, as of a lamb unblemished and spotless, the blood of Christ" (1 Pet. 1:18,19, emphasis added).

Every born-again Christian is a child of God and a new creation in Christ. Don't let incomplete repentance, a lack of faith in Him and unresolved conflicts keep you from experiencing your freedom in Christ. This lack of connectedness with God often results in depression.

HELP IS AVAILABLE

In Neil's book *Helping Others Find Freedom in Christ*, he describes the discipleship process that has helped thousands resolve their conflicts and find their freedom in Christ. Ultimately, God is our only hope and we must live in harmony with Him if we are going to be free from depression. These issues must be resolved and they can be. You can resolve these personal and spiritual conflicts on your own by going through the Steps to Freedom in Christ in appendix A.

Those who are severely depressed will also need the help and objectivity of a trained encourager. Such was the case of a woman who attended one of Neil's seminars in Europe. She shared the following testimony:

> I was born and raised in a very legalistic and abusive "Christian" home. Church attendance was mandatory, but the physical and emotional abuse I suffered at the hands of my parents distorted my concept of God. In our church was a large sign that said, "God is love." But I had no idea what love was. If what I experienced at home was supposed to be the love of God, then I wanted no part of it. I moved away from my parents to attend college and away from God. I finished my Ph.D. in psychology and worked as a professional counselor for 20 years. During this time I suffered continuously from depression. Finally I realized that I couldn't help myself, much less others, so I went into educational psychology and finally into vocational psychology.
>
> In desperation, I started to attend an international church. A Sunday School class was going through a video series by Neil Anderson. I learned who I was supposed to be in Christ and finally someone explained to me the battle that was going on in my mind. I found out that there were trained encouragers at the church who were taking people through the Steps to Freedom in Christ. I made an appointment with great apprehension and much fear. I didn't know what to expect but I knew I had nothing to lose and possibly much to gain.

It was an amazing encounter with God. I could feel the layers of self-righteousness, pride, rebellion, and sin come off. Every step was meaningful to me, but the biggest release came when I forgave my parents for their abuse and for distorting my concept of God. As soon as I was done, I knew I was free from years of living in bondage to the lies I have believed about God and myself. And I was connected to God in a living and liberating way. His Spirit was now bearing witness with my spirit that I was a child of God. I was set free. I never struggled with depression again.

THE GOD OF ALL COMFORT

GOD IS YOUR PROTECTION

You are my refuge and my shield; I have put my hope in your word (Ps. 119:114, *NIV*).

GOD IS ALWAYS AVAILABLE WHEN YOU NEED HELP

God is our refuge and strength, an ever-present help in trouble (Ps. 46:1, *NIV*).

GOD WILL NOT ABANDON YOU

I will never leave you nor forsake you (Josh. 1:5, *NIV*).

GOD WILL COMFORT YOU IN TIMES OF TROUBLE

Praise be to the God and Father of our Lord Jesus Christ, the Father of compassion and the God of all comfort, who comforts us in all our troubles, so that we can comfort those in any trouble with the comfort we ourselves have received from God (2 Cor. 1:3,4, *NIV*).

GOD HAS A PLAN FOR YOU

"For I know the plans I have for you," declares the Lord, "plans to prosper you and not to harm you, plans to give you hope and a future. Then you will call upon me and come and pray to me, and I will listen to you. You will seek me and find me when you seek me with all your heart" (Jer. 29:11,13, *NIV*).

GOD KNOWS YOU INTIMATELY

For you created my inmost being; you knit me together in my mother's womb. I praise you because I am fearfully and wonderfully made; your works are wonderful, I know that full well (Ps. 139:13,14, *NIV*).

GOD LONGS TO HELP THOSE WHO ARE HURTING

The Lord is close to the brokenhearted and saves those who are crushed in spirit (Ps. 34:18, *NIV*).

Note
1. Bell and McNeillie, eds., *The Diary of Virginia Woolf* (New York: Harcourt, 1984), p. 226.

CHAPTER FIVE

UNDERSTANDING YOURSELF

I am groaning under the miseries of a diseased
nervous System; a System of all others the most essential
to our happiness—or the most productive of our
misery...Lord, what is Man! Today, in the luxuriance of
health, exulting in the enjoyment of existence; In a
few days, perhaps in a few hours, loaded with conscious
painful being, counting the tardy pace of the lingering
moments, by the repercussions of anguish, and refusing
or denied a Comforter. Day follows night, and
night comes after day, only to curse him with life
which gives him no pleasure.

ROBERT BURNS [1]

See how great a love the Father has bestowed upon us,
that we should be called children of God; and such
we are. For this reason the world does not know us, because it
did not know Him. Beloved, now we are children of God,
and it has not appeared as yet what we shall be. We know
that, when He appears, we shall be like Him, because we
shall see Him just as He is. And everyone who has this
hope fixed on Him purifies himself, just as He is pure.

1 JOHN 3:1-3

Mental health is typically defined as being in touch with reality and relatively free from anxiety. Those are acceptable criteria for a secular world, but anyone caught in a spiritual battle will fail the test on both counts.

To illustrate, suppose a client made an appointment with a secular counselor and shared that he or she was hearing voices and seeing things that others weren't. The secular counselor would conclude that the client is out of touch with reality. One person in that counseling session is probably out of touch with reality, but it may not be the client!

One cannot deal with all reality without taking into account the Creator and the god of this world. The Bible presents the unseen spiritual world as more real than the natural world we see. Notice how Paul ties the idea of not losing heart (i.e., not being discouraged or depressed because of external circumstances) with the truth of our eternal nature and the reality of the spiritual world:

> Therefore we do not lose heart. Though outwardly we are wasting away, yet inwardly we are being renewed day by day. For our light and momentary troubles are achieving for us an eternal glory that far outweighs them all. So we fix our eyes not on what is seen, but on what is unseen. For what is seen is temporary, but what is unseen is eternal (2 Cor. 4:16-18, *NIV*).

We have tried to establish that depression is *primarily* a software (mental programming) problem rather than a hardware (brain or neurological) problem. The Christian psychiatrists we have talked to estimate that medication is probably essential in 10 percent of all the cases diagnosed as depression, from mild to severe. Medication is most often prescribed for those who are moderately to severely depressed.

If the problem is primarily due to the software, then how much of the problem is mental and how much is spiritual? Is it best to understand depression as a mental illness, or as a battle for the mind? Can we win the battle by repenting and believing in God, or is there also a need to resist the devil and take every thought captive to the obedience of Christ (see 2 Cor. 10:5)?

THE PRIMARY BATTLEFIELD: THE MIND

The answer is seldom either/or; it is usually both/and. Spiritual problems are also mental problems because the spiritual battle is waged in the mind. To solve the problem of depression, we need a complete answer that takes into account all reality. The least understood and therefore most often neglected piece of the puzzle is the spiritual battle that is going on in the minds of people around the world.

Scripture clearly warns us about the reality of the kingdom of darkness. Paul said, "I am afraid, lest as the serpent deceived Eve by his craftiness, your minds should be led astray from the simplicity and purity of devotion to Christ" (2 Cor. 11:3). He also wrote, "The Spirit explicitly says that in later times some will fall away from the faith, paying attention to deceitful spirits and doctrines [teachings] of demons" (1 Tim. 4:1).

We have counseled hundreds of people who are struggling with their thoughts, who have difficulty concentrating or reading their Bible, and many others who actually hear voices in their heads. In the large majority of cases, these common symptoms are evidence of a spiritual battle for their minds. This spiritual battle requires spiritual protection and weaponry. Again Paul writes:

> Finally, be strong in the Lord and in the strength of His might. Put on the full armor of God, that you may be able to stand firm against the schemes of the devil. For our struggle is not against flesh and blood, but against the rulers, against the powers, against the world forces of this darkness, against

the spiritual forces of wickedness in the heavenly places. Therefore, take up the full armor of God, that you may be able to resist in the evil day, and having done everything, to stand firm. Stand firm therefore, having girded your loins with truth, and having put on the breastplate of righteousness, and having shod your feet with the preparation of the gospel of peace; in addition to all, taking up the shield of faith with which you will be able to extinguish all the flaming missiles of the evil one (Eph. 6:10-16).

THE PRIMARY PROTECTION: ESTABLISHED IN TRUTH

The "heavenly places" (*NIV*, "realms") are a present reality. The phrase does not refer to heaven where God has His throne, nor does it refer to some physical planet such as Pluto or Mars that exists in the natural realm. It refers to the spiritual world or atmosphere in which we live. The god (ruler) of this world, "your enemy the devil prowls around like a roaring lion looking for someone to devour" (1 Pet. 5:8, *NIV*).

John says, "We know that we are of God, and the whole world lies in the power of the evil one" (1 John 5:19). Herein lies the problem and the answer in one verse. People are kept in spiritual bondage because of the lies they believe about God and themselves, and Satan is the father of lies (see John 8:44).

Jesus is the truth (see John 14:17), and the Holy Spirit is the Spirit of truth. He will guide you into all truth (see 16:13), and that truth will set you free (see 8:32). That is possible because we are children of God.

Every defeated Christian we have worked with, regardless of their presenting problem, had one thing in common. None of them knew who they were in Christ, nor understood what it meant to be a child of God. Almost all of them were questioning their salvation. If the Holy Spirit is bearing "witness with our spirit that we are children of God" (Rom. 8:16), then why weren't they sensing it? "Because you are sons, God has sent forth the Spirit of His Son into our hearts, crying, 'Abba! [or] Father!'" (Gal. 4:6). Where is the "Abba! Father!" in the depth of depression? He is there, but depressed people often don't sense His presence because of ignorance or lack of genuine repentance.

THE PRIMARY ISSUE: OUR IDENTITY AND POSITION IN CHRIST

The devil does not want you to know that you are a child of God and seated with Christ in heavenly places (see Eph. 2:6). From that position in Christ, we have authority over the kingdom of darkness. Every believer is alive in Christ and therefore united with Him:

In His death	Romans 6:3; Galatians 2:20; Colossians 3:1-3
In His burial	Romans 6:4
In His resurrection	Romans 6:5,8,11
In His ascension	Ephesians 2:6
In His life	Romans 5:10,11
In His power	Ephesians 1:19,20
In His inheritance	Romans 8:16,17; Eph. 1:11,12

ANXIETY AS A BATTLE FOR THE MIND

The second standard of mental health is to be relatively free from anxiety. Anxiety is fear without an apparent cause. Fear is not the same as anxiety, in that it is actually identified by its object. For instance, we fear other people, death, snakes or enclosed places, etc.

Many people are paralyzed by fears that seem to be irrational to others because they don't see the object of the fear, or they question its validity. When people fear something that others can't hear or see, it is usually called a panic or anxiety attack because they can't identify the object of their fear.

Again, such cases often prove to be a spiritual battle for the mind. These thoughts are very disturbing and very real. Others can't see or hear what suffering persons are going through because the object of their fear can't be seen or heard in a visual or auditory sense. Remember, we wrestle "not against flesh and blood" (Eph. 6:12). In other words, our enemy does not materialize in the physical realm because the battle is spiritual. It is also very, very real.

THE ORIGIN OF YOUR THOUGHTS

It is critical to distinguish between deceiving thoughts from the enemy and thoughts that are truly yours. If you think that tempting or accusing thoughts are your own, then you are going to draw some very bad conclusions about yourself. Understand that God cannot tempt you, but the devil will. "Let no one say when he is tempted, 'I am being tempted by God'; for God cannot be tempted by evil, and He Himself does not tempt anyone" (Jas. 1:13). Jesus will never accuse you, because there is "no condemnation for those who are in Christ Jesus" (Rom. 8:1). But the devil "deceives the whole world" (Rev. 12:9), and accuses the brethren day and night (see v. 10).

A very mature and godly pastor's wife discovered that she had cancer. Her doctors immediately put her on chemotherapy. Then she became very fearful. When I visited with her, she said, "I'm not sure if I am a Christian." I asked her why she would even question her salvation, and she said, "When I go to church I have these blasphemous thoughts go through my mind, and many times I struggle with evil and perverted thoughts."

"That's not you!" I told her, "Scripture teaches that you, 'joyfully concur with the law of God in the inner man'" (Rom. 7:22).

If such thoughts originated from the woman herself, then what would she logically conclude about herself? She reasoned, *If those thoughts were actually coming from my own nature, then I must not be a Christian.* Consequently, she was frightened about the prospect of dying. After all, how can a Christian think those kinds of thoughts?

Any Christian can *choose* to think them, but these thoughts don't originate from who they are in Christ. Because of this woman's maturity, I was able to help her get rid of those thoughts within an hour. She never questioned her salvation again.

FALSE IDENTITY OR TRUE?

Every Christian has tempting thoughts, but many don't understand the battle for their minds. Suppose a young man had a sexually tempting thought about another man. At first he may be a little surprised and would probably just brush it off. He certainly is not going to tell anybody. If the thoughts persist, he may start wondering why he is thinking these thoughts. "If I am thinking these thoughts, then maybe I am homosexual," he may conclude. If so, he just bought a false identity, and it could be years, if ever, before he shares what was going on in his mind. People struggling with depression are plagued with myriad thoughts that are not true.

True mental health is characterized by "the peace of God, which surpasses all comprehension," guarding "your hearts and your minds in Christ Jesus" (Phil. 4:7). It begins with a true knowledge of our heavenly Father and a true knowledge of who we are in Christ. If you knew and believed,

> That your heavenly Father loved you (see Eph. 3:14-19);
> That you now have eternal life in Christ (see John 3:16);
> That you are spiritually alive right now (see 1 John 5:11);
> That He would never leave nor forsake you (see Heb. 13:5);
> That He has completely forgiven you (see Col. 2:13,14);
> That He would supply all your needs (see Phil. 4:19);
> That you were a child of God (see Rom. 8:16);
> That there was no condemnation for those who are in
>   Christ Jesus (see Rom. 8:1);
> That you have an eternal purpose for being here
>   (see Eph. 2:10);

That you can do all things through Christ who strengthens
   you (see Phil. 4:13);

That God has not given you a spirit of fear, but of power
   and love and discipline (see 2 Tim. 1:7);

That the peace of God was guarding your heart and your
   mind in Christ Jesus (see Phil. 4:7);

then you would have the foundational beliefs necessary to establish
mental, emotional and spiritual health.

The most common deception associated with mental and
emotional illness is a distorted belief in God and yourself. If you
don't think that is true, then go to any mental ward in a hospital
and you will find some of the most
religious people you have ever met.
But when you question them about
their beliefs in God or themselves,
you will quickly discover that what
they believe is riddled with distortions and deception.

MENTAL STRONGHOLDS

Believing thoughts and feelings
about yourself that are not true
inevitably establishes mental strongholds over a period of time. We don't
want you to get the impression that
all the lies we have learned to believe
about ourselves and God come
directly from Satan. The world and
the flesh are also enemies of the

*Regardless of its
origin, we are to
take every thought
captive to the
obedience of Christ.
If what you are
thinking isn't true
or edifying, then
don't think it.*

soul. Most false beliefs about ourselves and God come from living
in a fallen world. They are patterns of the flesh that can only be
changed by renewing our minds to the truth of God's Word.

TAKING OUR THOUGHTS CAPTIVE

In one sense, it doesn't make any difference whether the thought you are now thinking came from your memory bank, the television set, another person, Satan or whether you just had a new thought yourself. The answer to what you are to do about it is the same. Regardless of its origin, we are to take *every* "thought captive to the obedience of Christ" (2 Cor. 10:5). If what you are thinking isn't true or edifying, then don't think it.

Telling people just to stop thinking negative thoughts is not a complete answer. You overcome negative thinking by choosing to think and believe the truth, as Paul says in Philippians 4:8: "Finally, brothers, whatever is *true*, whatever is noble, whatever is right, whatever is pure, whatever is lovely, whatever is admirable—if anything is excellent or praiseworthy—*think* about such things" (*NIV*, emphasis added). In other words, *we are not called to dispel the darkness; we are called to turn on the light.*

It is our experience that you can win the battle for your mind if you are free in Christ (i.e., if you have no unresolved conflicts between yourself and Him). But you can't if you have many unresolved personal and spiritual conflicts. Paul drives this point home in 1 Corinthians 3:2,3, when he tells Christians at Corinth that they were not able to receive the truth because there was jealousy and quarrels among them.

That is why, when we work with people, our first step is to help them resolve their conflicts, first through a process of repentance, which includes submitting to God and resisting the devil (see Jas. 4:7). *Establishing* freedom in Christ and *staying* free are two different issues, however. You maintain your freedom as you continue to believe the truth and live by faith. After giving us that list of what to think about in Philippians 4:8, Paul continues in verse 9 *(NIV)*, "Whatever you have learned or received or heard from me, or seen in me—put it into practice. And the God of peace will be with you."

You are not alone in your struggle to manage your thoughts. Every believer has to contend with the world, the flesh and the devil.

LIES WE OFTEN BELIEVE

The following statements are some of the most common lies that depressed people believe about themselves, life in general and their relationship with God:

"I'm worthless and would be better off dead."

"I have no value and no meaningful purpose for being here."

"I'll never amount to anything."

"No one loves or cares for me."

"My situation is hopeless. I see no way out but to die."

"I'm stupid, I'm dumb, I'm ugly."

"I'm a mistake."

"God doesn't love me and He won't help me."

"Life is the pits."

"My future is hopeless."

"Nobody can help me."

The list could continue with many other blasphemous thoughts about God, themselves and others.

To illustrate how destructive thoughts are developed over time, listen to the testimony of Cheryl Dankers, who was voted Mrs. Minnesota-America in 1996. Unlike the picture-perfect life that one might expect from a pageant queen, Cheryl's life was filled with trauma, rejection, depression, suicidal thoughts and years of emotional pain. She wrote the following letter to Hal:

Dear Dr. Baumchen,

It was such a pleasure to meet and work with you at those two benefits. Thank you for letting me share my story with you. I am still in awe of what God has taken me through these last 20 years.

I had a lot of allergy problems which were finally diagnosed when I was in second or third grade. It was very upsetting for my dad because they could no longer have big parties. I was too allergic to cigarette smoke. I remember my dad telling my mom, "Well, if she's so sick, put her in a hospital."

I excelled in school. I thought it was the only thing I could do well. I got nearly straight A's. However, I sank my sadness and social frustrations into bags of cookies, candy, potato chips, and gallons of ice cream and Kool-Aid. The neighborhood kids called me "Schultzie" after the "Hogan's Heroes" character who was overweight.

My parents partied a lot on weekends. There were many Sunday mornings when I woke up because dad was vomiting in the bathroom. My parents would have heated arguments, and many times dad threatened to leave. I remember my sister and I crying on his lap, begging him to stay. Dad lost a number of jobs because he quit or was fired. After he became a policeman in 1969, he started drinking less. However, he was very controlling and verbally abusive.

My parents attended most of my band concerts and were proud of my accomplishments in debate, although I felt they were overprotective. I had several very close friends throughout school, one of whom I am still very close to. Yet, I felt isolated and alone. I would throw parties and almost no one would come.

I went to Bemidji State University in the fall of 1976. During college, I developed a promiscuous lifestyle. Since this was the pre-AIDS era, protection was not always used. By the spring of 1977, I was feeling tremendous guilt and shame. I lost my motivation to work hard in my classes, and I had gone through two different roommates. I developed a friendship with a football player. When I would sit in rooms filled with marijuana smoke, he always defended my right to say no to drugs. So I considered him a friend. One very late night he knocked on my dorm room door. He had an intense look on his face, so I let him in to talk. Before

I knew what was happening, he was on top of me (he probably weighed close to 300 pounds). I kept telling him to stop and saying "NO! NO! NO!" But I was too ashamed to scream "Rape!" because I was afraid no one would believe me or help me. After he left, I took a long shower, trying to wash him off of me. The next day, he was gone. He had returned home.

I planned my suicide. Since I couldn't swim, I decided I should just start walking into Lake Bemidji. Eventually I would drown. I felt like I deserved a violent death. I wrote down the names of people close to me and gave a time frame of how long it would take until they would forget me. I thought I had let everyone down. I felt dirty, alone, ashamed and unworthy of God's love. Then I called out to God. I asked Him to rescue me and do something in my life that would stop me from ending it. Somehow I knew that God was with me, because I never contemplated suicide again.

Cheryl is describing a life filled with rejection, guilt and emotional pain. Those growing-up experiences caused her to think and therefore to feel that she was alone, dirty, ashamed and unworthy of God's love. Those negative beliefs had a very destructive influence in her life.

After college Cheryl was married, and her four and a half years of marriage were filled with threats of violence and emotional and sexual abuse. Then she was divorced, and life began to change for her. She writes:

A couple of weeks later, I signed a purchase agreement for a townhouse with an agent by the name of Mike Dankers. We started dating in July 1983. He said he was a Christian, and we started attending church at Grace Church Roseville with some of Mike's friends. During one of those first services, I invited Christ into my life. This time, I knew it was for real.

My life started changing right away. I was baptized, began teaching Sunday School, and most importantly, saw God's unconditional love for me in a way I had never seen it before. I knew He had always been with me, but now He was allowing me to experience Him. There was no turning back. Everything I had learned over the years made sense to me. God was alive and at work in my life. Mike and I were married in 1985.

In 1994, our church was going through some difficulties. We brought in Neil Anderson's series, "Resolving Personal and Spiritual Conflicts." During those seminars, I realized that I could forgive those who had harmed me.

In May 1995, our church had almost a day-long service in which people came forward to confess sin and recommit their lives to the Lord. God used this time to cleanse and heal so many in our church who had been hurting for many years. God used this opportunity to show me that, while I had been faithful in forgiving others in order to move on with my life, I also could forgive myself. I cried all day long, praising the Lord, and letting my gallons of tears wash away all the guilt, shame and sadness I had felt for so long.

Just over a year later, I was crowned Mrs. Minnesota-America. It was almost unbelievable. I was an overweight child who had hated herself. I had gone through so much trauma in my life that I didn't think I could ever be free. God cleansed all the self-inflicted hatred and made me see how internally beautiful I was in Christ. Then I was able to "clean up" the outside and serve Him faithfully wherever He leads.

Cheryl Dankers
Mrs. Minnesota-America, 1996

Free in Christ! Cheryl is no longer living beneath a load of guilt and shame. Now that her identity in Christ was firmly established, she was able to stand against the accusing and condemning messages from the world, the flesh and the devil. She could see herself the way God sees her—a new creation in Christ.

Nobody can fix your past. Not even God will do that. Nevertheless, the gospel assures us that we can be free from the past because we are not primarily a product of our past. We are primarily a product of Christ's work on the cross and His resurrection. We are no longer in Adam. Our primary identity is no longer in the flesh; it is in Christ. If that were not true, then all Christians would remain helpless victims of their past.

WEEDING OUT FALSE PERCEPTIONS

Realizing who we are in Christ and what it means to be a child of God is the basis for victorious living and an essential basis for overcoming depression. People cannot consistently behave in a way that is inconsistent with how they perceive themselves, nor can their feelings about themselves be any different from their perceptions about themselves.

For example, we will struggle with a poor self-image to the degree that we don't see ourselves the way God sees us. Such negative perceptions of ourselves are based on lies we have believed. They are like weeds in a field of grain. They stunt the growth of the good seed and rob the harvest. "Whatever a man sows, this he will also reap. For the one who sows to his own flesh shall from the flesh reap corruption, but the one who sows to the Spirit shall from the Spirit reap eternal life" (Gal. 6:7,8). If you sow a lie, you will reap corruption (garbage in, garbage out, remember?). You can't plant weeds, hoping to reap a harvest of grain!

TRUTH OR CONSEQUENCES

Holding false perceptions about ourselves has several predictable consequences:

1. False perceptions erode confidence and weaken our resolve. Many depressed people think they are losers, and choose to believe they can't do whatever it takes to overcome their problems. Of course, if they believe that lie, then they won't be able to overcome. Failures fail, losers lose and sinners sin; but children of God live righteous lives and do all things through Christ, who strengthens them.

John writes, "Dear friends, now we are children of God.... Everyone who has this hope in him purifies himself, just as he is pure" (1 John. 3:2,3, *NIV*). It is not what we do that determines who we are; it is who we are that determines what we do. That is why the Holy Spirit "bears witness with our spirit that we are children of God" (Rom. 8:16).

"Yet to all who received Him, to those who believed in his name, he gave the right to become children of God—children born not of natural descent, nor of human decision or a husband's will, but born of God" (John. 1:12,13, *NIV*).

2. False perceptions drive us to seek our own acceptance, security and significance. We try to accomplish this through appearance, performance and status. No matter how hard we try, we will still suffer from morbid introspection, hostile criticism, overt rejection and endless accusations. That is depressing! Acceptance, security and significance are already provided in Christ. Many Christians are endlessly looking for what they already have in Christ. Others are desperately trying to become someone they already are. "Coming to Him as to a living stone, rejected by men, but choice and precious in the sight of God, you also, as living stones, are being built up as a spiritual house for a holy priesthood" (1 Pet. 2:4,5).

3. False perceptions precipitate a fear of failure. To stumble and fall is not failure. To stumble and fall again is not failure. Failure comes when you say you were pushed.

There are no unforgivable failures in the kingdom of God, but there are many who are living far below their potential because they have never learned the truth of who they are in Christ. "There is therefore now no condemnation for those who are in Christ Jesus" (Rom. 8:1).

We probably learn more from our mistakes than we will ever learn from our successes. A mistake is only a failure when you fail to learn from it. "For though a righteous man falls seven times, he rises again" (Prov. 24:16, *NIV*). If you make a mistake, get back up and try again—and again and again.

Depressed people have a tendency to ask, "What do I stand to lose if I do try again?" They should be asking, "What do I stand to lose if I don't?" This is not a question of self-confidence. Our confidence is in God. Paul said that we "worship in the Spirit of God and glory in Christ Jesus and put no confidence in the flesh" (Phil. 3:3).

4. False perceptions cause us to seek the approval and affirmation of others. The need for affirmation and approval is universal. This need is so great that it should draw us to our heavenly Father because we are not going to get the need perfectly met in this world no matter how hard we try.

Jesus lived a perfect life, and everyone rejected Him. But He had the approval of His heavenly Father. Paul asks, "Am I now seeking the favor of men, or of God? Or am I striving to please men? If I were still trying to please men, I would not be a bond-servant of Christ" (Gal. 1:10). You will be a servant of humankind instead of God if you try to win their approval and seek their affirmation.

We don't do that which pleases God with the hope that He may some day accept us. We do those things because we already have His approval and affirmation in Christ. We don't labor in the vineyard with the hope that some day God may love us. We are already loved unconditionally by God because we are His children. That is why we labor in the vineyard.

Scripture warns us not to exalt ourselves (see Luke 14:7-11), and to be aware of those who stroke our egos. "For such people are not serving our Lord Christ, but their own appetites. By smooth talk and flattery they deceive the minds of naive people" (Rom. 16:18, *NIV*). Paul's written exhortation to the Thessalonians and to us is a reminder to be less concerned about the opinions of others and more concerned about what God thinks: "We speak, not as pleasing men but God, who examines our hearts. For we never came with flattering speech, as you know, nor with a pretext for greed—God is witness—nor did we seek glory from men, either from you or from others" (1 Thess. 2:4-6).

5. *False perceptions rob us of the courage to stand up for our convictions and beliefs.* A person who has a low sense of worth thinks, *My opinions don't matter. If I share what I really believe, others will only squash me.* Caving in to the fear of rejection undermines the courage to stand for our convictions.

Relationships become unhealthy when we begin to think, "I can't live without you or your accept-ance or your approval."

Depressed people frequently think of themselves as weak or cowardly. In the book of Daniel, three young men stood against the cultural trends and mandates of the land when they refused to bow down to the golden image of Nebuchadnezzar, king of Babylon. He put himself on a pedestal as tall as a water tower—but Nebuchadnezzar was about to be knocked off.

Courageous acts of independence and the fortitude to hold true to your convictions are only possible with an inner confidence in God. Believers find their strength not in themselves, but in the knowledge of who they are in Christ. "Finally, be strong in the Lord, and in the strength of His might" (Eph. 6:10).

6. *False perceptions lead to codependent relationships.* Every Christian is interdependent in a healthy sense because we absolutely need God and we necessarily need each other. We are under the conviction of God to love one another (i.e., to meet one another's needs). Relationships become unhealthy, however, when we begin to think, *I can't live without you or your acceptance or your approval.*

The letter from Cheryl Dankers revealed that she looked to

men in an unhealthy way to supply unmet dependency needs and her longing for love and approval. *The intense desire to have your emotional needs met from other people can often lead to compromising your own standards and values.*

7. *False perceptions make it difficult to receive ordinary compliments.* Affirmations, praise and compliments do not remove the terrible pain that depressed people feel. Because the pain did not go away with an expression of praise or gratitude, they wrongly conclude that it was not genuine.

Acceptance and affirmation accomplish more when directed toward the person's character, and when they reinforce who he or she really is in Christ. On the other hand, rejection and criticism of any kind contribute to the depressed state of an insecure person because they match existing false perceptions.

FROM THE BEGINNING

Ever since Adam chose to act independently of God, humankind has struggled to find its identity and craved the acceptance and affirmation of others. Because, in our sin, we were all spiritually dead (i.e., separated from God), we learned how to live our lives independently of God. We had neither the presence of God in our lives nor the knowledge of His ways. So we all tried to make a name for ourselves and determine our own purpose for being here.

Such futile pursuits were condemned by the prophets:

Thus says the Lord, "Let not a wise man boast of his wisdom, and let not the mighty man boast of his might, let not a rich man boast of his riches; but let him who boasts boast of this, that he understands and knows Me, that I am the Lord who exercises lovingkindness, justice, and righteousness on earth; for I delight in these things," declares the Lord (Jer. 9:23,24).

We do not come into this world possessing a built-in sense of identity, nor do we inherently feel good about ourselves. Without God's presence in our lives, we try to derive those basic needs from the world.

Most of our attitudes and beliefs about ourselves are assimilated from the environment in which we were raised. Nobody had perfect parents, because all parents make mistakes in raising their children. According to Dr. Gary Collins, children rarely are damaged by the minor errors all parents make, but real feelings of inferiority do come when parents:[2]

1. Criticize, shame, reject and punish repeatedly.
2. Set unrealistic standards and goals.
3. Express the expectation that the child will fail.
4. Punish repeatedly and harshly.
5. Avoid cuddling, hugging or affectionate touching.
6. Imply that children are a nuisance, stupid or incompetent.
7. Overprotect or dominate children so they fail later when forced to be on their own.

INADEQUATE SOLUTIONS

Because parents are imperfect, many people have had such experiences during their childhoods. In helping hundreds find their freedom in Christ, we have made the need to forgive parents from the heart a critical part of the process. When people pray and ask the Lord to reveal to their minds who they need to forgive, Mom and Dad are the first two people mentioned 95 percent of the time. But struggling people deserve to be warned of less adequate approaches.

SECULAR SELF-ESTEEM

I can't think of a topic that produces a bigger and more tangled mess with more inadequate solutions than identity and self-esteem.

Non-Christian counselors and therapists emphasize restoring a healthy self-image, building self-esteem and enhancing self-worth. This sounds good on the surface. Closer examination, however, reveals that the secular mind-set sometimes produces a person who is self-satisfied, self-indulgent sexually and self-reliant apart from God.[3]

Picking ourselves up by our own bootstraps and stroking one another's egos is not going to get it done.

America is besieged by a low sense of self-esteem. Rather than seeking quick-fix solutions from pop psychologists, we ought to encourage people to seek their self-worth through Christ. Imagine the consequences if we could get people to understand that their value is not self-determined, but has already been determined for them by God.[4]

Even among Christians we hear many inadequate solutions for attaining our identity and sense of worth. It has been suggested that a man gets his identity from his work, and a woman from bearing children. Perhaps some see that in Genesis 3, where the Bible says that the woman shall bear her child in pain and the man shall work by the sweat of his brow.

But that is a *fallen* identity. What happens if the man loses his job? Does he lose his identity? What happens if a woman never marries or can't have children? Does she lose her identity? Who we are has already been established by God in creation and redemption. What name could you make for yourself that would be better than calling yourself a child of God? From where does your identity and self-worth come?

SPIRITUAL GIFTS?

Do we get a sense of worth from spiritual gifts? No! Right in the middle of the most definitive teaching about spiritual gifts Paul says:

Those members of the body which we deem less honorable, on these we bestow more abundant honor, and our unseemly members come to have more abundant seemliness, whereas our seemly members have no need of it. But God has so composed the body, giving more abundant honor to that member which lacked (1 Cor. 12:23,24).

TALENTS?

Then do we get our sense of worth from talents? No! God has given some of us one talent, some two, and others five (see Matt. 25:14-30). We might ask, "God, how could you do that? Don't you know, Lord, that only the five-talent person could have any legitimate sense of worth?" That is not true. In fact, super-gifted and talented people often struggle more because they attempt to find their worth in their talents. That can draw attention to themselves when not used to edify the Body, the Church. The attempt can also distract them from developing their character and relationship with God, which is the source of true fulfillment.

INTELLIGENCE?

Surely our sense of worth must come from intelligence. No! "God has chosen the foolish things of the world to shame the wise" (1 Cor. 1:27). God has not distributed intelligence equally any more than He has gifts and talents. He has equally distributed Himself. Only in Christ is there equality:

> You are all sons of God through faith in Christ Jesus. For all of you who were baptized into Christ have clothed yourself with Christ. There is neither Jew nor Greek, there is neither slave nor free man, there is neither male nor female; for you are all one in Christ Jesus. And if you belong to Christ, then you are Abraham's offspring, heirs according to promise (Gal. 3:26-29).

APPEARANCE, PERFORMANCE OR SOCIAL STATUS?

Perhaps the most fickle of all false foundations are appearance, performance and social status. A fallen humanity labors under the following false equations:

Appearance + Admiration = A Whole Person
Performance + Accomplishments = A Whole Person
Social Status + Recognition = A Whole Person

Recognition is not the same as acceptance, and the respect given by others may be more for the position than the person. No matter how hard one tries, someone will come along and look better or outperform us. Talents and appearances will also fade with time. When we strive for the acceptance, recognition or admiration of others, then it is *they* who determine our worth. If they judge us unworthy, are we then worthless?

What a tragedy to put your identity and sense of worth in someone else's hands. Who is qualified to judge your worth? Who has the right to declare you to have value? Will another pot declare a pot seemly or unseemly? Only the Potter has the right to determine who we are. The value He placed on our lives cost Him His only begotten Son. The true equation is: You plus Christ makes you a whole person.

Certainly nothing is wrong in having gifts, talents, intelligence and appearance. They are life endowments given to us by our Creator. We are to be good stewards of such endowments. But if someone endowed us with a new car, we would not find our identity and sense of worth in the car. We hope we would understand that the giver had already found value in us; that is why he gave us the car. And even though no strings were attached to the gift, we would want to use the car in a way that shows appreciation for the gift. To abuse the free gift would be to insult the giver.

THE ONLY ANSWER IS CHRIST

Although Peter is speaking to wives, we believe the following is applicable to all God's children:

Your beauty should not come from outward adornment, such as braided hair and the wearing of gold jewelry and fine clothes. Instead, it should be that of your inner self, the unfading beauty of a gentle and quiet spirit, which is of great worth in God's sight (1 Pet. 3:3,4, *NIV*).

Our identity and sense of worth come from knowing who we are as children of God, then becoming the persons He created us to be. Nobody and nothing on planet Earth can keep you from being that, because it is God's will for your life. "For this is the will of God, your sanctification" (1 Thess. 4:3).

If Christians knew who they were in Christ, and their lives were characterized by love, joy, peace, patience, kindness, goodness, faithfulness, gentleness and self-control, would they feel good about themselves? Of course they would. Who can have that sense of self-worth? Every child of God has exactly the same opportunity, because those traits are the fruit of the Spirit (see Gal. 5:22,23), of which every Christian is a partaker.

Such characteristics cannot come by way of the world, the flesh or the devil. They can only come by abiding in Christ, and walking by faith and in the power of the Holy Spirit according to what God says is true.

Paul says, "My God shall supply all your needs according to His riches in glory in Christ Jesus" (Phil. 4:19). Our material needs are actually minimal. The most critical needs that must be met are the "being" needs; and they are the ones most wonderfully met in Christ.

The greatest need is life itself, and Jesus came that we might have life (i.e., spiritual life). Then there is the need to know who we are; and the Spirit bears witness with our spirit that we are children of God. Finally, we need to feel accepted, secure and significant. Neil wrote a book called *Living Free in Christ* to show how those needs can only be met in Christ. The following is the outline for the book, which not only reveals who we are, but how those needs are met:

IN CHRIST

I Am Accepted

John 1:12	I am God's child.
John 15:15	I am Christ's friend.
Romans 5:1	I have been justified.
1 Corinthians 6:17	I am united with the Lord, and I am one spirit with Him.
1 Corinthians 6:20	I have been bought with a price. I belong to God.
1 Corinthians 12:27	I am a member of Christ's Body.
Ephesians 1:1	I am a saint.
Ephesians 1:5	I have been adopted as God's child.
Ephesians 2:18	I have direct access to God through the Holy Spirit.
Colossians 1:14	I have been redeemed and forgiven of all my sins.
Colossians 2:10	I am complete in Christ.

I Am Secure

Romans 8:1,2	I am free from condemnation.
Romans 8:28	I am assured that all things work together for good.
Romans 8:31-34	I am free from any condemning charges against me.
Romans 8:35-39	I cannot be separated from the love of God.
2 Corinthians 1:21,22	I have been established, anointed and sealed by God.
Colossians 3:3	I am hidden with Christ in God.
Philippians 1:6	I am confident that the good work God has begun in me will be perfected.
Philippians 3:20	I am a citizen of heaven.
2 Timothy 1:7	I have not been given a spirit of fear, but of power, love and a sound mind.
Hebrews 4:16	I can find grace and mercy to help in time of need.
1 John 5:18	I am born of God and the evil one cannot touch me.

I Am Significant

Matthew 5:13,14	I am the salt and light of the earth.
John 15:1,5	I am a branch of the true vine, a channel of His life.
John 15:16	I have been chosen and appointed to bear fruit.
Acts 1:8	I am a personal witness of Christ.
1 Corinthians 3:16	I am God's temple.
2 Corinthians 5:17-21	I am a minister of reconciliation for God.
2 Corinthians 6:1	I am God's coworker (see 1 Corinthians 3:9).
Ephesians 2:6	I am seated with Christ in the heavenly realm.
Ephesians 2:10	I am God's workmanship.
Ephesians 3:12	I may approach God with freedom and confidence.
Philippians 4:13	I can do all things through Christ who strengthens me.

Notes

1. Robert Burns, *The Letters of Robert Burns* (Oxford: Oxford University Press, 1985), vol. 1, 1780-1789 (letter 374, December 3, 1789), 2nd ed., G. Ross Roy, ed., pp. 56-73.
2. Gary Collins, *Christian Counseling: A Comprehensive Guide* (Dallas, Tex.: Word Publishing, 1988), p. 318.
3. Neil T. Anderson and Charles Mylander, *The Christ-Centered Marriage: Discovering and Enjoying Your Freedom in Christ Together* (Ventura, Calif.: Regal Books, 1996), p. 108.
4. George Barna, *The Frog in the Kettle* (Ventura, Calif.: Regal Books, 1990), p. 229.

CHAPTER SIX

OVERCOMING
HOPELESSNESS

Heart! Thou and I are here sad and alone;
I say, why did I laugh? O mortal pain!
O Darkness! Darkness! ever must I moan!
To question Heaven and Hell and Heart in vain.
Why did I laugh? I know this Being's lease,
My fancy to its utmost blisses spreads;
Yet could I on this very midnight cease,
And the world's gaudy ensigns see in shreds;
Verse, Fame, and Beauty are intense indeed,
But Death intenser—Death is Life's high meed.

JOHN KEATS[1]

Why are you downcast, O my soul?
Why so disturbed within me?
Put your hope in God,
for I will yet praise him,
my Savior and my God.

PSALM 42:5,6, NIV

THE LIE OF HOPELESSNESS

Both Keats and the psalmist are not only depressed, but they are also in deep despair. They are overwhelmed by a sense of hopelessness. The hopelessness that accompanies depression was aptly described by one woman who said, "It feels like I am in a well 1,000 feet deep. From the bottom I look up and see a faint light the size of a pinhole. I have no ladder, no rope and no way out."

The hopelessness of depression is based on a lie. With God there is always hope, and it is based on truth. The difficulty is that when we are bound by the chains of hopelessness, this seems too good to be true. Consider the following parable:

A newly adopted child found himself in a big mansion. His new father whispered in his ear, "This is yours, and you have a right to be here. I have made you a joint heir with my only-begotten Son. He paid the price that set you free from your old taskmaster, who was cruel and condemning. I purchased it for you because I love you."

The young boy couldn't help but question this incredible gift. *This seems too good to be true. What did I do to deserve this?* he wondered. *I have been a slave all my life and I have done nothing to earn such a privilege!*

He was deeply grateful, however, and began to explore all the rooms in the mansion. He tried out some of the tools and appliances. Many other adopted people also lived in the mansion, and the boy began to form new relationships with his adopted brothers and sisters.

He especially enjoyed the buffet from which he freely ate. Then it happened! While turning away from the buffet table, he knocked over a stack of glasses and a valuable pitcher crashed to the floor and broke. Suddenly he began to think, *You clumsy, stupid kid! You will never get away with this. What right do you have to be here? You better hide before someone finds out, because they will surely throw you out!*

At first he was caught up with the wonder of living in the mansion with a whole new family and a loving father, but now he was confused. Old tapes laid down in early childhood began to play again in his mind. He was filled with guilt and shame. The self-condemning thoughts continued. *Who do you think you are, some kind of a privileged character? You don't belong here anymore, you belong in the basement! My old taskmaster was right about me—I don't belong here.* So, his mind filled with such thoughts, the boy descended into the basement.

The cellar was dreary, dark and despairing. The only light came from the open door at the top of the long stairs from which he came. He heard his father calling for him, but he was too ashamed to answer.

The boy was surprised to find others in the basement. Upstairs everybody talked to each other and joined in with daily projects that were fun and meaningful. In the basement, however, nobody talked to each other. They were too ashamed. Although no one liked it there, most felt that the basement was where they really belonged, anyway. They didn't see how they could ever walk in the light again. If they did, others would see their imperfections.

Old friends would occasionally come to the door and encourage them to come back upstairs where a place was prepared for them. Some "friends" were worse than others and would scold those in the basement, which only made it worse.

Not everyone stayed in the basement for the same reason. Some, like the boy, thought, *I deserve to be here. I was given a chance, but I blew it.* Others didn't think they could climb the stairs. Even if they mustered up the strength to try, the stairs would probably break under their weight. They always had a reason why they couldn't return to their father upstairs.

Some would muster the courage to go up for a short time, but they didn't stay long enough to resolve their conflicts and learn the truth that would enable them to stay. So they returned to the basement.

Still others were afraid that they would not be accepted. Their old taskmaster wouldn't accept them, so how could they expect this adoptive parent to welcome them back after what they had done?

At first, our newly adopted child groped around in the darkness, trying to find a way to survive. The longer he stayed in the basement, the more the memory of what it was like to live upstairs began to fade, along with his hope of ever returning. Those old tapes from early childhood questioned the love of this new father, and he began to question whether he was ever adopted in the first place.

The noise of people having fun upstairs irritated him. He remembered the light upstairs being warm and inviting, but now, whenever the basement door opened the light seemed penetrating and revealing. He recalled hearing his adopted father saying that most people loved the darkness rather than the light, for their deeds were evil.

The boy made a few half-hearted attempts to return to the light, but eventually he found a dark corner and lay down in it. To survive, he ate grubs and moss off the damp walls.

Then one day a shaft of light penetrated his mind, and reason returned. He began to think, *Why not throw myself on the mercy of this person who calls himself my father? What do I have to lose? Even if he makes me eat the crumbs that fall from the table, it would be better than this.* So he decided to take the risk of climbing those stairs and facing his father with the truth of what he had done.

"Father," he said, "I knocked over some glasses and broke a pitcher." Without saying a word, his father took him by the hand and led him into the dining room. To the boy's utter amazement, his father had prepared a banquet for him!

"Welcome home, Son," his father said. "There is no condemnation for those who are in my family!"

Oh, the deep, deep love of Jesus, and the matchless grace of God! The door is always open for those who are willing to throw themselves upon His mercy. "In love He predestined us to adoption as sons through Jesus Christ to Himself, according to the kind intention of His will, to the praise of the glory of His grace, which He freely bestowed on us in the Beloved" (Eph. 1:4-6). If people could accept our heavenly Father's grace and love, they would never confine themselves in the basement of depression or the grip of hopelessness.

Our heavenly Father doesn't want us to live self-condemned in the basement. He wants us to know that we are seated with Christ in heavenly places as joint heirs with Jesus. "Now if we are children, then we are heirs—heirs of God and co-heirs with Christ, if indeed we share in his sufferings in order that we may also share in his glory" (Rom. 8:17, *NIV*).

ACCEPTING GOD'S GRACE

How does one help a depressed person understand the grace of God? How can *anyone* fully understand the love and grace of God? Everything we have learned in the world has taught us that life is a jungle, and that only those who are mentally, emotionally and physically fit enough will survive. We learn that justice demands that we get what we deserve. It strikes a discordant note when we hear: "But when the kindness of God our Savior and His love for mankind appeared, He saved us, not on the basis of deeds which we have done in righteousness, but according to His mercy" (Titus 3:4,5).

Inspired by the Holy Spirit, Paul offers two prayers in the book of Ephesians. He first petitions God to open our eyes to who we are and what we have in Christ.

I pray that the eyes of your heart may be enlightened, so that you may know what is the hope of His calling, what are the riches of the glory of His inheritance in the saints, and what is the surpassing greatness of His power toward us who believe (Eph. 1:18,19).

In the second prayer, Paul is petitioning God on our behalf. Personalize this prayer by putting your name in the space allotted:

For this reason, I bow my knees before the Father, from whom every family in heaven and on earth derives its name, that he would grant (_____), according to the riches of His glory, to be strengthened with power through His Spirit in (_____)'s inner man; so that Christ may dwell in (_____)'s heart through faith; and that (_____), being rooted and grounded in love, may be able to comprehend with all the saints what is the breadth and length and height and depth, and to know the love of Christ which surpasses knowledge, that (_____) may be filled up to all the fullness of God (see Eph. 3:14-19).

Perhaps you wrongly think that you have exceeded some quota of iniquity, and that the grace of God is no longer available for you. Then consider the story of the Roman soldier who assisted with the crucifixion of Jesus. After participating in the sobering events of the day, he declared, "Surely he was the Son of God!" (Matt. 27:54, NIV). Hal wrote the following poem reflecting on the internal battle that must have waged in this soldier's mind as he pondered the Man on the Cross:

EXECUTIONER'S LAMENT

So I nailed another man onto a tree,
and won another round of it's you against me.
I've killed before; it's a small thing for me
to decrease my fear and uncertainty.

But this man's life revealed a plan
of hope and healing for every man.
For him to die in this sad way
seems I've only added to my own decay.

I plunged my spear into His side
and increased the speed at which He died.
From his eyes shot a pain-filled look,
which rocked my soul as the whole earth shook.

Who is this man? My fear dispel!
Criminal or Christ, I cannot tell.
From what I've heard His deeds suggest,
that of all men mortal He was the best.

But this only adds to my deep despair,
that Christ He was and I cannot bear:
that for all of time I shall remain,
he who tortured Christ and inflicted pain!

But as He hung upon the Cross,
my troubled life counted not for loss.
This pierced man's voice has pierced me through:
"Forgive them father, they know not what they do."

Upon mangled body my sins were laid,
not Wasted Life, but payment made.
How can this be? Yet, it swells inside,
my bonds were broke when for me He died!

Mercy poured out undeserved upon me
this crucified prisoner has set me free.
You've removed my pain, cleansed my heart from fraud
for surely this man was the Son of God!

All of us had our hands on the spear that was thrust into the side of Jesus. If you were the only one on planet Earth, He still would have gone to the Cross for you, and you would have put Him there! We are the reason He bled and died that we would have life and the forgiveness of sins. Does that make us guilty? No, it makes us a new creation in Christ and completely forgiven!

"He [God] made Him who knew no sin to be sin on our behalf, that we might become the righteousness of God in Him" (2 Cor. 5:21). You cannot do for yourself what Christ has already done for you. "For by grace you have been saved through faith; and that not of yourselves, it is the gift of God; not as a result of works, that no one should boast" (Eph. 2:8,9).

TURNING DOWN GOD'S GIFT
Some people refuse to accept this free gift of life because they do not feel worthy. But understand that this is not true humility; it is a sure road to defeat and hopelessness.

Many have then reasoned, *I believe that He died for the sins I have already committed, but what about the sins I commit in the future?* What if I broke the glasses and the pitcher after I was invited to live with my new family? When Christ "died to sin, once for all" (Rom. 6:10), how many of your sins were then future? All of them were! This is not a license to go on sinning. It is a glorious truth that enables us to know that we are truly forgiven and can now live a righteous life because we are "dead to sin, but alive to God in Christ Jesus" (v. 11).

Without the grace of God and Christ's death on the cross, we *would* be guilty before a Holy God, and we could do nothing about it. Every attempt to live a righteous life in our own strength would fail. But the penalty for the sins of the world has been paid in full, and the payment is applied to our account when we trust in Christ.

Then why do so many of us feel so guilty? After we receive forgiveness of sins, guilt is just a feeling based on a lie or a humanly developed conscience—in which case the guilt is only psychological. The conscience is a part of the mind, and is not the same as the convicting work of the Holy Spirit. Even nonbelievers have a conscience, and they will feel shame or guilt when it is violated.

The process of renewing the mind will bring the conscience in conformity to the nature and character of God. The devil first tempts us to sin. Then, as soon as we do, he becomes the accuser, saying, "You will never get away with this," or "How can you even consider yourself a Christian if you do those kinds of things?" But the Lord has forgiven our sins and defeated the devil, as Paul so clearly reveals:

> And when you were dead in your transgressions and the uncircumcision of your flesh, He made you alive together with Him, having forgiven us all our transgressions, having canceled out the certificate of debt consisting of decrees against us and which was hostile to us; and He has taken it out of the way, having nailed it to the cross. When He had disarmed the rulers and authorities, He made a public display of them, having triumphed over them through Him (Col. 2:13-15).

DISCERNING THE SPIRIT'S TRUTH AND SATAN'S LIES

The Lord will not tempt us, but He will test us to perfect our faith. He will also convict us of sin to cleanse us from all unrighteousness. How then do we know the difference between the convicting work of the Holy Spirit and the accusations of the devil or a condemning conscience that has been programmed by the world? Paul gives one answer in 2 Corinthians 7:9,10:

> I now rejoice, not that you were made sorrowful, but that you were made sorrowful to the point of repentance; for you were made sorrowful according to the will of God,...For the sorrow that is according to the will of God produces a repentance without regret, leading to salvation; but the sorrow of the world produces death.

The word "sorrow" is used for the convicting that comes from God as well as the false guilt produced by the world, the flesh and the devil. Both experiences may feel the same, but the end result is totally different. The conviction God sends us leads to repentance without regret.

This is a wonderful truth we have witnessed many times. I have never seen any person regret going through the Steps to Freedom in Christ and resolving their personal and spiritual conflicts through repentance and faith in God. What stays with them afterward is the freedom they achieved, not the pain from the past. It was nailed to the Cross.

Peter betrayed Christ by denying Him three times. Later he came under the conviction of the Holy Spirit and became the spokesperson for the Early Church. Judas betrayed Christ, came under the sorrow of the world and hanged himself.

NOT LIVING UP TO THE GOOD NEWS

During the Civil War, General Sherman burned Atlanta, then waged war against the civilians of the South during his long march toward the Atlantic coast. His theory was that soldiers fight wars, but civilians support the soldiers and pay for war. He wanted to defeat the South's ability to support the war. He broke the back of the war effort the moment they felt defeated, hopeless, useless and helpless, and no longer believed the war could be won.

This is exactly what Satan wants us to believe, with the demonic intent that we will be demoralized in the spiritual battle between good and evil. But our war with the world, the flesh and the devil has already been won! We just have to believe it.

Slavery in the United States was abolished on December 18, 1865, by the Thirteenth Amendment to the Constitution. How many slaves were there on December 19? In reality, none; but many still lived like slaves—because they hadn't learned the truth. Others knew and even believed that they were free, but chose to live as they had been taught under slavery.

Several plantation owners were devastated by this proclamation of emancipation. "We're ruined!" they cried. "Slavery has been abolished. We've lost the battle to keep our slaves." But Satan, the chief spokesman against the truth, slyly responded, "Not necessarily. As long as these people *think* they're still slaves, the Emancipation Proclamation will have no practical effect. We don't have a legal right over them anymore, but many of them don't know it. Keep your slaves from learning the truth, and your control over them will not even be challenged."

"But, what if the news spreads?"

"Don't panic. We have another bullet to fire. We may not be able to keep them from hearing the news, but we can still keep them from understanding it. They don't call me the father of lies for nothing. We still have the potential to deceive the whole world. Just tell them that they misunderstood the Thirteenth Amendment. Tell them that they are going to be free, not that they are free already. The truth they heard is just positional truth, not actual truth. Some day they may receive the benefits, but not now."

"But they'll expect us to say that. They won't believe us."

"Then pick out a few persuasive ones who are convinced that they're still slaves, and let them do the talking for you. Remember, most of these free people were born slaves and have lived like slaves all their lives. All we have to do is to deceive them so that they still think like slaves. As long as they continue to do what slaves do, it will not be hard to convince them that they must still be slaves. They will maintain their slave identity because of the things they do. The moment they try to profess that they are no longer slaves, just whisper in their ears, 'How can you even think you are no longer a slave when you are still doing things that slaves do?' After all, we have the capacity to accuse the brethren day and night."

Years later, many have still not heard the wonderful news that they have been freed, so naturally they continue to live the way they have always lived. Some have heard the good news, but evaluated it by what they are presently doing and feeling. They reason, *I'm still living in bondage, doing the same things I have always done. My experience tells me that I must not be free. I'm feeling the same way I was before the proclamation, so it must not be true. After all, your feelings always tell the truth.* So they continue to live according to how they feel, not wanting to be hypocrites!

One former slave hears the good news, and receives it with great joy. He checks out the validity of the proclamation, and finds out that the highest of all authorities has originated the decree. Not only that, but it personally cost the authority a tremendous price, which he willingly paid, so that he could be free. His life is transformed. He correctly reasons that it would be hypocritical to believe his feelings, and not believe the truth. Determined to live by what he knows to be true, his experiences begin to change rather dramatically. He realizes that his old master has no authority over him and does not need to be obeyed. He gladly serves the one who set him free.[2]

We are no longer sinners in the hands of an angry God. We are saints in the hands of a loving God.

The gospel is the "Emancipation Proclamation" for all sinners. Because of the Fall, we were all enslaved to sin. We were dead in our "trespasses and sins" (Eph. 2:1), "and were by nature children of wrath" (v. 3). The good news is that we are no longer slaves to sin. We are now alive in Christ and dead to sin (see Rom. 6:11). We have been set free in Christ. We are no longer sinners in the hands of an angry God. We are saints in the hands of a loving God. We are forgiven, justified, redeemed and born-again children of God.

You may not feel like it, you may not act like it and others may tell you that you are not, but you have been justified in Christ. "Therefore having been justified by faith, we have peace with God through our Lord Jesus Christ" (Rom. 5:1).

TAKE GOD AT HIS WORD

According to Hebrews 6:13-20, God stakes His own credibility on the fact that our hope is in Him:

> When God made his promise to Abraham, since there was no one greater for him to swear by, he swore by himself, saying, "I will surely bless you and give you many descendants." And so after waiting patiently, Abraham received what was promised. Men swear by someone greater than themselves, and the oath confirms what is said and puts an end to all argument. Because God wanted to make the unchanging nature of his purpose very clear to the heirs of what was promised, he confirmed it with an oath. God did this so that, by two unchangeable things in which it is impossible for God to lie, we who have fled to take hold of the hope offered to us may be greatly encouraged. We have this hope as an anchor for the soul, firm and secure. It enters the inner sanctuary behind the curtain, where Jesus, who went before us, has entered on our behalf *(NIV)*.

The two unchangeable things are God's promise and the oath confirming the promise. Our hope in God is a solid anchor for our souls, and the answer to hopelessness and depression. If God cannot lie, then the basis for our hope is found in the truth of His nature, character and word.

HOPELESSNESS FROM FAULTY PERCEPTIONS

Although God cannot change, our perception of Him can change; and that will greatly affect how we feel. To illustrate this, look at how Jeremiah became depressed because his perceptions about God were all wrong:

I am the man who has seen affliction because of the rod of His wrath. He has driven me and made me walk in darkness and not in light. Surely against me He has turned His hand repeatedly all the day. He has caused my flesh and my skin to waste away, He has broken my bones. He has besieged and encompassed me with bitterness and hardship. In dark places He has made me dwell, like those who have long been dead (Lam. 3:1-6).

Jeremiah believes that God is the cause of his physical and emotional hardships. He actually believes that God is out to get him, when in fact He is out to restore him. Instead of being led by God, Jeremiah feels that he is being driven to dark places where God has abandoned him. Jeremiah is in the basement! Listen to his feelings of entrapment, hopelessness and fear:

He has walled me in so that I cannot go out; He has made my chain heavy. Even when I cry out and call for help, He shuts out my prayer. He has blocked my ways with hewn stone; He has made my paths crooked. He is to me like a bear lying in wait, like a lion in secret places. He has turned aside my ways and torn me to pieces; He has made me desolate. So I say, "My strength has perished, and so has my hope from the Lord" (vv. 7-11,18).

Jeremiah was depressed because his perception of God was wrong. God wasn't the cause of his affliction. God didn't set up the circumstances to make his life miserable. God isn't a wild beast waiting to chew people up. But Jeremiah thought He was, and consequently he lost all hope in God. Then suddenly everything changed:

I remember my affliction and my wandering, the bitterness and the gall. I well remember them, and my soul is downcast within me. Yet this I call to mind and therefore I have hope: Because of the Lord's great love we are not consumed, for his compassions never fail. They are new every morning; great is your faithfulness. I say to myself, "The Lord is my portion; therefore I will wait for him." The Lord is good to those whose hope is in him, to the one who seeks him; it is good to wait quietly for the salvation of the Lord (vv. 19-26, *NIV*).

Nothing had changed externally in Jeremiah's experience. The only thing that changed was his perception of God. He had won the battle for his mind by recalling what he knew to be true about God. Hope returns when we choose to believe in the true nature and character of God.

This is why it is so necessary for us to worship God. Our heavenly Father is not an egomaniac who needs His ego stroked every Sunday morning. He is totally secure within Himself. He doesn't need us to tell Him who He is. We worship God because we need to keep the divine attributes of God constantly on our minds. We don't worship God to change Him; we worship God to change ourselves, as Jeremiah did.

FAITH AS AN ANTIDOTE FOR HOPELESSNESS

The writer of Hebrews said, "Faith is being sure of what we hope for and certain of what we do not see" (Heb. 11:1, *NIV*). Hope is the parent of faith, which is the evidence of things not seen. Martin Luther wrote:

Everything that is done in the world is done in hope. No husbandman would sow one grain of corn if he hoped not it would grow up and become seed; no bachelor would marry a wife if he hoped not to have children; no merchant or tradesman would set himself to work if he did not hope to reap benefit thereby.[3]

This truth can be illustrated in many practical ways. Suppose you hoped to catch the next bus, which was scheduled to come at 11:00 A.M. You leave your home at 10:45 A.M., giving yourself enough time to walk at a leisurely pace. So you walk by faith to the bus stop, hoping the bus would be on time and that the schedule was right.

If the bus were late and the schedule were wrong, your hope would be dashed. You would lose faith in the public transportation system. If you fell behind schedule and thought you had no hope of catching the next bus, you would not proceed by faith. That would be foolish.

If you thought there were no hope for any promotion at work, you might look around for other positions. If you had no hope of finding the grocery store open on Sunday at 6:00 A.M., you wouldn't drive there.

What if you believed there were no hope of being loved, no hope of eternal life, no hope of change, no hope for the future, no hope for joy in your life? You would probably be depressed and not very willing to continue living by "faith."

Biblical hope is not wishful thinking. Hope is the present assurance of some future good that is solidly based on the true nature and character of God. Remember, our hope is in God, not in humankind nor in the circumstances of life. His word is true. His promises can be claimed with confidence and counted on. He cannot break His covenant, which assures us of His presence within us and the forgiveness of our sins (see Heb. 8:8-13).

Matthew Henry said, "The ground of our hope is Christ in the world, but the evidence of our hope is Christ in the Heart."[4] Paul wrote, "God willed to make known what is the riches of the glory of this mystery among the Gentiles, which is Christ in you, the hope of glory" (Col. 1:27). It is Christ's presence within us that changes our mood and our perception of reality. "Why are you in despair, O my soul? And why have you become disturbed within me? Hope in God, for I shall again praise Him for the help of His presence" (Ps. 42:5).

CHALLENGES TO HOPE

A sense of hopelessness is an emotional reaction to how we perceive ourselves, the circumstances surrounding us and the future. As we have seen, the resulting emotional state may not be based on reality nor perceived truthfully from God's perspective. The world is also filled with naysayers, negative circumstances and obstacles we don't see.

Against these challenges, a biblical hope must be established and maintained if we are going to experience freedom from depression. To guide us through the maze of life, we must know the truth of God's Word and be guided by the Holy Spirit. To illustrate, listen to Neil's first entry in his daily devotional:[5]

A young pilot had just passed the point of no return, when the weather changed for the worse. Visibility dropped to a matter of feet as the fog descended to the earth. He couldn't trust in his own sensual perceptions, because he had no idea of where he was nor what direction he was headed. Putting total trust in the instruments was a new experience to him. Before he became a pilot, he had always trusted in his own natural instincts and perceptions of reality. The ink was still wet on the certificate verifying that he was qualified for instrument flying.

He wasn't worried about the flying; however, it was reaching his destination which was a crowded metropolitan airport that he couldn't see and one he had never seen before. He would be within radio contact within minutes. Until then, he was alone with his thoughts. Flying alone with no visibility, he was aware how easy it would be to become disoriented and panic. Twice he reached for the radio to broadcast, "Mayday, Mayday!" Instead he forced himself to go over and over the words of his instructor who had practically forced him to memorize the rule book. He didn't see the need for it at the time, but now he was thankful.

Finally the voice of the air traffic controller was heard. Trying not to sound apprehensive, the young pilot asked for landing instructions. "I'm going to put you on a holding pattern," the controller responded. *Oh, great!* thought the pilot. However, he knew that reaching his destination was in the hands of a person he couldn't see. He had to draw upon his previous instruction and training, and trust the voice of the air traffic controller. The words of the old hymn, "Trust and obey for there's no other way," took on new meaning. Aware that this was no time for pride, he informed the controller, "This is not a seasoned pro up here. I would appreciate any help you could give me." "You got it," he heard back.

For the next 45 minutes, the controller gently guided the pilot through the blinding fog. Course and altitude corrections came periodically, as the young pilot realized the controller was guiding him around obstacles, and away from potential collisions. With the words of the rule book firmly placed in his mind, and the gentle voice of the controller, he reached his destination. The controller assumed that the instructions of the flight manual were understood by the young pilot. His guidance could only be based on that. Such is the case of the Holy Spirit who guides us through the maze of life with the knowledge of God's will established in our hearts.

MAINTAINING HOPE UNDER FIRE

It is easy to throw in the towel when our health is failing and the circumstances are negative. The definition of a fanatic is someone who has lost his way so he doubles his efforts. One of the most common characteristics of burnout is the loss of hope.[6] Unless we want to be depressed, it is essential to maintain our hope when facing difficult circumstances.

Nehemiah was called by God to rebuild the protective walls around Jerusalem. In addition to facing seemingly insurmountable odds, Nehemiah was jeered by Sanballat and Tobiah, who set out to create a sense of hopelessness:

> When Sanballat heard that we were rebuilding the wall, he became angry and was greatly incensed. He ridiculed the Jews, and in the presence of his associates and the army of Samaria, he said, "What are those feeble Jews doing? Will they restore their wall? Will they offer sacrifices? Will they finish in a day? Can they bring the stones back to life from those heaps of rubble—burned as they are?" Tobiah the Ammonite, who was at his side, said, "What they are building—if even a fox climbed up on it, he would break down their wall of stones!" (Neh. 4:1-3, *NIV*).

Have you ever been in a situation that seems impossible, and matters become worse when your efforts are ridiculed? What did Nehemiah do? He prayed, posted a guard and kept working (see Neh. 4:9-23), and he was successful in rebuilding the walls.

But the enemy never gives up. He just changes strategies. Nehemiah's enemies saw one chink in the armor, but he was equal to the challenge:

> When word came to Sanballat, Tobiah, Geshem the Arab and the rest of the enemies that I had rebuilt the wall and not a gap was left in it—though up to that time I had not set the doors in the gates—Sanballat and Geshem sent me this message: "Come, let us meet together in one of the villages on the plain of Ono." But they were scheming to harm me; so I sent messengers to them with this reply: "I am carrying on a great project and cannot go down. Why

should the work stop while I leave it and go down to you?"
Four times they sent me the same message, and each time
I gave them the same answer (6:1-4, *NIV*).

The devil will be persistent, but we must never let him set the
agenda. We must not negotiate with the enemy, nor allow him to distract us from our calling in life. No one and nothing can keep us
from being the people God created us to be. In the face of opposition,
our answer is always the same: "I am a child of God, saved by the
blood of the Lord Jesus Christ, and I choose to live my life by faith
according to what God said is true in the power of the Holy Spirit."
The next time the devil sends you a message, send him back
this answer:

> We know that anyone born of God does not continue to
> sin; the one who was born of God keeps him safe, and the
> evil one cannot harm him. We know that we are children of
> God, and that the whole world is under control of the evil
> one. We know also that the Son of
> God has come and has given us
> understanding, so that we may
> know him who is true (1 John 5:18-
> 20, *NIV*).

In this world, we are always going to
face negative circumstances and the
inevitable loss of health. Our hope does
not lie in our ability to overcome these
obstacles in our own strength and
resources, but in God's strength and
resources.

*Our hope does not
lie in our ability
to overcome these
obstacles in our
own strength and
resources, but in
God's strength
and resources.*

Nor does our hope lie in the eternal
preservation of our physical bodies. Our
ultimate hope lies in the Resurrection:

Therefore, since we have this ministry, as we received mercy,
we do not lose heart, but we have renounced the things hidden because of shame, not walking in craftiness or adulter-
ating the word of God, but by the manifestation of truth
commending ourselves to every man's conscience in the
sight of God (2 Cor. 4:1,2).

Paul then shows how we do not lose hope in the midst of negative
circumstances and failing health:

But we have this treasure in jars of clay to show that this all-
surpassing power is from God and not from us. We are
hard pressed on every side, but not crushed; perplexed, but
not in despair; persecuted, but not abandoned; struck
down, but not destroyed. We always carry around in our
body the death of Jesus, so that the life of Jesus may also be
revealed in our body. For we who are alive are always being
given over to death for Jesus' sake, so that his life may be
revealed in our mortal body. Therefore we do not lose heart.
Though outwardly we are wasting away, yet inwardly we are
being renewed day by day. For our light and momentary
troubles are achieving for us an eternal glory that far out-
weighs them all. So we fix our eyes not on what is seen, but
on what is unseen. For what is seen is temporary, but what
is unseen is eternal (2 Cor. 4:7-11,16-18, *NIV*).

Dr. Victor Frankl, the late Austrian psychiatrist, was among
those imprisoned by the Nazis during World War II. He observed
that prisoners did not continue to live very long after they lost
hope. Even the slightest ray of hope—the rumor of better food, a
whisper about an escape—helped some of the camp inmates to continue living even under systematic horror.[7]
There is not enough darkness in all the world to put out the
light of one small candle. Truth always shines through the dark-

ness. Let us close this chapter with a testimony we received of how light shining in the darkness set one captive free.

I was raised in a good family and had a very good childhood. I received Christ into my life when I was 20, and married a Christian woman when I was 22. We had three children and I worked in the same excavating business that my father and grandfather owned.

When I was 31, I decided to start my own business. The first two years went great and life seemed to be very good. There isn't much work in the winter months because of the weather. In the third spring of my new business, I learned that my mother had Lou Gehrig's disease which has no known cure. That spring was incredibly wet which made it almost impossible to get any work done. The bills piled up and for the first time in my life I started to feel depressed.

I always felt that I was in control of my life, but now everything I did seemed to make it worse. I felt guilty that I couldn't be with my mother who lived 800 miles away. We fell further behind in our bills and then my wife suffered a miscarriage. It seemed like I had lost control of everything. The depression got worse and I started to think of suicide.

The next season we started so far behind that I didn't see any way to catch up with my bills, and my mother was getting worse. The fact that she wasn't a Christian weighed heavily on me. Then, praise God, my father led himself and my mother to Christ. Finally something good happened. Shortly later she died, but I still missed her.

When the bill collectors called, all I could think of was to kill myself. I could sense no hope. In the past I could always fix things, but now I couldn't. I finally decided to end it all. On my way down the steps to get a gun, two questions came to my mind. First, "Which is more important, having your bills paid by the insurance money, or your children having a father?" Second, "Which is more important, having your bills paid, or your wife having a husband?" At that moment I knew I didn't want to kill myself, but those condemning and suicidal thoughts just wouldn't go away.

I met with my pastor regularly, but I still couldn't see any hope. Then I met with a friend who had gone to a "Living Free in Christ" conference. He showed me in Ephesians 1:18-21 that I have Christ in me and the same power that raised Him from the dead. He asked me if I thought there was anything that power couldn't do. Of course not! He then explained how the battle was in my mind and how I could win that battle by taking every thought captive to the obedience of Christ. From that time on I have not been depressed nor entertained any thoughts of suicide. I finally found the hope I had been looking for.

A few weeks later, my friend moved away. There was so much more that I wanted to learn, so I bought *Victory over the Darkness*, *The Bondage Breaker*, and *Helping Others Find Freedom in Christ*. I read them all on my way to Washington, D.C., to attend the Promise Keepers event called "Stand in the Gap." The transformation has been incredible. My wife tells me she has a new husband. When I read God's Word it comes alive. When I listen to my pastor preach, I often cry because the Word of God touches my heart. My life will never be the same because of the freedom that Christ has given me.

Notes

1. John Keats, "Why Did I Laugh Tonight?" lines 5-14, *The Complete Poetical Works and Letters of John Keats*, ed. R. George Thomas (Oxford, England: Oxford University Press, 1978), p. 193.

2. Neil T. Anderson, *Living Free in Christ* (Ventura, Calif.: Regal Books, 1993), pp. 56-58.

3. Frank Mead, *The Encyclopedia of Religious Quotations* (Grand Rapids: Fleming H. Revell, 1965), p. 234.

4. Sherwood Wirt and Kersten Beckstrom, *Living Quotations for Christians* (New York: HarperCollins, 1974), p. 114.

5. Neil and Joanne Anderson, *Daily in Christ* (Eugene, Oreg.: Harvest House, 1993), devotional for January 1.

6. Minirth, Hawkins, Meier and Flournoy, *How to Beat Burnout* (Chicago: Moody Press), p. 135.

7. George Sweeting, *Great Quotes & Illustrations* (Dallas, Tex.: Word Books, 1985), p. 143.

CHAPTER SEVEN

OVERCOMING HELPLESSNESS

The pain is unrelenting, and what makes the condition intolerable is the foreknowledge that no remedy will come—not in a day, an hour, a month, or a minute. If there is mild relief, one knows that it is only temporary; more pain will follow. It is hopelessness even more than the pain that crushes the soul. So the decision-making of daily life involves not, as in normal affairs, shifting from one annoying situation to another less annoying— from discomfort to relative comfort, or from boredom to activity—but moving from pain to pain. One does not abandon, even briefly, one's bed of nails, but is attached to it wherever one goes.

NOVELIST WILLIAM STYRON,
IN *THE DARKNESS VISIBLE*[1]

I don't give tuppence for the man who goes into the pulpit to tell me what my duty is; but I give all I have to the man who tells me from whence my help cometh.

T. R. GLOVER

I lift up my eyes to the hills—
where does my help come from?
My help comes from the Lord,
the Maker of heaven and earth.

PSALM 121:1,2, *NIV*

People who struggle with depression frequently complain about feelings of helplessness. They can point to a series of life circumstances over which they had no control. These often include job loss, marital conflict, the death of a loved one, divorce, serious illness or injury. Most aspects of these situations were in fact beyond their ability to control. Because they have no control over these events, they begin to believe that they are inadequate, incompetent and powerless. Consequently they feel helpless. Although Scripture says they can do all things through Christ who strengthens them (see Phil. 4:13), they are overwhelmed by the belief that they are unable to affect their world or keep from being affected by the world that has overtaken them!

God did not create His children helpless or emotionally paralyzed. Helplessness creeps in when we don't know or don't believe the truth. It is all the more insidious because it did not "come with the package" of our humanity. Because helplessness is something we "learn," it is very hard to unlearn.

LEARNED HELPLESSNESS

Dr. Martin Seligman, a researcher, conducted some fascinating experiments that linked helplessness with depression.[2] He constructed an environment in which dogs were administered a shock in a kennel where they could not escape by jumping or hiding. Dogs that endured this treatment "learned" that they were helpless. Nothing the dog tried would reduce the pain. These dogs were conditioned to just accept the shock as an inevitable consequence of living!

Seligman then demonstrated that dogs who were exposed to this treatment had more trouble avoiding an *escapable* shock than dogs who had not been previously conditioned by such training. Additionally, those dogs that were conditioned *not* to avoid painful consequences developed the characteristics of depression. They had difficulty eating, sleeping and grooming themselves. They moved more slowly and appeared less alert.

Many other experiments have revealed the same thing. Fleas were put inside a jar with a piece of glass on the top. Any attempt to leave the jar only resulted in bumping into the glass. It didn't take long to condition these fleas to believe that they could not leave the jar. When the glass top was removed, they never even tried to leave because they were conditioned to "believe" that they could not.

In another experiment, a glass divider was put inside a fish tank, which moved all the fish to one side. Food was put on the other side of the divider. After a few times of bumping into the glass, the fish no longer tried. Even when the glass divider was removed, the fish remained on their side of the tank.

Have you ever been to a circus and noticed an elephant that was staked to the ground? How could that little stake keep that big elephant immobile? It couldn't, but the elephant doesn't know that. When elephants are very young, and not strong enough to pull up the stakes, they are staked to the ground just as they will be as adults. As they grow older and bigger, they could easily dislodge the stake, but they don't believe they can, so they don't even try. They are conditioned to stop trying when they meet the slightest resistance.

It is important to understand that, ultimately, helplessness is a distortion of the truth. The elephants who were initially made to feel helpless were only youngsters; it was a distortion of the truth when they later believed they were still helpless.

But these are animals, and we are people. How can these experiments apply to us?

HELPLESS PEOPLE AND THE LIES THEY BELIEVED

Scripture abounds with illustrations of learned helplessness.

AS GRASSHOPPERS IN THEIR OWN EYES

The Israelites had been enslaved in Egypt for 400 years when God revealed to Moses His plans to set them free. God challenged Moses:

"Therefore, say to the Israelites: 'I am the Lord, and I will bring you out from under the yoke of the Egyptians. I will free you from being slaves to them, and I will redeem you with an outstretched arm and with mighty acts of judgment. I will take you as my own people, and I will be your God. Then you will know that I am the Lord your God, who brought you out from under the yoke of the Egyptians. And I will bring you to the land I swore with uplifted hand to give to Abraham, to Isaac and to Jacob. I will give it to you as a possession. I am the Lord'"(Exod. 6:6-8, *NIV*).

Years of conditioning created in the Israelites a sense of learned helplessness, even when God Himself said He would deliver them.

Pack your bags, Israelites! God is about to set you free! He knows your plight. He loves you, and wants to redeem you and bring you back to the land of your dreams. But listen to the Israelites' response to this good news: "Moses reported this to the Israelites, but they did not listen to him because of their discouragement and cruel bondage" (v. 9, *NIV*). Years of conditioning created in the Israelites a sense of learned helplessness even when God Himself said He would deliver them.

When God did deliver them from Egypt anyway, the people stalled in the wilderness. They became greatly discouraged and wanted to go back. They rebelled and complained about Moses' leadership. About this time, "The Lord spoke to Moses saying, 'Send out for yourself men so that they may spy out the land of Canaan, which I am going to give to the sons of Israel; you shall send a man from each of their fathers' tribes, every one a leader among them'" (Num. 13:1,2). They came back to Moses and Aaron and the whole Israelite community and gave this report:

"We went into the land to which you sent us, and it does flow with milk and honey! Here is its fruit. But the people who live there are powerful, and the cities are fortified and very large. We even saw descendants of Anak there."...Then Caleb silenced the people before Moses and said, "We should go up and take possession of the land, for we can certainly do it." But the men who had gone up with him said, "We can't attack those people; they are stronger than we are." And they spread among the Israelites a bad report about the land they had explored. They said, "The land we explored devours those living in it. All the people we saw there are of great size. We saw the Nephilim there (the descendants of Anak come from the Nephilim). We seemed like grasshoppers *in our own eyes*, and we looked the same to them" (Num. 13:27-33, *NIV*, emphasis added).

The people believed the bad report and rebelled against Moses and Aaron. But Joshua and Caleb said to the entire Israelite assembly:

"The land we passed through and explored is exceedingly good. If the Lord is pleased with us, he will lead us into that land, a land flowing with milk and honey, and will give it to us. Only do not rebel against the Lord. And do not be afraid of the people of the land, because we will swallow them up. Their protection is gone, but the Lord is with us. Do not be afraid of them" (14:7-9, *NIV*).

Unfortunately, the Israelites again believed the bad report rather than the truth. The Lord delivered them into the Promised Land anyway, but because of their disobedience they would be delayed in the wilderness for another 40 years.

A GIANT OF A LIE, A YOUTH WITH THE TRUTH

Even after they arrived in the land God gave them, the Israelites would still encounter many obstacles (as we will today). At one time, the Philistines challenged God's people to a winner-take-all match between their champion, Goliath, and anyone the Israelites chose. They were paralyzed by fear until David came along and said, "Who is this uncircumcised Philistine, that he should taunt the armies of the living God?" (1 Sam. 17:26). Then David said to Saul:

"Let no man's heart fail on account of him [Goliath]; your servant will go and fight with this Philistine....Your servant has killed both the lion and the bear; and this uncircumcised Philistine will be like one of them, since he has taunted the armies of the living God....The Lord who delivered me from the paw of the lion and from the paw of the bear, He will deliver me from the hand of this Philistine" (1 Sam. 17:32,36,37).

Even more impressive is what David said to the giant:

"You come to me with sword, a spear, and a javelin, but I come to you in the name of the Lord of hosts, the God of the armies of Israel, whom you have taunted. This day the Lord will deliver you up into my hands, and I will strike you down and remove your head from you. And I will give the dead bodies of the army of the Philistines this day to the birds of the sky and the wild beasts of the earth, that all the earth may know that there is a God in Israel, and that all this assembly may know that the Lord does not deliver by sword or by spear; for the battle is the Lord's and He will give you into our hands" (vv. 45-47).

In their learned helplessness the Israelites saw the giant in relationship to themselves, whereas David saw him in relationship to God. The spies also saw the giants in the land in relationship to themselves, but Joshua and Caleb saw through the eyes of faith. They knew that the battle is the Lord's.

We must believe the same if we are ever going to experience any victory in this life. In Christ, God has given us the "Promised Land." Jesus has pulled up the stakes that are keeping us immobilized. He has taken the glass partition away. God is with us, and nothing is impossible for Him. We can be like Joshua and Caleb and believe that we are never helpless with God, or we can be like those who choose to believe they are as helpless now as they were before they believed in Christ.

ROOTS OF HELPLESSNESS

Most learned helplessness is the result of early childhood experiences. Lacking the presence of God in our lives and the knowledge of His ways, we learned how to survive, how to defend and protect ourselves.

Many people have felt defeated from the beginning because the messages they received from the world were often negative: "You can't do that, you'd better let me do it"; "You're not big enough or smart enough"; "You'll never amount to anything"; "It's a dog-eat-dog world out there, so be careful and watch your backside." Upon hearing these kinds of messages, it is no wonder that we start to believe *in our own helplessness.*

It has been estimated that 95 percent of the world's population is pessimistic by nature. Even the weatherman says, "There will a 35 percent chance of rain tomorrow." He never says there will be a 65 percent chance of sunshine. The news anchors don't tell us about the good things that happened that day, they only tell the bad news. Three news helicopters and 25 policemen will follow a fugitive in a car pursuit for hours, but nobody follows the good guys who set about their day encouraging others. That cannot help but give the general population a distortion of reality.

Blessing snatchers can be found everywhere. "Oh, I see you bought that brand of car. I bought one once, and it was a lemon." Even in churches, people are prone to point out the imminent dangers and the sad state of affairs in the world, rather than to encourage one another to live above difficult circumstances by having great confidence in God. "I heard that you have just become a Christian. Congratulations—now you have an enemy you never had before!"

OVERCOMING HELPLESSNESS

PROPER FOOD AND REST

We mentioned earlier the research by Dr. Henn (as reported by Papolos), which concluded that just as neurochemistry affects behavior, changes in behavior affect neurochemistry. In such cases, a physical intervention may need to take place to jump-start the process of recovery. Such may have been the case in the Bible account of the prophet Elijah, as he fled from the wicked Queen Jezebel.

Elijah showed incredible confidence in God and was even recognized by the king's men as the "man of God" (2 Kings 1:9,11,13). Elijah had witnessed the incredible power of God displayed against the prophets of Baal (see 1 Kings 18). But when Jezebel heard of it, she responded, "So may the gods do to me and even more, if I do not make your life as the life of one of them by tomorrow about this time" (1 Kings 19:2). Elijah was afraid, and ran for his life. When he came to Beersheba, in Judah, he left his servant there while he went a day's journey farther into the desert.

Why did Elijah flee? This great man of God believed a lie, just as any one of us can. Then he cried out in despair, "'I have had enough, Lord,'...'Take my life; I am no better than my ancestors.' Then he lay down under the tree and fell asleep" (1 Kings 19:4,5, *NIV*).

Elijah was exhibiting all the classic signs of depression. He was afraid and fatigued, and felt that he was a helpless failure and all alone. That can potentially happen to the best of us—especially after a mountain-top experience. We are most vulnerable when we are brimming with confidence but our energy is sapped from victoriously fighting the good fight. That confidence in God could easily turn to self-confidence when we let down our guard.

"Therefore let him who thinks he stands take heed lest he fall" (1 Cor. 10:12).

Back to Elijah, in the midst of his depression: "Behold, there was an angel touching him, and he said to him, 'Arise, eat.' Then he looked and behold, there was at his head a bread cake baked on hot stones, and a jar of water. So he ate and drank and lay down again" (1 Kings 19:5,6). God in His mercy prescribed some food and rest for His discouraged servant.

When our electrolytes are depleted and our bodies are malfunctioning for lack of nutrition, then we need to address these deficiencies through good nutrition, rest and exercise.

WHAT ABOUT DIET SUPPLEMENTS?

Many health-food experts recommend supplementing our diets with amino acids for depression. The most common is DLPA (DL-phenylalanine), which is available in capsules at health-food stores. It is nontoxic, but it may increase blood pressure. Authorities usually suggest taking DLPA along with vitamin C, vitamin B6 and fruit or fruit juice about 45 minutes before breakfast.

Taken on an empty stomach, DLPA is absorbed into the blood, then the brain, which uses it to synthesize more of the neurotransmitters that increase wakefulness and energy. Another amino acid, L-tyrosine, has a similar effect on brain chemistry.

A common herbal treatment for depression is St. John's wort. Researchers have shown that this herb can improve the mood and the quality of sleep in depressed people. It can be bought over the counter, but we recommend that you consult a nutrition-trained doctor or health-food expert for proper dosage.

God created many fruits and vegetables that were intended to be cultivated and harvested to preserve human life. Isn't St. John's wort created by God? Probably many other natural cures were created by God that are waiting to be discovered. Because of the pressures of living in these last days, the proper balance of rest, exercise and diet is even more essential. Couple that with the fact that the soils that produce our grains are becoming more and more depleted of their mineral content. Thus it may be more necessary than ever to supplement our diets with vitamins and minerals.

Another nutritional remedy that should be considered for depression is vitamin B12. A B12 deficiency is notorious for causing a variety of changes in the way the nervous system functions. This deficiency can be corrected in some patients through a B12-rich diet or nutritional supplements, but often this will not be sufficient. That is because the deficiency is frequently caused by the person's inability to absorb the nutrient in the intestines. So the vitamin needs a more direct route into the body through monthly injections, which have helped many people who had symptoms of depression. Blood tests can verify B12 deficiency if they are specifically asked for.

PHYSICAL FITNESS

After Elijah had eaten and rested, he was visited again. "The angel of the Lord came again a second time and touched him and said, 'Arise, eat, because the journey is too great for you.' So he arose and ate and drank, and went in the strength of that food forty days and forty nights to Horeb, the mountain of God" (1 Kings 19:7,8).

This suggests the importance of exercise, a third ingredient of good physical and mental health. We don't want to read anything into the story of Elijah beyond what Scripture warrants, but it does suggest that he was physically fit.

Modern research indicates that aerobic exercise may be one of the best antidepressants yet to be discovered. Aerobic exercises are not particularly strenuous, but a certain energy level must be maintained for at least 30 minutes for them to be effective. Your pulse rate should double, your breathing should accelerate and you should work up a good sweat. In addition to the well-known positive effect they have on the cardiovascular system, aerobic exercises increase the production of endorphins, which are the brain's own molecules associated with natural "highs." Aerobic exercises are most effective when combined with good nutrition.

Another important health consideration was implied when the angel said to Elijah that the journey was "too great" for him. Many people suffer from post-adrenaline depression. We explained in an earlier chapter that we get an adrenaline rush in response to demanding external circumstances. When these pressures become excessive, then ordinary stress becomes *distress*. Our ability to physically cope is diminished, and sometimes our systems break down. That is why many people experience an emotional low after an exhausting event.

This kind of reactionary depression is common for people who have just experienced a demanding week of work. Sundays can become very depressing. The authors often feel this after a long conference, which is usually one continuous adrenaline rush.

Running for 40 days and 40 nights is not exactly observing the Sabbath. We all need to recognize the need for rest and recovery. People who are facing an especially demanding schedule should consider taking an extra dosage of B-complex vitamins to prepare for it, and for the post-adrenaline letdown.

Good mental health cannot be totally separated from our physical health, which must be maintained by practicing good nutrition, exercise and diet. Many people who are struggling with depression are not physically healthy. One will have an effect on the other, and you cannot always establish which came first. Did someone's poor health contribute to depression, or did the depressive state contribute to poor health? We do not have to determine that to help someone because the proper prescription must deal with the whole person.

We are not suggesting that, in Elijah's case, the angel did nothing more than prescribe good nutrition and rest to enable Elijah to run for 40 days and nights. Scripture clearly shows that Elijah's problem began when he believed a lie. Nevertheless, God dealt with him as a whole person.

STICKING TO WHAT GOD REQUIRES

God wasn't finished with Elijah yet. Elijah needed to correct his sense of "learned helplessness" with some straight truth, so God gave him a little object lesson about His divine nature, and what He really required of Elijah:

> There he went into a cave and spent the night. And the word of the Lord came to him: "What are you doing here, Elijah?" He replied, "I have been very zealous for the Lord God Almighty. The Israelites have rejected your covenant, broken down your altars, and put your prophets to death with the sword. I am the only one left, and now they are trying to kill me too." The Lord said, "Go out and stand on the mountain in the presence of the Lord, for the Lord is about to pass by." Then a great and powerful wind tore the mountains apart and shattered the rocks before the Lord, but the Lord was not in the wind. After the wind there was an earthquake, but the Lord was not in the earthquake. After the earthquake came a fire, but the Lord was not in the fire. And after the fire came a gentle whisper. When Elijah heard it, he pulled his cloak over his face and went out and stood at the mouth of the cave. Then a voice said to him, "What are you doing here, Elijah?" (1 Kings 19:9-13, *NIV*).

God asked Elijah the same question again, and again Elijah defended his motives and actions by protesting that he had fled to the wilderness because he was the only true prophet of God left. The truth is, God didn't send him there, and Elijah wasn't the only one left. There were 7,000 others who had not bowed their knees to Baal (see 1 Kings 19:18).

God was not asking Elijah to bring in His kingdom program or bring judgment upon those who did not keep His covenant. He was asking Elijah, as He asks us, to trust Him and follow Him wherever He leads. He would bring judgment in due time, and establish His kingdom His way and in His timing. That is not for us to decide nor for us to accomplish. Our response to God is to trust and obey.

Our own perceived service for God may be the greatest enemy of our devotion to Him, and a hotbed for depression. We must resist the temptation to do God's work for Him. We are not instructed to petition God to bring judgment upon the disobedient in the form of winds, earthquakes and fire. If anything, we are called to pray for mercy, that God would withhold His judgment. "I searched for a man among them who should build up the wall and stand in the gap before Me for the land, that I should not destroy it; but I found no one" (Ezek. 22:30).

God finally instructs Elijah to "go back the way you came" (1 Kings 19:15, *NIV*). In other words, "Get back on track, and don't isolate yourself from other people." Elijah found himself alone in the desert because he believed the lies of the enemy. Although he was very zealous for God's work, he was assuming sole responsibility for doing it himself. This is often referred to as the Elijah complex. "I alone am left, and I must vindicate the word and reputation of God." If you want to feel helpless, then try doing God's work for Him!

FAITHFULNESS VS. SUCCESS

The story of Elijah reminds us of a parable passed around the Internet:

One night a man was asleep in his cabin when he was suddenly awakened by the appearance of the Savior. His room was filled with light. The Lord said, "I have work for you to do." He showed the man a large rock, and told him to push against that rock with all his might. This the man did, and for many days he toiled from sunup to sundown, with his shoulder set squarely against the cold, massive surface of the rock, pushing with all his might. Each night the man returned to his cabin sore and worn out, wondering if his whole day had been spent in vain.

Seeing that the man was showing signs of discouragement, Satan decided to enter the picture. He placed thoughts in the man's mind, such as, "Why kill yourself over this project? You're never going to move that rock." Or "Boy! You've been at it a long time and you haven't even scratched the surface," etc., etc. The man began to get the impression that the task was impossible and that he was an unworthy servant because he wasn't able to move the massive stone.

These thoughts discouraged and disheartened him and he started to ease up on his efforts. *Why kill myself?* he thought. *I'll just put in my time, expending a minimum amount of effort and that will be good enough.* And that he did, or at least planned on doing, until one day he decided to take his troubles to the Lord.

"Lord," he said, "I have labored hard and long in Your service, putting forth all my strength to do that which You have asked me. Yet, after all this time, I have not even nudged that rock half a millimeter. What is wrong? Am I failing You?"

"My son," the Lord answered, "when long ago I asked you to serve Me and you accepted, I told you to push against the rock with all your strength. That you have done. But never once did I mention that I expected you to move it, at least not by yourself! Your task was to push!

"Now you come to Me all discouraged, thinking that you have failed and ready to quit. But is that really so? Look at yourself. Your arms are strong and muscled; your back sinewed and brown. Your hands are calloused and your legs have become massive and hard. Through opposition you have grown much and your ability now far surpasses that which you used to have.

"Yet, you haven't succeeded in moving the rock; and you come to Me now with a heavy heart and your strength spent. I, my son, will move the rock. Your calling was to be obedient and to push, and to exercise your faith and trust in My wisdom. And this you have done."

If we can do all things through Christ who strengthens us, what *are* those "all things"? In other words, what is God's will for our lives? Paul clearly tells us, "This is the will of God, your sanctification" (1 Thess. 4:3).[3] This means that we are to conform to the image of God, and this we can do only by His grace. We don't have any power to change ourselves; that also must come from Him. Allowing ourselves to be influenced by the world, the flesh and the devil will interrupt the sanctifying process.

We will also curb the process when trying to change the world becomes our primary focus. On the other hand, if our goal is to become the person God created us to be, no other person nor anything on planet Earth can prevent that from happening. Not even Satan can stop us.

For example, how should we respond when the government turns a deaf ear to the Church, or when other people show contempt for the Lord? Is it our job to take on the government, or try to change those who are blasphemous? Those who try will only become angry controllers or very depressed. We are called by God to submit to governing authorities and pray for them (see Rom. 13:1-6; 1 Tim. 2:1,2). We are also to accept one another as Christ has accepted us (see Rom. 15:7). That does not mean we approve of sin or allow others to determine who we are. All Christians must learn how to establish scriptural boundaries to protect themselves from further abuse.[4]

ENCOURAGEMENT VS. DISCOURAGEMENT

Word got around heaven that the devil was holding a fire sale. Some of his best weapons were going on the auction block. A couple of curious angels thought they would check out some of the items to see what the devil was up to. There, displayed on pedestals, were many of his devilish tricks.

Of course the primary tools of his trade, temptation, accusation and deception, were not for sale. They sat prominently on display for all to see. They were the parents of all the other tools. On display were petty gossip, jealousy, arrogance, gluttony, lust and many other well-known tricks of the devil that have caused defeat to many of God's children. Satan's pitchmen (those little devils) were anxious to sell these tools and to disperse them more widely in God's kingdom for others to use.

One of the angels noticed that one pedestal was empty, and asked the little devils why. "Oh, the weapon that goes there is discouragement," they said. "It is not for sale because it is always in constant use and is our most effective weapon. Most of God's children already own it anyway!"

It is a sin to take away another person's courage when they can do all things through Christ, who strengthens them.

THE CAN-DO SPIRIT

It is a sin to take away another person's courage when they can do all things through Christ, who strengthens them (see Phil. 4:13). Those who sow the seeds of helplessness and discouragement will reap the harvest of depression. On the other hand, those who sow encouragement will reap a rich spiritual harvest. Dale Carnegie once said:

If you want to change people without giving offense or arousing resentment, use encouragement. Make the fault you want to correct seem easy to correct; make the thing you want the person to do seem easy to do....If you and I will

inspire the people with whom we come in contact to a real-
ization of the hidden treasure they possess, we can do far
more than change people. We can literally transform them.[5]

Dale Carnegie was well known for teaching the "power of positive
thinking." Many other motivational speakers have also tied into
that well-known axiom, and people have generally benefited from
it. There is no question that what we choose to think determines
what we do. You can't do anything without first thinking it. "For as
he thinks within himself, so he is" (Prov. 23:7). Someone wrote the
following poem, which illustrates this principle:

> If you think you are beaten—you are.
> If you think you dare not—you won't.
> If you want to win but think you can't,
>   It's almost a cinch you won't.
> If you think you'll lose—you've lost.
> For out of the world we find,
> That success begins with a fellow's will,
>   It's all in the state of mind.
> Life's battles don't always go,
>   To the stronger or faster man,
> But sooner or later the man who wins,
>   Is the one who thinks he can.

Christians have been somewhat reluctant to buy into this "power
of positive thinking," and in some cases for good reason. Thinking is a
function of the mind, and it cannot exceed the mind's inputs and
attributes. Any attempt to push the mind beyond its limitations will
only result in moving from the world of reality to the world of fantasy.

However, one has to be impressed with what people can do if
they will only believe in themselves. Most people are living far below
their human potential. It is estimated that most people use only five
percent of their brain capacity.

EVEN THE SKY ISN'T THE LIMIT

Some pastors in the 1950s were saying humankind would never reach the moon. But when Russia launched *Sputnik*, the United States rose to the challenge. Within a few short years, we had not only surpassed the Russians, but Neil Armstrong had actually set foot on the moon. It inspired a lot of confidence in what humans could do if they only believed they could.

About the time the Apollo space program was shutting down, a new program was envisioned. Originally it was called "Shuttle Bus." The idea was to create a reentry rocket or capsule that could be used again and again. When the government issued proposals and requested bids from aerospace companies, the technology to build such a craft didn't exist. But flushed with the success of the Apollo space program, supporters of the program actually believed it could be done, given enough time and money. Today, launching a space shuttle is so commonplace that the public is hardly aware of it.

There seems to be no limit to what humans can do. Endowed by the Creator with incredible mental and physical powers, we have launched satellites that make global communication commonplace. We have learned how to transplant hearts, kidneys, livers and other organs, allowing people to live far longer than they ever have. Some have climbed the highest peaks, descended to the lowest depths of the ocean and probed outer space, going where no man has ever gone before. Others keep chopping inches and seconds off world records that were deemed impossible decades ago.

YET THERE ARE LIMITS

But there really is a limit to what finite humans can do. We still haven't solved the problems of poverty, war, crime and corruption. In spite of all our accomplishments, faith in science as the hope for humanity has actually diminished in this post-modern era.

Enter the New Age. Out with humanism and in with "spiritism." Of course, people as finite creatures are limited, we are told, but what if we are really gods, and only need to become aware of our divine nature? There would be no limit to what we could do. We wouldn't need a Savior; we would only need to be enlightened. We could create reality with our own minds. If we believed hard enough, it would become true.

This kind of thinking is nothing more then old-fashioned occultism dressed up in New Age clothing. It seems that if its practitioners are just called "channelers" instead of mediums, and if they speak of "spirit guides" instead of demons, a naive public will buy it! We have come a long way, yet returned to the beginning—all the way back to the Garden of Eden, where Satan whispered the ultimate lie: "For God knows that in the day you eat from it *your eyes will be opened, and you will be like God,* knowing good and evil" (Gen. 3:5, emphasis added).

To have "knowledge" of good and evil implied to Adam and Eve that they could be the origin or determiner of what is good or evil, and what is true or untrue. When they ate the fruit of the forbidden tree, they were saying, "We reject God as the One who determines what is right and wrong. We will determine for ourselves what is good for us and what is true." They played right into the hands of the devil, who is the deceiver and the father of lies.

In a distorted way, Satan was right. Adam and Eve *acted* like gods in determining for themselves what is true and what is right. But what they determined wasn't right, and rather than embracing the truth that would preserve their lives and freedom, they believed a lie that led to death and bondage to sin.

Today Satan is up to his same old tricks, and they are dangerous because they are built on a half-truth. We are not gods, and we don't create reality with our minds. Believing anything doesn't make it true, no matter how hard we try. God is the ultimate reality. He is the truth, which means that what He says is true. It is for that reason we believe it. Both the humanist and the spiritist are playing god, and are creating disastrous results.

Yet we *are* created in the image of God. We are not helpless, because, by the grace of God, we can respond in a responsible way to the reality of this world. We have access to a greater power than human potential: *the power of believing the truth*. If we knew the truth as revealed in God's Word, and chose to believe it, it would set us free from artificial limitations. We would rarely, if ever, feel discouraged or helpless.

If man can accomplish what he has while exalting himself as the object of his faith, imagine what he could accomplish if the object of his faith were God! Jesus said, "With men this is impossible, but with God all things are possible" (Matt. 19:26).

We do not determine what is included in the "all things" Jesus refers to. We cannot decide for ourselves all that we can do, or what is true, then claim this verse to say, "I believe it so I can do it." That would be playing god again. Every believer has to assume responsibility for being "transformed by the renewing of your mind. Then you will be able to test and approve what God's will is—his good, pleasing and perfect will" (Rom. 12:2, *NIV*).

The real issue is: Do you believe that God's will is good, pleasing and perfect for you? When we were dead in our trespasses and sins, we lacked the presence of God in our lives. In such a state we wanted and needed much more than we had, but we were unable to obtain it on our own. Without the knowledge of God's ways we developed a "learned helplessness."

APPLYING "I CAN" THOUGHTS PRACTICALLY
Paul wrote to the Romans:

> And we rejoice in the hope of the glory of God. Not only so, but we also rejoice in our sufferings, because we know that suffering produces perseverance; perseverance, character; and character, hope. And hope does not disappoint us, because God has poured out his love into our hearts by the Holy Spirit, whom he has given us. You see, at just the right time, when we were still powerless, Christ died for the ungodly (Rom. 5:2-6, *NIV*).

Jesus defeated the devil and made us brand-new creations in Himself. He set us free from our past. We have to destroy those old strongholds that say *I can't*, and replace them with the truth that we *can* in Christ.

We have to destroy those old strongholds that say I can't, and replace them with the truth that we can in Christ.

The human tendency is to say, "This marriage is hopeless," then think the solution is to change or try to change our spouse. The same holds true for any depressing situation. The answer is neither to try to change the situation nor let the situation determine who you are. The answer is to work with God in the process of changing yourself.

According to Paul, your hope does not lie in avoiding the trials and tribulations of life, because they are inevitable. Your hope lies in persevering through those trials and becoming more like Christ. The hope that comes from proven character will never disappoint you. Only through proven character will we positively influence the world.

Imagine the terrible emotional pain when a spouse leaves or a child runs away. Anybody could become disappointed, discouraged or depressed by these difficult circumstances. Many times this is because the essence of our question is, *How can I win back the one I lost?* And the unspoken question underlying that, all too often, is, *How can I control my spouse or child, or arrange the circumstances so that I can manipulate him or her into coming back?* That kind of control or manipulation may have been the reason the person left in the first place.

The fruit of the Spirit in such a case is neither spouse control nor child control. God does not ensure that external circumstances will always be bent to accommodate our desires. The fruit of the Spirit is self-control.

It would be better to ask yourself, *If I haven't committed myself to be the spouse or parent that God called me to be, would I now?* That is the only thing within your power to change, and it is by far the best thing you could do to win back the other person. But even if you don't, you can come through the crisis having proven your character.

These trials and tribulations are what God uses to refine our character and conform us to His own image. The hope that comes from proven character will never disappoint. If our hope lies only in favorable circumstances, or trying to alter something that we have no right or ability to change or control, then we are going to suffer a lot of disappointment in this fallen world. An unknown author said it well in these lines:

"Disappointment—His appointment,"
change one letter, then I see
That the thwarting of my purpose
is God's better choice for me.
His appointment must be blessing,
tho' it may come in disguise.
For the end from the beginning
open to His wisdom lies.
"Disappointment—His appointment,"
no good will He withhold,
From denials oft we gather
treasures of His love untold.
Well He knows each broken purpose
leads to fuller, deeper trust,
And the end of all His dealings
proves our God is wise and just.
"Disappointment—His appointment,"

Lord, I take it, then, as such.

Like clay in hands of a potter,

yielding wholly to Thy touch.

My life's plan is Thy molding;

not one single choice be mine;

Let me answer unrepining—

"Father, not my will, but Thine."

God never promises to take the person out of the slum, but He does promise to take the slum out of the person. He may even call some of us to go to the slum for the sake of ministry. It is the eternal plan of God...

> To grant those who mourn in Zion, giving them a garland instead of ashes, the oil of gladness instead of mourning, the mantle of praise instead of a spirit of fainting. So they will be called oaks of righteousness, the planting of the Lord, that He may be glorified (Isa. 61:3).

TWENTY CANS OF SUCCESS[6]

Someone once said that success comes in "Cans," and failure in "Cannots." Here are 20 cans of success you would do well to memorize:

1. Why should I say I can't when the Bible says I can do all things through Christ who gives me strength (Phil. 4:13)?
2. Why should I worry about my needs when I know that God will take care of all my needs according to His riches in glory in Christ Jesus (Phil. 4:19)?
3. Why should I fear when the Bible says God has not given

me a spirit of fear, but of power, love and a sound mind (2 Tim. 1:7)?

4. Why should I lack faith to live for Christ when God has given me a measure of faith (Rom. 12:3)?

5. Why should I be weak when the Bible says that the Lord is the strength of my life and that I will display strength and take action because I know God (Ps. 27:1; Dan. 11:32)?

6. Why should I allow Satan control over my life when He that is in me is greater than he that is in the world (1 John 4:4)?

7. Why should I accept defeat when the Bible says that God always leads me in victory (2 Cor. 2:14)?

8. Why should I lack wisdom when I know that Christ became wisdom to me from God, and that God gives wisdom to me generously when I ask Him for it (1 Cor. 1:30; Jas. 1:5)?

9. Why should I be depressed when I can recall to mind God's lovingkindness, compassion and faithfulness, and have hope (Lam. 3:21-23)?

10. Why should I worry and be upset when I can cast all my anxieties on Christ, who cares for me (1 Pet. 5:7)?

11. Why should I ever be in bondage when I know that there is freedom where the Spirit of the Lord is (Gal. 5:1)?

12. Why should I feel condemned when the Bible says there is no condemnation for those who are in Christ Jesus (Rom. 8:1)?

13. Why should I feel alone when Jesus said He is with me always, and will never leave me nor forsake me (Matt. 28:20; Heb. 13:5)?

14. Why should I feel like I'm cursed or have bad luck when the Bible says that Christ rescued me from the curse of the law that I might receive His Spirit by faith (Gal. 3:13,14)?

15. Why should I be unhappy when I, like Paul, can learn to be content whatever the circumstances (Phil. 4:11)?

16. Why should I feel worthless when Christ became sin for me so that I might become the righteousness of God (2 Cor. 5:21)?

17. Why should I feel helpless in the presence of others when I know that if God is for me, who can be against me (Rom. 8:31)?

18. Why should I be confused when God is the author of peace and He gives me knowledge through His Spirit, who lives in me (1 Cor. 2:12; 14:33)?

19. Why should I feel like a failure when I am more than a conqueror through Christ, who loved me (Rom. 8:37)?

20. Why should I let the pressures of life bother me when I can take courage knowing that Jesus has overcome the world and its problems (John 16:33)?

Notes

1. William Styron, *Darkness Visible: A Memoir of Madness* (New York: Random House, 1990), p. 62.

2. Demitri and Janice Papolos, *Overcoming Depression* (New York: Harper Perennial, 1992), p. 89.

3. We recommend two of Neil Anderson's books: *Walking in the Light* (Nashville: Thomas Nelson Publishing, 1992) to help you know and understand God's will for your life; and *The Common Made Holy*, which Neil coauthored with Dr. Robert Saucy (Eugene, Oreg.: Harvest House, 1997). This book on sanctification comes with a study guide to help you understand how we can conform to the image of God.

4. We recommend the book *Boundaries*, by Dr. Henry Cloud and Dr. John Townsend, to help you set up scriptural boundaries to protect yourself from further abuse (Grand Rapids: Zondervan Publishing Co., 1992).

5. Sherwood Wirt and Kersten Beckstrom, *Living Quotations for Christians* (New York: HarperCollins, 1974), p. 65.

6. Neil Anderson, *Victory over the Darkness* (Ventura, Calif.: Regal Books, 1990), pp. 115-117.

CHAPTER EIGHT

DEALING WITH LOSS

As I looked, the poplar rose in the shining air
Like a slender throat,
And there was an exaltation of flowers,
The surf of apple tree delicately foaming.
All winter, the trees had been silent soldiers,
A vigil of woods, their hidden feelings
Scrawled and became scores of black vines,
Barbed wire sharp against the ice-white sky.
Who could believe then in the green,
Glittering vividness of full-leafed summer?
Who will be able to believe, when winter again begins
After the autumn burns down again, and the day is ashen,
And all returns to winter and winter's ashes,
Wet, white, ice, wooden, dulled and dreary, brittle or frozen,
Who will believe or feel in mind and heart
The reality of the spring and of birth,
In the green warm opulence of summer,
And the inexhaustible vitality and immortality of the earth?

DALMORE SCHWARTZ
"THE DECEPTIVE PRESENT"[1]

How completely satisfying to turn from our limitations
to a God who has none. Eternal years lie in His heart.
For Him time does not pass, it remains; and those who
are in Christ share with Him all the riches of limitless
time and endless years. God never hurries. There are no
deadlines against which He must work. Only to know
that is to quiet our spirits and relax our nerves. For
those out of Christ, time is a devouring beast.

A. W. TOZER[2]

Roxanne and David had been married for five years. David was a successful businessman who was deeply devoted to his wife and children. One Sunday afternoon, as David packed his bags for his next trip out of town, the couple started to quarrel. Roxanne was bothered by a minor demand David had placed on her. Words were exchanged, a brief apology came and life went on. Later that day the couple chatted quietly as they rode together to the airport. Roxanne kissed David as he boarded the plane. He turned, smiled and waved as he entered the loading tunnel to the waiting aircraft.

Roxanne never saw David alive again. The trip to his destination and the meetings were uneventful. David then boarded the airplane and headed home. The aircraft developed mechanical problems and attempted to land in a crippled condition. The pilot and an off-duty pilot who happened to be on board were responsible for saving some of the lives on board. David, however, was thrown from the aircraft and killed, along with many other passengers. It was a terrible catastrophe.

Roxanne was torn with pain, and went through many turbulent reactions to her loss. Scrambling for some explanation for why the tragedy had happened, she began to blame herself. *If I hadn't complained or argued with David, he would still be alive,* she reasoned. Blaming herself for his death only compounded her sense of loss.

THE RESPONSE OF SADNESS

The melancholy that followed Roxanne's loss is called *reactive depression.* This emotional response to any crisis of life is the most common form of depression. But the crisis itself did not cause the depression. Our mental perception of external events based on what we believe, and how our minds have been programmed, are what determine how we feel and react to any crisis.

People typically go through a very predictable cycle when they experience a crisis, as depicted in the following diagram:

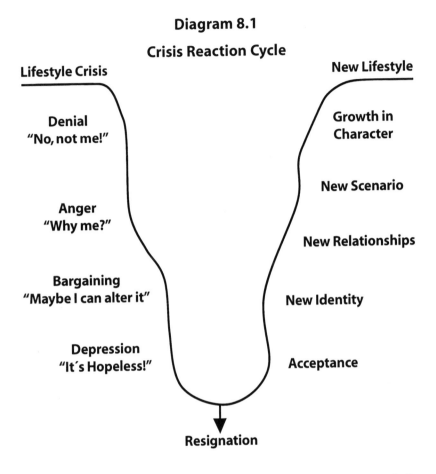

Diagram 8.1

Crisis Reaction Cycle

Lifestyle Crisis   New Lifestyle

Denial   **Growth in**
"No, not me!"   **Character**

                                                    New Scenario

Anger
"Why me?"   **New Relationships**

Bargaining
"Maybe I can alter it"   **New Identity**

Depression
"It's Hopeless!"   **Acceptance**

Resignation

Most of us settle into a lifestyle we assume will continue indefinitely, or hopefully improve. We make plans for the weekend and summer vacations, assuming that life will go on as scheduled. Daily events are scheduled with the hope that we will still be alive, our health will be okay, and that all the conditions necessary for life to go on as it is will be favorable. According to the poet Dalmore Schwartz, quoted at the beginning of this chapter, it is hard for us even to imagine in the summer of our souls what it will be like in the winter of our discouragement. We don't even want to think about it.

Some people take a fatalistic approach to tomorrow. They say with Solomon, when he limited his view to things under the sun,

"That which has been is that which will be....So there is nothing new under the sun" (Eccles. 1:9). Such people make no realistic plans, and consequently they end up having no meaningful future.

Others, even Christians, presume upon the future. James has some sobering advice for those who do that:

> Now listen, you who say, "Today or tomorrow we will go to this or that city, spend a year there, carry on business and make money." Why, you do not even know what will happen tomorrow. What is your life? You are a mist that appears for a little while and then vanishes. Instead, you ought to say, "If it is the Lord's will, we will live and do this or that." As it is, you boast and brag. All such boasting is evil. Anyone, then, who knows the good he ought to do and doesn't do it, sins (Jas. 4:13-17, *NIV*).

The good, which we ought to do, is the Lord's will, so we must choose to live a responsible life one day at a time. The will of God will not take you where the grace of God cannot keep you.

In the Sermon on the Mount, Jesus tells us not to worry about tomorrow. If God takes care of the lilies of the fields and the birds of the air, will He not much more provide for you? Jesus asks (see Matt. 6:30). Because your heavenly Father knows your needs, "Seek first His kingdom and his righteousness, and all these things shall be added to you. Therefore do not be anxious about tomorrow; for tomorrow will care for itself. Each day has enough trouble of its own" (vv. 32-34).

This does not mean we don't make plans for tomorrow. We have to do some planning to live responsibly. However, the primary purpose for setting goals and making plans for the future is to give us meaningful direction for our lives today. Because we don't have control over many circumstances that can totally disrupt those plans, we need to say, "Lord willing, tomorrow we will do whatever, and regardless of what tomorrow holds, we will trust Him." This requires us to mentally and emotionally prepare for impermanence.

PREPARING FOR IMPERMANENCE

Nothing will be as it is five years from now. There is no permanence; there is only change. Tennessee Williams said, "We are all terrorized by the idea of impermanence." The Lord tried to prepare His disciples for this reality when He told them three times "that the Son of Man must suffer many things and be rejected by the elders and the chief priests and the scribes, and be killed, and after three days rise again. And He was stating the matter plainly" (Mark 8:31,32).

The disciples' first response was denial. Peter actually rebuked the Lord (see Mark. 8:32). When He told them a second time what was going to happen to Him, they didn't understand what He meant, and were afraid to ask (see 9:32). They didn't want to talk about it.

Finally, as Jesus and His fearful disciples approached Jerusalem, He told them a third time what was going to happen (see 10:32-34). His purpose for telling them in advance was to teach them the principle that the Messiah must die to purchase salvation for humankind, and to give them hope when they faced persecution. He wanted to assure them that even though He would be killed, He would rise again.

Hope does not lie in the possibility of permanence, or in avoiding trials and tribulations. Hope lies in the proven character that comes from persevering through them. Neither does our hope lie in the eternal preservation of our physical bodies. Our hope lies in the Resurrection.

To survive the crises of life, we must have an eternal perspective, because time, as Tozer said, is a devouring beast for those who are outside of Christ. Without such a perspective, we cannot see the hope of summer during the emotional winters of our soul. The "deceptive present" masks the possibility of any hope for tomorrow. The psalmist's statement, "Precious in the sight of the Lord is the death of His godly ones" (Ps. 116:15), doesn't make sense from a time-bound perspective. But it makes complete sense from an eternal perspective.

STAGES OF GRIEF

Grief and reactive depression can arise from any crisis that interferes with well-intentioned or meaningful plans. It could be the loss of a job, our health, our spouse or other loved one, or the end of our dreams. Such losses sow the seeds of depression when we fail to see that our times are in His hands. Let us examine here the first three stages of grief as diagrammed on the preceding chart—the phases people often go through on the way to the depths of depression.

DENIAL: *NO, NOT ME!*

The first response is often denial, a refusal to accept the crisis or the loss. Some may find it too painful to face the truth. They consciously or subconsciously think, *This is all a bad dream or a trick that someone is playing on me. I refuse to even consider this as real.* Or they may consciously choose to not entertain thoughts that it actually happened. *I'll deal with this tomorrow or maybe next month.* Others are incredulous. They wonder, *How could this be happening to me? I'm a good person.* They may make many attempts to recover what is lost, or go on living as though it never happened.

A very depressed graduate student was laid off from his engineering job. He couldn't face the shame of telling his spouse, even though the downsizing of his company had nothing to do with his competence. So he got dressed the next Monday morning drenched in denial, and went to work as he normally did. By Wednesday his old employer had to call the police.

ANGER: *WHY ME?*

Denial can last for 30 seconds or 30 years. When people finally face the truth, they feel angry or resentful because what happened to them wasn't fair. They think, *Why is this happening to me?* Their anger can be directed toward others, including God, who they think caused the crisis. Those who feel guilty or ashamed direct their anger toward themselves, as when Roxanne blamed herself for her husband's death.

BARGAINING: *MAYBE I CAN ALTER IT.*

After their anger has simmered, some start to bargain. They reason, *Maybe I can alter the situation or undo the events that led up to this crisis.* They become depressed when they discover they can't do anything to change what happened, nor can they reverse the consequences. They believe the situation is hopeless and they are helpless to do anything about it. They tried to undo it all, but couldn't. Now they're not sure if they can go on living with the present circumstances. The tragic loss seems too much to bear. It is the winter of the soul. How can one even possibly imagine what summer is like again?

A TIME TO MOURN

It is natural, normal and certainly not sinful to mourn the loss of anything that is morally good or even morally neutral. It is inordinate, destructive or inappropriate grief that can lead to serious depression. It is normal to grieve the loss of a loved one; but note how Paul would help us guard against destructive grief over a loved one who has died in the Lord:

> But we do not want you to be uninformed, brethren, about those who are asleep, that you may not grieve, as do the rest who have no hope. For if we believe that Jesus died and rose again, even so God will bring with Him those who have fallen asleep in Jesus (1 Thess. 4:13,14).

We are protected from destructive grief when our hope lies in the finished work of Christ, not in the things of this world that we have no right or ability to control. We grieve for that which we have lost because we have become attached to certain people, places, ideas and things. The extent of the grief is determined by the degree of attachment we had, whether appropriate or otherwise.

IN LOSING, WE WIN

Paul was deeply attached to the Pharisaic traditions and customs of his people, and he had worked hard to achieve his status in life. For him to give all that up would require a massive intervention by God.

It came suddenly on the Damascus road. Paul was struck down and blinded by the power of God. All his hopes for a successful future were dashed in a moment. "Why, God?" he must have asked. "Why did you do this to me? Nobody has been more zealous for You than I." To make matters worse, his only hope would come from the Church he had so ervently persecuted. Reflecting on this later in life, Paul wrote:

Our hope lies in the finished work of Christ, not in the things of this world which we have no right or ability to control.

> But whatever things were gain to me, those things I have counted as loss for the sake of Christ. More than that, I count all things to be loss in view of the surpassing value of knowing Christ Jesus my Lord, for whom I suffered the loss of all things, and count them but rubbish in order that I may gain Christ (Phil. 3:7,8).

Jim Elliot said, "He is no fool who gives up what he cannot keep in order to gain that which he cannot lose." There is nothing on planet Earth that we cannot lose. This is the central teaching of all four Gospels. "For whoever wishes to save his life [Greek *psyche*] shall lose it; but whoever loses his life [*zoe*] for My sake shall find it. For what will a man be profited, if he gains the whole world, and forfeits his soul?" (Matt. 16:25,26).

The first reference to life (*psyche*) in this passage refers to the soulish life that comes from humans. The second reference to life (*zoe*) refers to the spiritual life that comes from God. He who finds his life within himself will eventually lose it. He who finds his life in God will keep it for all eternity.

In other words, those who find their identity, security and sense of worth in the natural order of things will lose it. We cannot take it with us. Whatever name we made for ourselves, whatever fame we achieved, whatever earthly position we attained, whatever treasures we were able to amass—all will be left behind. Attachments to this world subtract from our attachment to Christ.

On the other hand, nothing can separate us from the love of God, and we will suffer no debilitating loss that we cannot endure if we find our life, identity, acceptance, security and significance in Christ.

Destructive reactive depression signifies an overattachment to people, places, ideas and things that we have no right or ability to control. It indicates that we simply will not let go of something we are going to lose anyway, or have already lost.

In Africa, monkeys are caught by hollowing out a coconut shell and attaching a chain to it. The other end of the chain is tied to a tree or a stake in the ground. Then the hunters put some favorite monkey food in the hollowed-out shell. The monkey comes along and puts his fist into the shell to get the food. But when he makes a fist around the food, he can no longer extract his hand from the shell. Then the hunters simply detach the chain from the tree or stake and walk off with the monkey.

"Why doesn't the monkey just let go?" you ask. I don't know. Why don't we?

EXPLANATORY STYLES

Difficult times befall us all on the road to wholeness and maturity. Some people bounce back rather quickly, but others struggle for weeks or months, and some never recover from their loss. Most people learn how to accept and grow through childhood mistakes, adolescent embarrassments, young adult misunderstandings and adult problems of all kinds. Some have had more than their share of afflictions. God must have known that they had broad shoulders, or was preparing them for a special ministry of helping others through their crises.

Why do some recover faster than others when faced with the same crisis? Does one have greater health or greater support from others? The major difference in our ability to recover is found in the way we perceive events that befall us. Our beliefs about these events, ourselves and God will determine if we respond in fear, despair or faith.

We interpret trials and tribulations through the grid of our previous learning experiences. We attempt to explain what happened and why it happened. How we explain difficult circumstances and painful events is drawn from our beliefs about God, ourselves, others and the way we think the world works.

Some of the most enlightening research responsible for the theory of explanatory styles was conducted by Martin Seligman, the same person who did the pioneering research on learned helplessness (see chapter 7). Seligman asked:

How do you think about the cause of the misfortunes, small and large, that befall you? Some people, the ones who give up easily, habitually say of their misfortunes: "It's me, it's going to last forever, it's going to undermine everything I do." Others, those who resist giving in to misfortune, say: "It was just circumstances, it's going away quickly anyway, and besides, there's much more in life."[3]

According to Seligman, we have all developed explanatory styles to deal with crisis events. These explanatory styles determine how soon and even whether we will recover from losses. These explanatory styles are made up of the following three constructs.

PERMANENCE: *IT WILL LAST FOREVER.*

The speed of our recovery is greatly affected by whether we think the consequences of the crisis will have a short-term or a long-term effect on us. If we think our problems today will negatively affect us all our lives, then we will become pessimistic, believe that the situation is hopeless and consequently feel depressed.

This kind of thinking is so commonplace that we are hardly aware of it. Suppose a husband thinks, *My wife is cranky. She must be in a bad mood.* That is a short-term problem, and it will have very little lasting effect upon her husband. He may decide to avoid confrontation until the mood passes. But if the husband thinks, *My wife is cranky. She is an irritable person,* he is viewing the situation as a long-term problem. His response could vary from:

"I'm going to ignore her." That is denial.
"I'm going to try controlling her." That is anger.
"I'm going to try appeasing her." That is bargaining.
"I'm going to try to change her." That will be depressing!
"I'm going to avoid her." That is resignation.
"I'm going to love her and learn to live with her." That is acceptance.

When people reach the stage of depression on the crisis cycle, they are at a major crossroad. They can believe that their predicament is permanent and resign, or they can see it as impermanent and come to reach that point of acceptance, saying, "I can't change what happened, but by the grace of God I can change myself. I can come through this crisis a better person."

A young couple attending seminary came to see me. They had

tried every possible means to have children. Their disappointment with God was written all over their faces. They had all but given up on any hope of having children. They had one other option, but it was very expensive and a very unnatural means of child reproduction.

Theirs was a reactionary depression. At first they had been angry toward God, then they had tried bargaining with Him. "Lord, will you let us have children if we promise to go to the mission field?" All they heard from heaven was silence. I suggested the possibility that they weren't supposed to have children of their own.

"You mean just give up," she said.

"No, that would be resignation," I responded. "I think you should consider trusting God again, and accepting His will for your life. There may be reasons why you shouldn't have children, reasons that we don't know about. We only see one little piece of a giant puzzle, but God sees the whole picture. If God has laid it on your heart to have children, then maybe He wants you to consider adoption as an alternative, or possibly He is calling you to work with children."

The crises of life are not intended by God to destroy us, but they do reveal who we are. They expose our character and reveal what we believe in.

There are many crisis events and losses that cannot be altered, and that will result in our having to live with their consequences all our lives. Such events include losing a spouse to death or losing a leg to injury. The loss is permanent, but it doesn't have to negatively affect us permanently. How we respond to the loss will determine whether the crisis makes us or breaks us. The crises of life are not intended by God to destroy us, but they do reveal who we are. They do expose our character and reveal what or whom we believe in.

Difficult circumstances are opportunities to adjust our course of life. When a pilot encounters turbulent air while flying he may consider going higher or lower, but stopping is a poor option. Someone once said that a bend in the road is not the end of the road unless you fail to make the turn.

Joni Eareckson Tada must have felt that her life had come to the end of the road when she found herself paralyzed after a swimming accident. In an interview recorded in June 1993 on a Focus on the Family broadcast, she said, "I wanted to end my life, and the frustration I felt at not being able to do that only intensified my depression. I was so desperate, I begged one of my friends to help me end it all." Thank God that she couldn't, and thank God that He enabled Joni to make the bend in the road and become a blessing to millions.

The future belongs to the Church, not to the lost. "For momentary, light affliction is producing for us an eternal weight of glory far beyond all comparison" (2 Cor. 4:17). The Lord never sees our troubles as permanent; to Him they are momentary. To the troubled nation of Israel, He said, "For I know the plans that I have for you...plans for welfare and not for calamity to give you a future and a hope" (Jer. 29:11).

Even when the children of Israel failed Him badly, God showed mercy toward them and restored what was lost: "I will make up to you for the years that the swarming locust has eaten," (Joel 2:25). God will make it right in the end.

When we are in the darkness of depression, it is easy to believe the lie that God's favor is only momentary and His anger will last forever. But the truth is, "His anger is but for a moment, His favor is for a lifetime; weeping may last for the night, but a shout of joy comes in the morning" (Ps. 30:5).

Winter is not permanent, even though you can't sense the warmth of summer. You must choose to believe that summer comes. When you think your crisis is permanent, then consider again the words of Jeremiah in Lamentations 3:19-23:

> I remember my affliction and my wandering, the bitterness and the gall. I well remember them, and my soul is down-

cast within me. Yet this I call to mind and therefore I have hope: because of the Lord's great love we are not consumed, for his compassions never fail. They are new every morning; great is your faithfulness *(NIV)*.

PERVASIVENESS: *IT WILL RUIN MY WHOLE LIFE.*

The "grid" of pervasiveness refers to the extent to which a crisis can affect other areas of one's life. An example of pervasive thinking is to conclude that if we failed in one endeavor, then we must be a total failure, or to think that our lives are over if we were turned down or rejected by someone on whom we based our whole future.

To illustrate, take Sandy, who went through a painful breakup with her boyfriend. She mourned the loss of a loved one with whom she hoped to spend the rest of her life. *Would anyone ever want to marry me?* she wondered.

Sandy cried incessantly for the first two and a half days, and on and off after that. She didn't want to be around anybody, and she began missing work. Her "explanatory style" led Sandy to think her employer would eventually discover her to be inadequate anyway, so why bother trying? Her friends called, but she often didn't return their calls; and when she did she was cold and distant. The loss she was experiencing in one area of her life was projected onto every other area. Consequently, she felt there was no hope for her.

Don't let one loss infiltrate other aspects of your life. If you experience loss, it does not mean you are a loser in life. If you fail to accomplish one goal, you are not a failure. If you get laid off at work, it doesn't mean you are an irresponsible dad or a bad husband or an incompetent Sunday School teacher.

The tendency of this kind of thinking is to rest our whole sense of worth on one relationship, experience, idea or plan. When plans or relationships don't last or fail to materialize, we wrongly deem ourselves failures.

PERSONALIZATION: *IT'S ME! IT'S ALL MY FAULT!*
The third construct in explanatory styles is to take personal responsibility for something we didn't cause or couldn't control. In personalization, the depressed person feels responsible for another person's anger, for the downsizing of a corporation, for bad weather, for not knowing the future and for a host of other uncontrollable circumstances and situations.

Little children become depressed when their parents get divorced because they think it is their fault. Many perfectionists struggle with depression because they have a tendency to blame themselves for everything. One little crisis upsets their idealized world and they can't help but think, *It's my fault.* They become so driven to achieve their self-made goals that they become supersensitive to any failure or crisis.

Personalization distorts the perception of reality. When a crisis erupts at work, some immediately think, *What did I do now?* They may go home and obsessively review the incident, looking for what they did wrong. They live on "if onlys." "If only I had done that, she would never have left me"; "If only I had joined the Navy when I had a chance."

Much of the identity of such people rides on the successful outcome of life events. The fact is, they have it backward. Their identity and their future rests on identifying who they are in Christ and the truth that there is now no condemnation for those who are in Him (see Rom. 8:1).

Many of these people were wrongly accused in early childhood, and they have come to believe they have a part to play in every negative thing that happens. Paul says, "Let no one keep defrauding you of your prize by delighting in self-abasement" (Col. 2:18).

Others are just victims of the accuser, Satan, who accuses them day and night. They never understood the battle for their minds, nor learned how to take every thought captive to the obedience of Christ.

Blaming ourselves for every crisis in life and for every slight imperfection is a sure way to perpetuate a failure identity and depression. On the other hand, blaming others is a sure way to become bitter, angry, proud, self-serving and abusive. Self-exaltation is as bad as self-condemnation. "For through the grace given to me I say to every man among you not to think more highly of himself than he ought to think; but to think so as to have sound judgment, as God has allotted to each a measure of faith" (Rom 12:3). It doesn't do any good to blame others, and it doesn't do any good to blame ourselves. Neither pride nor false humility is a proper response to the trials and tribulations of life.

GETTING OUT OF THE RUT

It's my fault that our company didn't get the contract (personalization). Now I'll never get the promotion I wanted (permanence). I'm a total failure in life (pervasiveness)! The constructs of personalization, permanence and pervasiveness dominate the way depressed people think. How can we change these "grids" that distort our perception of reality?

If you experience loss in one area, don't generalize it into a total life crisis. Keep it specific. If you experience a crisis today, don't allow it to affect you tomorrow. Keep short accounts. If the world is disintegrating around you, don't accept the blame when it's not appropriate!

If you are suffering the consequences of a bad decision, then change what you can, minimize your losses and move on. If you have committed a willful act of sin, then own up to it. "If we confess our sins, He is faithful and righteous to forgive us our sins and to cleanse us from all unrighteousness" (1 John 1:9).

Depression is an intertwining of body, soul and spirit, all of which are regulated by what we believe. Jesus said, "You shall know the truth, and the truth shall make you free" (John 8:32). Choosing to believe the truth and living by faith is the essential prerequisite for living an emotionally healthy and productive life.

The converse is also true. Believing a lie and thinking unwholesome thoughts will fuel depression and lead to bondage. You can change what you believe and how you think, and that must happen if you are going to be free from depression.

CHANGING WRONG BELIEFS

The story is told of a frog who was hopping around a pasture. It had rained the day before, and the soil was very damp. A truck had driven through the pasture and cut deep ruts in the ground. Unintentionally, the frog bounced into one of those ruts and got stuck. It made a halfhearted attempt to hop out, but didn't make it. The rut was too deep.

The next day a few of the frog's friends came looking for it, and they found it stuck in a rut. They encouraged it to try again to jump out, but the frog said it was hopeless. It was permanently stuck in a rut, it thought, and now wasn't good for anything. The frog further thought, *It was probably my fault that it rained the other day. That was just God's way of getting even with me for not being a better frog.* For five straight days the other frogs came by to encourage the stuck frog, but it remained stuck in its rut.

But on the sixth day, the frog's friends were surprised to see the frog hopping around the field. They ask how it managed to get unstuck. "Oh," it said, "a big truck came along and I *had* to get out of there!"

Fortunately, we don't have to stay in the rut of accepting fatalistically any of the three preceding "explanatory styles." We can change these grids:

From:	To:
Personal: "I'm the problem"	Impersonal: "It's a problem"
Pervasive: "In everything"	Specific: "In this one thing"
Permanent: "Forever"	Temporary: "For a season"

How do we get unstuck? The first step is to define the crisis and then put it into perspective. We can never change if we deny the crisis.

IS THE LOSS REAL OR IMAGINARY?

Analyzing the crisis helps to determine if the perceived loss is real or only imagined. Many people have gone all the way to the bottom of the crisis cycle only to find out that what they had believed or heard wasn't true. This can easily happen in early stages of diagnosing physical illnesses. One lady was so sure that her husband was going to die from cancer that she was already bargaining with God to save his life when she found out it wasn't cancer at all.

It is possible to go through all the stages of anger, bargaining and depression when the crisis is only a feared or potential loss. Suppose a man is very concerned about his job. His company just laid off a few good men, and now he is wondering if he is next. Then one day he just "knows" that it's going to happen. He begins to think, *That isn't fair! I'm a good employee. How could they do that to me?*

For the next several days he is angry about being fired. Then he starts to think, *Maybe if I volunteer for overtime they won't fire me.* So he begins to do just a little more than the others, hoping the boss will notice his efforts. But nobody seems to notice that he is making the extra effort. After a while he starts to get depressed about work. Now he is thinking, *It doesn't make any difference how I work, they are going to lay me off anyway.*

We can choose to mentally dwell upon facts or assumptions. The soul does not need facts to turn speculation into worry, worry into fear, and fear into despair. The emotional result is the same whether it is real or imagined.

Every real loss that is acknowledged will result in some degree of mourning. Denying the loss only robs us of the comfort we need. Jesus said, "Blessed are those who mourn, for they shall be comforted" (Matt. 5:4). Christians are real people who bleed when they are cut and cry when they are hurt. It takes time to adjust to the loss.

BEWARE OF EXCESSIVE ATTACHMENT

Excessive grief about any loss can turn into a depression. It may indicate that too much value was placed on one or more attachments. This requires an honest evaluation of the loss in light of eternity, and a decision to let go of the past and grab hold of God—as Paul exhorts us:

> Not that I have already obtained all this, or have already been made perfect, but I press on to take hold of that for which Christ Jesus took hold of me. Brothers, I do not consider myself yet to have taken hold of it. But one thing I do: Forgetting what is behind and straining toward what is ahead, I press on toward the goal to win the prize for which God has called me heavenward in Christ Jesus. All of us who are mature should take such a view of things. And if on some point you think differently, that too God will make clear to you. Only let us live up to what we have already attained (Phil. 3:12-16, *NIV*).

AVOID BLAME AND GUILT
Casting blame or feeling guilty are inappropriate responses to loss, and will only prolong the grieving period. We must accept the cards that have been dealt to us, realizing that God "causes His sun to rise on the evil and the good, and sends rain on the righteous and the unrighteous" (Matt. 5:45).

EVALUATE WHAT YOU HAVE AND WHO YOU ARE
We are all in this boat together, and none of us will make the journey without facing many trials and tribulations. Even if you lived a perfect life, you would still experience considerable loss. But never forget: What you have to gain in Christ is far greater than any loss you will be called to endure. We don't bargain with God. We humbly submit to Him. And we pray the serenity prayer:

> God, grant me the serenity
> To accept the things I cannot change,
> The courage to change the things I can,
> And the wisdom to know the difference.

Recovery from any crisis is going to precipitate a deeper evaluation of who we really are. We may have placed too much of our identity in the things we do and not enough in who we are in Christ. The wife who found her identity in marriage and motherhood will experience far greater loss when her husband leaves her than the woman who already deeply understood what it means to be a child of God. The man who finds his identity in his job will suffer great loss when he loses it.

Neil received the following letter from a pastor:

> I have been reading your two books, *Victory over the Darkness*, and *The Bondage Breaker*. I wanted to thank you for giving me two tools that I really needed. I'm the founding pastor of this church, having begun 15 years ago. I am in the first steps of recovering from a church split. I have never known pain like this before, but I am finding it to be a tremendous time of learning and growth in the Lord. Your "Victory" book has been especially helpful in that [it helped me to realize that] I have tried to find too much of my identity in what I do as a pastor and not enough in who I am as a saint.

Such crises not only help us clarify who we are and why we are here, but they also precipitate the need for new relationships and the need to construct a new scenario for our lives. These changes were probably necessary for our growth in the Lord, but we would never have made those changes if we had not been forced to do so.

Buzz Aldrin, the second man to walk on the moon, said, "My depression forced me, at the age of 41, to stop and, for the first time, examine my life."[4] We can easily get stuck in the same old ruts until God brings a truck along and we have to move. That is just God's way of disciplining us for our good. Listen to the words of Hebrews 12:7-11:

Endure hardship as discipline; God is treating you as sons. For what son is not disciplined by his father? If you are not disciplined (and everyone undergoes discipline), then you are illegitimate children and not true sons. Moreover, we have all had human fathers who disciplined us and we respected them for it. How much more should we submit to the Father of our spirits and live! Our fathers disciplined us for a little while as they thought best; but God disciplines us for our good, that we may share in his holiness. No discipline seems pleasant at the time, but painful. Later on, however, it produces a harvest of righteousness and peace for those who have been trained by it *(NIV)*.

God wants us to share in His holiness. The purpose of His discipline is to produce godly character. In addition, we will all be victimized as the inevitable consequence of living in a fallen world. Whether we remain victims is our choice. We have the potential to come through every crisis a better person than we were before. Our resultant lifestyle will be higher and more godly than it was.

So in the winter of your discouragement, lift up your eyes to heaven. Recall that your hope is in God, and that you will again experience the warmth of summer and the harvest of fall.

Notes

1. Kay Jamison, *Touched with Fire* (New York: Free Press Paperbacks, 1993), p. 136.
2. George Sweeting, *Great Quotes and Illustrations* (Dallas, Tex.: Word Books, 1985), pp. 65, 66.
3. Martin Seligman, *Learned Optimism* (New York: Pocket Books, 1990), pp. 65, 66.
4. Buzz Aldrin, "Return To Earth," cited in *Current Biographic Yearbook*, 1993.

CHAPTER NINE

SUFFERING FOR RIGHTEOUSNESS' SAKE

*I think we've lost the knowledge that happiness is
overrated, that in a way, life is overrated. We've lost
somehow, a sense of mystery about us, about our purpose,
our meaning, and our role. Our ancestors believed in
two worlds and understood this world to be the solitary,
poor, nasty, brutish, and short one. We are the first
generation of man that actually expected to find happines.
here on earth and our search for it has caused such
unhappiness. The reason? If you do not believe in another
higher world, if you believe in only the flat, material
world around you, if you believe that this is your only
chance for happiness, if that is what you believe, then
you are not disappointed when the world does not give
you a good measure of its riches—you are despairing.*

PEGGY NOONAN
SPEECH WRITER FOR PRESIDENTS
REAGAN AND BUSH

*Beloved, do not be surprised at the fiery ordeal
among you, which comes upon you for your testing, as
though some strange thing were happening to you; but to
the degree that you share the sufferings of Christ, keep
on rejoicing; so that also at the revelation of His glory,
you may rejoice with exultation. If you are reviled for
the name of Christ, you are blessed, because the Spirit
of glory and of God rests upon you.*

1 PETER 4:12-14

We live in a fallen world, and life on this planet isn't always fair. We want things to go our way, but they often don't. We want justice to prevail, but that will not perfectly happen in this lifetime. God will make it right in the end, but until then we will have to live with many injustices. Many Christians struggle with depression because they have never understood the role that suffering has in our sanctification, and that suffering is an inevitable consequence of living in a fallen world.

We are tempted to think that Christians shouldn't have to suffer if they live a righteous life. Early Christians, however, suffered greatly at the hands of the religious establishment. After being beaten for sharing what they believed, "They went on their way from the presence of the Council, rejoicing that they had been considered worthy to suffer shame for His name" (Acts 5:41). "Indeed, all who desire to live godly in Christ Jesus will be persecuted" (2 Tim. 3: 12).

Furthermore, persecution is not just a thing of the past. More Christians were martyred for their faith in 1997 than in any other year in Church history.

Scripture uses many terms to describe suffering, including affliction, anguish, distress, grief, misery, pain, tribulation and chastisement. In addition, various metaphors also depict suffering—e.g., refining fire (see Isa. 48:10; 1 Pet. 1:6,7), overflowing waters (see Isa. 43:2) and birth pangs (see John 16:20-22; Rom. 8:18-22).

J. I. Packer defines this anguish as "getting what you do not want while wanting what you do not get."[1] Such is the lot of everyone, and it plays a significant role in the understanding and treatment of depression.

Although most of us would rather not face it, suffering and anguish are a part of the process of conforming to the image of God. Many Christians are depressed because they believe they shouldn't have to suffer—which isn't true. Suffering plays a critical role in our sanctification.[2]

WHY DO WE SUFFER?

First, Christians will suffer for the sake of righteousness. We will share in the glory of Christ only if we "share in his sufferings" (Rom. 8:17, *NIV*). "If we endure, we shall also reign with Him" (2 Tim. 2:12). "For just as the sufferings of Christ are ours in abundance, so also our comfort is abundant through Christ" (2 Cor. 1:5). Much of the suffering of the believer is in relation to living for Christ in a hostile world. "Trials" are destined to come "in spreading the gospel of Christ" (1 Thess. 3:2, *NIV*). "We must go through many hardships to enter the kingdom of God" (Acts 14:22, *NIV*).

Second, suffering will also come as the consequence of our own sin and as the chastisement of our heavenly Father. David felt the heavy hand of God in the form of physical and mental suffering as a result of his sin (see Ps. 32:3-5). Even apart from sin, our heavenly Father will discipline us in order to share in His holiness. "All discipline for the moment seems not to be joyful, but sorrowful; yet to those who have been trained by it, afterwards it yields the peaceful fruit of righteousness" (Heb. 12:11). Even the sinless Christ was perfected through suffering (see Heb. 2:9; 5:8).

Finally, suffering comes simply from our human frailty as part of a fallen world. The decaying of the "outer man" and the accompanying afflictions are part of our normal existence in the present life which is "subject to a thousand troubles and under sentence of death."[3] The bonds of intimacy, if not broken through sin, are surely broken through death—resulting in a profound suffering of love lost in a fallen world.

Along with all of creation, "we ourselves, who have the firstfruits of the Spirit, groan inwardly as we wait eagerly for our adoption as sons, the redemption of our bodies" (Rom. 8:23, *NIV*). Despite our natural aversion to pain and suffering, Scripture tells us that they are hard realities and even a necessity in the life of the believer. In Packer's words, "suffering Christianly is an integral aspect of biblical holiness, and a regular part of business as usual for the believer."[4]

THE VALUE OF SUFFERING

Physical pain is a necessary warning signal. As one physician states, "Pain is a sign that action should be taken; it implies that if action is not taken, the survival chances of the organism are going to decrease."[5] Even lack of proper bodily nourishment is felt as pain.

Suffering in the Christian life can be a sign of sickness, warning us that further deterioration in the condition is inevitable unless something is changed. Suffering may therefore be God's way of trying to motivate us to the necessity of change, as C. S. Lewis's well-known statement suggests: "God whispers to us in our pleasures, speaks in our conscience, but shouts in our pains."[6]

Sometimes it takes great suffering to get our attention. As someone has said, "Small trials often make us beside ourselves, but great trials bring us again back to ourselves." Such was the case of the prodigal son. It was only after his food ran out and he said, "I am dying here with hunger" that he "came to his senses," repented and returned to his father (Luke 15:17-20).

For good or ill, suffering, grief and depression often bring us to the heart of life. The darkness of despair, "like Plato's cave, is the place where all men come to know themselves."[7]

SUFFERING BUILDS CHARACTER

The trials and tribulations of life do not break us; they only reveal who we are. The fact that suffering builds character is evident in Scripture. Even the suffering of Jesus produced something in His own life. He was made "perfect through suffering" (Heb. 2:10, *NIV*); "He learned obedience from the things which He suffered" (Heb. 5:8).

There is no suggestion in these statements of prior disobedience or sinful flaws in Christ. His suffering, rather, occurred through the Incarnation, when Jesus, who was fully God, became fully human. The development of His humanity from infant to adult gave us a model we ought to follow. His experience of suffering made Him a compassionate High Priest who could come to the aid of suffering people (see Heb. 4:15,16). It also taught Him the fullness of what it meant to obey and to determine to follow His Father's will no matter how high the cost.

In His developing humanity, Jesus learned the chain of moral values that come to us through adversity: "Knowing that tribulation brings about perseverance; and perseverance, proven character; and proven character, hope" (Rom. 5:3,4). If it was "fitting that God...should make the author of...[our] salvation perfect through suffering" (Heb. 2:10, *NIV*), how much more that He should use the same process on us.

The hardship and pain of Christ is felt by every one of His true sons and daughters:

> Our fathers disciplined us for a little while as they thought best; but God disciplines us for our good, that we may share in his holiness. No discipline seems pleasant at the time, but painful. Later on, however, it produces a harvest of righteousness and peace for those who have been trained by it (Heb. 12:10,11, *NIV*).

All godly character is summed up in love, according to the apostle's description in 1 Corinthians 13. Godly love flows only from those who, because they have died to self-centeredness, can live for others. Putting to death that old self that wants its way inevitably involves pain. It does not die easily, and there is no painless way to die. Growth in true character that is the expression of love inevitably entails suffering. "To render back the will which we have so long claimed for our own, is in itself, wherever and however it is done, a grievous pain."[8]

SUFFERING DRAWS US TO GOD

Our love of God is often tainted with our love of the good things He gives us. Suffering strips away any pretense from our relationship with God. It weans us from all that is not God, that we might learn to love Him for *who* He is, rather than for *what* He gives. Augustine says, "God wants to give us something, but cannot, because our hands are full—there's nowhere for Him to put it." Suffering empties our hands so that God can give us Himself, the true treasure of life.

C. S. Lewis wrote:

> Now God, who has made us, knows what we are and that our happiness lies in Him. Yet we will not seek it in Him as long as He leaves us any other resort where it can even plausibly be looked for. While what we call "our own life" remains agreeable, you will not surrender it to Him. What then can God do in our interests but make "our own life" less agreeable to us, and take away the plausible sources of false happiness?[9]

SUFFERING HELPS US UNDERSTAND GOD AND HIS WORK

We live in a world of moral conflict. Biblical history reveals a battle between good and evil that has brought much suffering. Even God shares in this suffering because of what sin has done to His creation. As the prophet reveals, God also suffers in the suffering of His people: "In all their affliction He was afflicted" (Isa. 63:9). This reality of evil and the true nature of God's love for us would not be known except through the experience of suffering: "The only way in which moral evil can enter into the consciousness of the morally good, is as suffering."[10] Lewis says, "A bad man, happy, is a man without the least

Your suffering in depression can testify of God's sustaining grace to others, both believers and unbelievers, and thus be used to draw them to God.

inkling that his actions do not 'answer,' that they are not in accord with the laws of the universe."[11]

Your suffering in depression can be an opportunity to testify of God's sustaining grace to others, both believers and unbelievers, and thus be used to draw them to God. Doctors and nurses are far more impressed with godly patients who hold up well under suffering and face death without fear, than with begging, pleading Christians who have no sense of their immortality.

No matter what the source of our suffering, whether directly from God's discipline, from the hand of another person or simply from the natural evil that is part of the fallen world, it is all under the control of God. In His infinite wisdom and love He allows suffering to come our way for His ultimate glory, our growth in character and for our witness in this world. Peter Kreeft raises a question that is worth keeping in mind in the experience of all suffering.

Perhaps we suffer so inordinately because God loves us so inordinately and is taming us. Perhaps the reason why we are sharing in a suffering we do not understand is because we are the objects of a love we do not understand...perhaps we are even becoming more real by sharing in sufferings that are the sufferings of God, both on earth, as part of Christ's work of salvation, and in heaven, as part of the eternal life of the Trinity which is the ecstatic death to self that is the essence of both suffering and joy.[12]

ONLY WHAT YOU CAN BEAR

The full reasons for all our sufferings may never be fully known to us in this life. But be assured that God always has a limit on the suffering He allows for each of us. Just as He clearly set limits on the suffering Satan could bring on Job, so He does for each of us. Some, such as Job and Paul, obviously have broader shoulders upon which God allows more suffering to rest for righteousness' sake.

Suffering always comes with a temptation to respond in the sin of unbelief, either in despondency that says "God has forsaken me and there is no hope," or in the anger of rebellion—"I hate you, God, for letting this happen, so forget You. I'm going to go my own way from now on." Satan has scored another victory when the victim believes such a lie and walks away from his only source of hope.

Our heavenly Father assures us He will not allow any suffering that we cannot bear:

> No temptation [testing or trial] has seized you except what is common to man. And God is faithful; he will not let you be tempted beyond what you can bear [or beyond your strength]. But when you are tempted, he will also provide a way out so that you can [or have the strength to] stand up under it (1 Cor. 10:13, *NIV*).

This promise assures us that God places a limit on our suffering that is not beyond what we can bear in each circumstance. He knows our strength and weakness in every area of our lives—physically, emotionally and spiritually—and says that, with His grace, He will not allow any suffering on any occasion that we cannot handle. The will of God will never take you where the grace of God will not sustain you.

GOD'S PROVISIONS IN SUFFERING

It is clear by the reference to standing up under suffering that the way out that God provides does not mean an *immediate* cessation of the sufferings. The promise of Scripture is not that God will keep us from all suffering or even remove it quickly, but that He will supply certain provisions so we can "stand up under it." Trusting in God's faithfulness and promise of a way out is what makes it possible to endure suffering.

GRACE AND COMFORT

God promises to provide the grace and comfort necessary for us to faithfully endure suffering. The psalmist does not say, "Cast your cares on the Lord and go free from care," but rather, "Cast your cares on the Lord and he *will sustain you*" (Ps. 55:22, *NIV*, emphasis added). Similarly, we are not told that the causes of our anxieties will be removed, but that in their midst we can experience the peace of God (see Phil. 4:6,7).

In the midst of his imprisonment and trial, Paul testifies that "the Lord stood with me, and strengthened me" (2 Tim. 4:17). Not only God's strength but His comfort is available in our sufferings. He is the "Father of mercies and God of all comfort; who comforts us in all our affliction" (2 Cor. 1:3,4). The Greek word for "comfort" may also be translated "encouragement." It is used here in its basic sense of "standing beside a person to encourage him when he is undergoing severe testing."[13] The present tense of the verb tells us that our God comforts us at *all* times, constantly and unfailingly in *all* our sufferings.

JOY IN SUFFERING

James says, "Consider it all joy, my brethren, when you encounter various trials" (1:2). But the idea of joy as a result of trials and suffering is not unique to this verse. Paul says, "We also rejoice in our sufferings" (Rom. 5:3, *NIV*). Similarly, Peter said: "Rejoice that you participate in the sufferings of Christ, so that you may be overjoyed when his glory is revealed" (1 Pet. 4:13, *NIV*). All these passages share something of Jesus' pronouncement, in the Sermon on the Mount, of a state of blessedness (being fortunate, happy or divinely privileged) on the poor, the mourning, the hungry and the persecuted (see Matt. 5:3,4,6,10-12).

These references to joy or blessedness in trials and suffering are not for the suffering in itself, but for the outcomes that are associated with it. Joy in trials of suffering is possible because we know that "the testing of your faith produces endurance," and that we are to "let endurance have its perfect result, that you may be perfect [or mature] and complete, lacking in nothing" (Jas. 1:3,4; see also Rom. 5:3). In the word picture drawn by Peter, trials produce a genuine faith like gold from a refiner's fire that will result "in praise and glory and honor at the revelation of Jesus Christ" (1 Pet. 1:6,7).

For this joy to be present, there must be appreciation and even gratitude for what God is doing. "You must thank God in the midst of your pain. Tell Him you trust Him. Praise Him for what He can do, for what He *is* doing. As you do so pressures will lift. You will be given a garment of praise to replace a spirit of heaviness."[14]

HOPE AND ASSURANCE

We cannot find joy in the midst of trials and suffering without hope. In the references cited, joy was present because of the anticipated future glory. The right attitude in suffering is therefore to focus on our hope.

Remember that biblical hope is not wishful thinking, but the present assurance of some future good. We do live in a vale of tears, but this is not the end. There is a new day coming for the Christian, a day that is described as fullness of joy where there will be "no more death or mourning or crying or pain, for the old order of things [with its trials and suffering] has passed away" (Rev. 21:4, *NIV*).

The suffering itself helps to engender this perspective of hope that is so critical for overcoming depression. There is a grand circle in the thinking of Paul in Romans 5 in which hope stands at both ends, and tribulation in the middle. We rejoice in the hope of the glory of God (see Rom. 5:2, *NIV*), and we glory in our sufferings because we know that suffering leads to a sanctifying process that terminates in hope—"suffering produces perseverance; perseverance character; and character, hope" (Rom. 5:3,4, *NIV*).

Hope not only undergirds our steadfastness in trials and enables joy, but it is also strengthened by such trials. As John Murray says, "We glory in tribulations because they have an eschatological orientation—they subserve the interests of hope."[15]

We can accept the sufferings that come our way if we understand their purpose, and if we have the hope that God will make it right in the end. We can put up with any "how" if we know the "why." Sometimes, however, the "why" is elusive, which brings us to a topic that speaks to many people who are depressed because of suffering.

THE PERCEPTION OF GOD'S ABSENCE

What if you couldn't sense God's presence—if the consciousness of His blessings were for some reason suspended? What would you do if you were faithfully following God, when suddenly all external circumstances turned sour? That was the case, remember, with Job.

Job was enjoying the benefits of living righteously, when one day it was all taken away. Health, wealth and even family were all gone! Our minds would spin with questions. "What did I do to deserve this?" "Did I miss a turn in the road?" "Is this what I get for living a righteous life?" "Where is God?" "God, why are you doing this to me?" Like Job, you would be tempted to curse the day you were born.

It is a marvelous life when we sense the presence of God, live victoriously over sin and know the truth that sets us free. Thank God for the mountaintop experiences when the circumstances of life are favorable. But are they always?

Something like Job's experience of being stripped of all awareness of God's blessings has happened twice to me (Neil) and my family.[16] Both times preceded significant changes in my ministry. If it weren't for the message given in Isaiah 50:10,11, I'm not sure we would have survived those trials:

Who is among you that fears the Lord, that obeys the voice of His servant, that walks in darkness and has no light? Let him trust in the name of the Lord and rely on his God. Behold, all you who kindle a fire, who encircle yourselves with firebrands, walk in the light of your fire and among the brands you have set ablaze. This you will have from My hand; and you will lie down in torment.

Isaiah is talking about a believer when he asks, "Who is among you that fears the Lord?" He is talking about a believer, someone who obeys God, and yet walks in darkness. Isaiah is not talking about the darkness of sin, nor even the darkness of this world (i.e., the kingdom of darkness). He's talking about the darkness of uncertainty, a blanket of heaviness that hovers like a dark cloud over our very being...when the assurance of yesterday has been replaced by the uncertainties of tomorrow...when He has suspended His conscious blessings.

In such a state, even attending church may be a dismal experience. Friends seem more like a bother than a blessing. Could this happen to a true believer? What is the purpose for such a dark time? What is a person to do during these times?

WALK IN THE LIGHT OF PREVIOUS REVELATION

First, the passage in Job tells us that we are to keep on walking. In the light, we can see the next step and the path ahead is clear. We know a friend from an enemy, and we can see where the obstacles are. The Word has been a lamp unto our feet, providing direction for our steps. In our anguish we may begin to wonder if that is true. Darkness has overcome us. We are embarrassed by how feelings oriented we are. Every natural instinct tells us to drop out, sit down, stop! But the text encourages us to keep on living by faith according to what we know to be true.

Our first encounter with such a period of darkness came after my wife, Joanne, discovered that she was developing cataracts in both eyes. In the late 1970s they would not do lens implants for anyone under age 60. We had no alternative but to watch each of her eyes cloud over until she could barely see.

Then doctors surgically removed the lenses from her eyes. Thick cataract glasses were prescribed until she could be fitted with contact lenses. All this took place over a two-year period, and was very traumatic for Joanne. Being a pastor's wife is pressure enough, but this additional trauma was more than she could bear.

So for Joanne's sake, I started to consider a way to serve the Lord other than being a senior pastor. I felt led to pursue the field in which I had begun work on my first doctoral degree, even though I had no idea what God had in store for me. Just the assurance that I was putting Joanne ahead of my desire to pastor gave her a sense of hope.

But since our church was in the middle of a building program, I needed to stay until the project was completed. Within months after dedicating our new buildings, God released me from that pastorate. I was nearing the completion of my doctoral studies, and facing the major task of a dissertation. I also wanted to finish a second seminary degree.

Sensing God's release, I began one of the most difficult educational years of my life. In one year I completed 43 semester units, 17 of them consisting of language studies in Greek and Hebrew. In the middle of that year I took my comprehensive exams, and by the end of the year finished my doctoral dissertation. I also taught part-time at Talbot School of Theology. It was a difficult year, to say the least. But if you take a year off for education, you want to accomplish as much as you possibly can.

We started that year with the assurance that $20,000 would be made available for my education, interest free. The plan was to pay off the loan when we sold our home. Not having to sell our house allowed us to keep our children in the same school for that year. After I completed my education, I was confident that God would have a place for us. So I proceeded with a great deal of anticipation to finish my doctorate and a second master's degree. For the next six months our life together unfolded as planned. Then God turned out the lights.

Apparently the second half of the promised $20,000 wasn't going to come in. Having no other source of income, our cupboards became bare. I had no job, and my educational goals were only half completed. I always considered myself a faithful provider, but now I was on the brink of not being able to provide for the basic needs of my family. Six months earlier, I had been so certain of God's calling; but now the darkness of uncertainty had settled in.

It all culminated two weeks before my comprehensive exams. Only 10 percent of the doctoral candidates had passed the previous testing, which took place on two consecutive Saturdays, so there was a lot of pressure. If I didn't pass the exams, I couldn't start my dissertation. I had already invested three years of my life and $15,000 in the program. Now I didn't even know where my next meal was coming from.

I had equity in my home, but interest rates at the time were so high that houses simply weren't selling. The tension to create my own "light" was overwhelming. I looked into a couple of ministry opportunities, but I knew they weren't for me, and I couldn't accept them. The problem wasn't an unwillingness to work; I would have sold hot dogs to provide for my family. It wasn't a problem of pride; I just wanted to know God's will!

I began to wonder if I had made the wrong decision. God's leading was so clear the past summer. Why was I walking in darkness now? It was as though God had dropped me into a funnel, and it got darker and darker. When I thought it couldn't get much darker, I hit the narrow part! Then at the darkest hour God dropped us out of the bottom of that funnel and everything became clear.

It was about two o'clock on a Thursday morning when the dawn broke. Nothing changed circumstantially, but everything changed internally. I remember waking up with a great deal of excitement and a sense of joy. My startled wife awoke, wondering what was going on; but she, too, could sense that something had taken place. There was a conscious awareness of God in a remarkable way. No audible voices or visions were alerting us, only God in His quiet and gentle way was renewing my mind.

My thought process went something like this: *Neil, do you walk by faith or do you walk by sight? Are you walking by faith now? You believed Me last summer, do you believe Me now? Neil, do you love Me, or do you love My blessings? Do you worship Me for who I am, or for the blessings I bring? What if I suspended My conscious presence in your life? Would you still believe in Me?*

I knew then in a way I had never known before. In my spirit I responded, *Lord, you know I love You, and of course I walk by faith, not by sight. Lord, I worship You because of who You are, and I know that You will never leave me nor forsake me. Forgive me, Lord, that I ever doubted Your place in my life or questioned Your ability to provide all our needs.*

Those precious moments can't be planned or predicted. They are never repeatable. What we have previously learned from the Bible becomes incarnate during these times. Our worship is purified and our love clarified. Faith moves from a textbook definition to a living reality. Trust is deepened when God puts us in a position where we have no other choice but to trust Him. We will either trust or compromise our faith.

The Bible gives us the only infallible rules of faith and knowledge of God, but we learn to live by faith in the arena of life. This is especially true when circumstances are not working favorably for us. The Lord has a way of stretching us through a knothole, and just before we are about to break in half, suddenly we slip through to the other side. But we will never go back to the same shape we were in before.

The next day everything changed. The dean at Talbot School of Theology called to ask if I had taken another position. He asked me not to accept anything until we had the opportunity to talk. That Friday afternoon he offered me the position I held for the next 10 years.

On Friday night a man from my previous ministry stopped by at 10 o'clock. When I asked him what he was doing at our home at that hour of the night, he said he wasn't sure. I invited him in with the assurance that, "We'll figure out something." I half jokingly asked him if he'd like to buy my house, and he responded, "Maybe I would." The next Tuesday he and his parents made an offer on our house, which we accepted. Now we could sell our house because we knew the destination of our next move.

Nothing had changed externally before that morning, but everything changed internally. God can change in a moment what circumstances can never change. My wife and I had previously made this commitment that helped sustain us during such times: *We will never make a major decision when we are down.* That commitment alone has kept me from resigning after difficult board meetings or pulpit messages that bombed.

The point is, never doubt in darkness what God has clearly shown you in the light. We are to keep on walking in the light of previous revelation. If it was true six months ago, it's still true. If we're serious about our walk with God, He will test us to determine if we love Him or only His blessings. He may cloud the future so we can learn to walk by faith, not by sight or by feelings.

Understand in such times that God has not left us. He has only suspended His "conscious" presence so that our faith will never rest on our feelings, or be established by unique experiences, or fostered by blessings.

If our physical parents found themselves in difficult circumstances and couldn't afford any Christmas presents when we were young, would we stop loving them? Would we stop looking to them for direction and support? If God's ministry of darkness should envelop you, keep on walking in the light of previous revelation.

Don't create your own light. The natural tendency when we don't see it God's way, is to do it our way.

DON'T CREATE YOUR OWN LIGHT

The second lesson we learn from Isaiah is, *Don't light your own fire.* In other words, don't create your own light. The natural tendency when we don't see it God's way is to do it our way. Notice the text again: "Behold, all you who kindle a fire, who encircle yourselves with firebrands, walk in the light of your fire" (Isa. 50:11). God is not talking about the fire of judgment; He is talking about fire that creates light. Notice what happens when people create their own light: "And among the brands you have set ablaze. This you will have from My hand; and you will lie down in torment." Essentially, God is saying, "Go ahead, do it your way. God will allow it, but misery will follow."

Let us illustrate from the Bible. God called Abraham out of Ur into the Promised Land. In Genesis 12, a covenant was made in which God promised Abraham that his descendants would be more numerous than the sands of the sea or the stars in the sky.

Abraham lived his life in the light of that promise, then God turned out the light. So many months and years passed that his wife Sarah could no longer bear a child by natural means. God's guidance had been so clear before, but now it looked as though Abraham would have to assist God in its fulfillment.

Who could blame Abraham for creating his own light? Sarah supplied the match by offering her handmaiden to Abraham. Out of that union came another nation that has created so much conflict that the whole world now lies in torment. Jew and Arab have not been able to dwell together peacefully to this day. All this as a result of Abraham's trying to provide his own light.

God superintended the birth of Moses and provided for his preservation. Raised in the home of Pharaoh, he was given the second most prominent position in Egypt. But God had put into Moses' heart a burden to set his people free. Impulsively, Moses pulled out his sword, attempting to help God set His people free. He killed an Egyptian taskmaster, and God turned out the lights.

Abandoned to the back side of the desert, Moses spent 40 years tending his father-in-law's sheep. Then one day, he turned aside to see a burning bush that wasn't consumed, and God turned the light back on.

I'm not suggesting that we may have to wait 40 years for the cloud to lift. In our life span, that would be more time than an average person's faith could endure. But the darkness may last for weeks, months and, possibly, for some exceptional people, even years. God is in charge, and He knows exactly how small a knothole He can pull us through. We must only remember: "The One forming light and creating darkness, causing well-being and creating calamity; I am the Lord who does all these" (Isa. 45:7).

Let me share our second period of darkness. Five years after Joanne's surgery to remove the lenses from both eyes, her doctor suggested that she have a lens implant. So much progress had been made that implanting a lens was done as outpatient surgery. At first Joanne was reluctant. In addition, our insurance wouldn't pay at first, calling the surgery "cosmetic," but it finally came around. Joanne's doctor and I convinced her it was the best thing to do.

The surgery was successful, but Joanne emerged from the anesthesia in a phobic state. She had been anesthetized in surgery before, so I couldn't understand why she was so fearful now. I certainly could understand her apprehension before surgery, because cutting into one's eyeball is not something you look forward to. Just the thought of it can send shivers down your spine. So her emotional state before surgery was somewhat troubled.

But why was she traumatized after the surgery? Could the anesthetic itself have caused her emotional state? Or could the nature of her postoperative care have been a factor? The cost for medical care has pushed many hospitals into day surgeries that leave no time for rest or recovery after such a traumatic experience.

The nurses had to ask for my assistance in helping Joanne come out of the anesthesia. Joanne was just one of several patients that day, and I think part of their motivation was to clear a bed for other patients. Most people need more emotional care than that. If she had been permitted to recover from her experience gradually and spend at least one night in the hospital, she might have recovered a lot better. Bringing Joanne home that afternoon was an ordeal for both of us. She just couldn't stabilize emotionally.

The possibility that this was also a spiritual battle became evident the next day. Joanne thought she had a foreign object in her eye that had to come out. This made no rational sense at all because the surgery had been successful. She could see with 20/30 vision.

I didn't understand the battle for our minds then as I do today. Since then, I have seen young women struggling with eating disorders have such thoughts. Along with Paul, who said, "I find then the principle that evil is present in me, the one who wishes to do good" (Rom. 7:21), such people believe they have evil present in them and they have to get it out. That is the lie behind their purging, defecating and cutting themselves. But the evil is not their blood, feces or food. And the evil that Joanne was fighting was not the physical kind; it was the lie of Satan, which came at a very vulnerable moment.

It is painful to recall this because much of what followed could have been avoided. Joanne's struggle with anxiety led to sleeplessness and finally depression. She went from her eye doctor to her primary care doctor, to her gynecologist and finally to a psychiatrist. Because they could find nothing physically wrong with Joanne, they assumed she was a head case or a hormone case. They tried hormones, antidepressants and sleeping pills, but nothing seemed to work. She lost her appetite and her weight dropped significantly. She was hospitalized five times.

THIS, TOO, WILL PASS

The attempts to get medical help became exceedingly expensive. Our insurance ran out, and we had to sell our house to pay the medical bills. Joanne couldn't function as a mother or wife. My daughter, Heidi, wasn't sure whether she could handle it if her mother were to die. My son, Karl, withdrew into himself. I got caught in a role conflict like never before. Was I Joanne's pastor, counselor or discipler, or was I supposed to be just her husband?

I decided there was only one role I could fulfill in her life, and that was to be her husband. If someone was going to "fix" my wife, it would have to be someone other than myself. My role was to hold her every day and say, "Joanne, someday this will pass." I was thinking it would be a matter of weeks or months, but it turned into a long, 15-month ordeal. The funnel got narrower and narrower. Isaiah 21:11,12 had great meaning to me: "One keeps calling to me from Seir, 'Watchman, how far gone is the night? Watchman, how far gone is the night?' The watchman says, 'Morning comes but also night.'"

A ministry of hope must be based on the truth that morning comes. No matter how dark the night, morning comes. And it is always the darkest before the dawn. In our darkest hour, when I wasn't even sure whether Joanne was going to live or die, morning came.

Joanne had all but given up on any medical hope. A doctor who remained in private practice was recommended to her. He immediately took Joanne off the medication she was on, and prescribed a much more balanced approach that dealt with depression but also her general health, including good nutrition.

At the same time, we had a day of prayer at Biola University where I taught. I had nothing to do with the program other than to set aside special time for prayer in my own classes. Our undergraduate students had a communion service that evening. Because I taught at the graduate level, I normally wouldn't have gone. But because work had detained me on campus, I decided to participate.

I sat on the gym floor with the undergraduate students and took communion. I am sure nobody in the student body was aware that it was one of the loneliest and darkest times of my life. I was deeply committed to doing God's will, and I was walking as best I could in the light of previous revelation, but I felt incredibly frustrated. There was nothing I could do to change Joanne or the circumstances.

MORNING COMES

I can honestly say that I never once questioned God, nor felt bitter about my circumstances. For some time, the Lord had been preparing my heart and leading me into a ministry that sets captives free. Somehow I knew that the nature of my ministry was related to what my family was going through, but I didn't know what to do about it.

Should I abandon what I was doing to help others in order to spare my family? God was blessing my ministry in unprecedented ways, but my family wasn't being blessed. He had stripped us of everything we owned. All we had left was each other and our relationship to God. When there was nowhere else to turn, morning came!

If God has ever spoken to my heart, He did in that communion service. There were no voices or visions. It was just the quiet and gentle way He has in renewing our minds. It didn't come by way of the pastor's message, or the testimonies of the students; but it did come in the context of taking communion.

The essence of my thought process went like this:

Neil, there's a price to pay for freedom. It cost My Son His life. Are you willing to pay the price?

Dear God, I answered inwardly, *if that's the reason, I'm willing, but if it's some stupid thing I'm doing, then I don't want to be a part of it anymore.*

I left with the inward assurance that it was over. The circumstances hadn't changed, but in my heart I knew that morning had come.

Within a week, Joanne woke up one morning and said, "Neil, I slept last night." From that point on, she knew she was on the road to recovery. She never looked back, but continued on to full and complete recovery. At the same time, our ministry took a quantum leap forward.

BROKENNESS: THE KEY TO MINISTRY

What was the point of all this? Why did we have to go through such a trial?

SEEING IN THE DARK

First, you learn a lot about yourself in times of darkness. Whatever was left of my old nature that gave simplistic advice such as "Why don't you read your Bible?" or "Just work harder" or "Pray more" was mercifully stripped away.

Most people going through dark times want to do the right thing, but many can't or at least don't believe they can, and don't know why. Brokenness can give us a kind of "night vision," helping us to realize our limitations and deepen our roots in the eternal streams of life while severing ties with temporal things that don't last.

WEEPING INSTEAD OF INSTRUCTING

Second, we learn compassion in God's ministry of darkness. We learn to wait patiently with people, and *weep* with those who weep, not *instruct* those who weep. We learn to respond to the emotional needs of people who have lost hope. Instruction will come later. I think I was a caring person before, but nothing like I am now, because of God's gracious way of ministering to me.

We had some "friends" like those who tried to help Job, who tried to advise us in our time of darkness, and I can tell you it hurts. What Job needed in his hour of darkness was a few good friends who would just sit with him. They did for one week, but then their patience ran out.

The meaningful help we received was from the church, people who just stood by us and prayed. If God took away every external blessing, and reduced our assets to nothing more than meaningful relationships, would that be enough for us?

Most people of the world have learned to be content with food and clothing because they have no other choice. Paul said, "I know how to get along with humble means, and I also know how to live in prosperity; in any and every circumstance I have learned the secret of being filled and going hungry, both of having abundance and suffering need" (Phil. 4:12). That is an important lesson to learn.

Again, as was the case with Job, our final lot was far better than it was at the beginning. Within two years God replaced everything we lost, only this time it was far better in terms of home, family and ministry. Be encouraged that God makes everything right in the end.

DISCOVERING LIFE THROUGH DEATH

Third, I believe God brings us to the end of our resources so that we may discover His. We don't hear many sermons about brokenness in our churches these days. It's the great omission, and that's why we can't fulfill the Great Commission.

In all four Gospels, Jesus taught us to deny ourselves, take up our cross daily and follow Him. When it was time for the Son of Man to be glorified, He said: "Truly, truly, I say to you, unless a grain of wheat falls into the earth and dies, it remains by itself alone; but if it dies, it bears much fruit" (John 12:24). I don't know any painless way to die to ourselves. But I do know that it is necessary, and that it is the best possible thing that could ever happen to us.

"For we who live are constantly being delivered over to death for Jesus' sake, that the life of Jesus also may be manifested in our mortal flesh" (2 Cor. 4:11). If we are relying on degrees, diplomas, status and self-confidence, God is going to strip us of our self-sufficiency.

Joseph was no good for God in Pharaoh's court until all earthly possessions and positions were stripped from him. Chuck Colson was no good for God in the White House, but he was when he had to go to prison. I had a lot of hard-earned attributes, including five earned degrees, but I wasn't much good for God until suffering had its perfect result.

I can't set anybody free, but God can. Every book I have written and every tape I have recorded was accomplished after this period of brokenness. It was the birth of "Freedom in Christ Ministries," which has spread around the world. "No pain, no gain," says the bodybuilder. That is also true in the spiritual realm. Back to Isaiah's second point: Don't create your own light. Man-made light is very, very deceptive.

A LESSON IN TRUST

The final point Isaiah makes is that those who fear God must "Trust in the name of the Lord and rely on his God" (Isa. 50:10). The purpose of walking in darkness is a lesson in trust.

Possibly the greatest sign of spiritual maturity is the ability to postpone rewards. The ultimate test would be to receive nothing in this lifetime, but look forward to receiving our reward in the life to come. Listen to how the writer of Hebrews expressed it:

> All these died in faith, without receiving the promises, but having seen them and having welcomed them from a distance, and having confessed that they were strangers and exiles on this earth. For those who say such things make it clear that they are seeking a country of their own (Heb. 11:13,14).

Verses 39 and 40 read, "And all these, having gained approval through their faith, did not receive what was promised, because God had provided something better for us, so that apart from us they should not be made perfect."

God's will for your life is on the other side of a closed door, and you may never know what it is unless you resolve an issue on this side of the door. If God is God, He has the right to decide what is on the other side of the door. If we don't give Him that right, and insist on doing our own thing, then we will play our games and decide our own destiny on this side of the door. We get our way, but we miss our calling. "There is a way which seems right to a man, but its end is the way of death" (Prov. 14:12).

If I had known beforehand what my family would have to go through to get where we are today, I probably wouldn't have come through that door. But looking back we can all say, "We're glad we came." That's why God doesn't show us beforehand what's on the other side of the door.

Remember: God makes everything right in the end. It may not even be in this lifetime, as it wasn't for the heroes mentioned in Hebrews 11. But I believe with all my heart that when life is done, looking back, we will all say that the will of God is good, acceptable and perfect.

Notes

1. J. I. Packer, *Rediscovering Holiness* (Ann Arbor, Mich.: Servant Publications, 1992), p. 249.

2. Much of this discussion on suffering is presented in Neil's book *The Common Made Holy*, coauthored by Dr. Robert Saucy (Eugene, Oreg.: Harvest House, 1997).

3. C. K. Barrett, *A Commentary on the Second Epistle to the Corinthians* (New York: HarperCollins, 1973), p. 146.

4. Packer, op. cit., p. 250.

5. Gordon R. Lewis, "Suffering and Anguish," *Zondervan Pictorial Encyclopedia of the Bible*, Merrill C. Tenny, ed. (Grand Rapids: Zondervan, 1976), p. 5:532.

6. C. S. Lewis, *The Problem of Pain* (New York: Macmillan, 1962), p. 93.

7. John Freccero, *Dante: The Poetics of Conversion*, Rachel Jacoff, ed. (Cambridge, Mass.: Harvard University Press, 1986), p. 70.

8. C. S. Lewis, op. cit., p. 91.

9. C. S. Lewis, *The Joyful Christian: 127 Readings from C. S. Lewis* (New York: Macmillan, 1977), p. 210.

10. H. W. Robinson, *Suffering: Human and Divine* (New York: Macmillan, 1939), p. 139.

11. Lewis, *The Problem of Pain*, p. 93.

12. Peter Kreeft, *Making Sense Out of Suffering* (Ann Arbor, Mich.: Servant Publications, 1986), p. 78.

13. Philip Edgcumbe Hughes, *Paul's Second Epistle to the Corinthians* (Grand Rapids: Eerdmans, 1962), p. 11.

14. John White, *The Fight* (Downers Grove, Ill.: InterVarsity Press, 1976), p. 116.

15. John Murray, *The Epistle to the Romans*, vol. 1 (Grand Rapids: Eerdmans, 1959), p. 164.

16. Neil first shared this story in his book *Walking in the Light*, published by Thomas Nelson.

CHAPTER TEN

A COMMITMENT TO FREEDOM FROM DEPRESSION

The root of the evil lies in the constitution itself,
in the fatal weakening of families from generation
to generation....The root of the evil certainly lies
there, and there's no cure for it.[1]

VINCENT VAN GOGH

What then shall we say to these things? If God is for us,
who is against us? He who did not spare His own Son,
but delivered Him up for us all, how will He not also
with Him freely give us all things? Who shall separate us
from the love of Christ? Shall tribulation, or distress, or
persecution, or famine, or nakedness, or peril, or sword?
But in all these things we overwhelmingly conquer
through Him who loved us. For I am convinced that
neither death, nor life, nor angels, nor principalities,
nor things present, nor things to come, nor powers, nor
height, nor depth, nor any other created thing, shall be
able to separate us from the love of God, which is
in Christ Jesus our Lord.

ROMANS 8:31,32,35,37-39

The apostle John records the story of a man who had been lame for 38 years. The Lord singled him out at the pool of Bethesda, where many other blind, lame and paralyzed people were gathered.

The people who were there believed that an angel would occasionally stir the waters, and that anybody who was in the pool at the time would be healed. But this poor man could never get to the pool before the waters stopped stirring. "When Jesus saw him lying there and learned that he had been in this condition for a long time, he asked him, 'Do you want to get well?'"(John 5:6, NIV).

That is either the cruelest question in the New Testament or one of the most profound. Obviously, it is the latter because the Lord asked it. The lame man answered:

"I have no one to help me into the pool when the water is stirred. While I am trying to get in, someone else goes down ahead of me." Then Jesus said to him, "Get up! Pick up your mat and walk." At once the man was cured; he picked up his mat and walked (John 5:7-9, NIV).

The context reveals that the man really didn't want to get well. He never asked Jesus to be healed, and he always had an excuse why others could get to the pool and he couldn't. Later, Jesus found him in the Temple and said to him, "See, you are well again. Stop sinning or something worse may happen to you" (5:14, NIV). Then the man actually went away and told the Jews that it was Jesus who had made him well, turning Him in for healing him on the Sabbath!

Applying this incident to the problem of depression, here are 10 commitments to be made if you can answer yes to Jesus' question, "Do you want to get well?"

COMMIT YOURSELF TO COMPLETE RECOVERY

Create in me a clean heart, O God, and renew a steadfast spirit within me. Restore to me the joy of Thy salvation, and sustain me with a willing spirit (Ps. 51:10,12).

Do you want to get well as much as this psalm indicates King David did? Are you willing to humble yourself and seek the help you need from God and others? Are you willing to face the truth and walk in the light? Do you want a partial answer or the whole solution?

We ask these tough questions for your sake. More than 50 percent of those struggling with depression never ask for help or seek treatment for their depression. There are adequate answers for depression, but you have to want it more than anything else in the world, and be willing to do whatever it takes to be free.

There are adequate answers for depression, but you have to want it more than anything else in the world, and be willing to do whatever it takes to be free.

The key to any cure is commitment. We are not offering a Band-Aid, a quick fix or a partial answer. We believe that if you will follow the procedure in this chapter in the order in which it comes, you will have a comprehensive and adequate answer for your depression.

Recovery begins by saying, "I have a problem and I need help." Your diligence in reading to this point demonstrates your commitment to seek the help you need to gain total victory. We have a God of all hope. He is "our refuge and strength, an ever-present help in trouble" (Ps. 46:1, *NIV*). The story of the lame man reveals that God is fully capable of healing someone even against his will and regardless of his faith. Rest assured that your heavenly Father will be faithful in all that He has said and in all that He is. "Jesus Christ is the same yesterday and today, yes and forever" (Heb. 13:8).

COMMIT YOURSELF TO PRAYER

Do not be anxious about anything, but in everything, by prayer and petition, with thanksgiving, present your requests to God. And the peace of God, which transcends all understanding, will guard your hearts and your minds in Christ Jesus (Phil. 4:6,7, *NIV*).

We are asking you to *pray*, not to "Get tough and try harder." That kind of advice and attitude could itself lead to burnout and depression.

Human effort alone will not be an adequate answer. Besides, adding one more thing to your plate would only contribute to your crisis. Instead, we are encouraging you to trust God by submitting yourself to Him and His ways, and by seeking a holistic answer through the godly counsel and assistance of others.

If you have the desire to get well, and if you are willing to assume your responsibility for your own attitudes and actions, then we believe there is hope for you. E. Stanley Jones said:

I laid at Christ's feet a self of which I was ashamed, couldn't control, and couldn't live with; and to my glad astonishment He took that self, remade it, consecrated it to kingdom purposes, and gave it back to me, a self I can now live with gladly and joyously and comfortably.[2]

He alone can bind up the brokenhearted and set the captive free. God can do wonders with a broken heart if you give Him all the pieces. The world will encourage you to seek every possible natural explanation and cure first. When that is not successful, people will say, "There is nothing more that we can do but pray." Scripture has a different order. "But seek first His kingdom and His righteousness; and all these things shall be added to you" (Matt. 6:33).

The first thing a Christian should do about anything is pray. May we suggest the following prayer to begin your process of recovery:

Dear heavenly Father, I come to You as Your child. I declare my total dependence upon You, and acknowledge that apart from Christ I can do nothing. Thank You for sending Jesus to die in my place in order that my sins could be forgiven. I praise You for Your resurrection power that raised Jesus from the grave in order that I too may have eternal life.

I choose to believe the truth that the devil has been defeated, and that I am now seated with Christ in the heavenlies. Therefore I choose to believe that I have the power and the authority to do Your will and be the person You created me to be. I submit my body to You as a living sacrifice, and ask You to fill me with Your Holy Spirit. I desire nothing more than to know and do your will, believing that it is good, perfect, and acceptable for me. I invite the Spirit of truth to lead me into all truth that I may be set free in Christ.

I choose from this day forward to walk in the light and speak the truth in love. I acknowledge my pain to You, and confess my sins, doubts and lack of trust. I now invite You to search my heart, try my ways, and see if there is any wicked way within me, then lead me into the everlasting way by the power and guidance of Your Holy Spirit. In Jesus' precious name I pray. Amen.

COMMIT YOURSELF TO AN INTIMATE RELATIONSHIP WITH GOD

Come to me, all you who are weary and burdened, and I will give you rest. Take my yoke upon you and learn from me, for I am gentle and humble in heart, and you will find rest for your souls. For my yoke is easy and my burden is light (Matt. 11:28-30, *NIV*).

A whole answer will require first and foremost the presence of God in your life. Jesus is not just a "higher power"; He is our Lord and our Savior who took upon Himself the form of a man and dwelt among us. He was tempted in every way and suffered a humiliating and agonizing death so that we could have access to our heavenly Father.

Now this same Jesus says, "Come. Come to Me." We are not being invited to a physical church structure or program; we are being invited into the very presence of God. We need His presence in our lives because He is our life. We can do no other than what is recorded in Hebrews 10:22-25:

> Let us draw near to God with a sincere heart in full assurance of faith, having our hearts sprinkled to cleanse us from a guilty conscience and having our bodies washed with pure water. Let us hold unswervingly to the hope we profess, for he who promised is faithful. And let us consider how we may spur one another on toward love and good deeds. Let us not give up meeting together, as some are in the habit of doing, but let us encourage one another—and all the more as you see the Day approaching *(NIV)*.

The greatest crisis humankind has ever suffered was when Adam and Eve lost their relationship with God. The ultimate answer is to reestablish an intimate relationship with Him who is our only hope. What Adam and Eve lost was life, and what Jesus came to give us was life.

We possess that spiritual and eternal life the moment we are born again. That relationship was established by the blood of the Lord Jesus Christ and His resurrection. We need to maintain that relationship by living in harmony with our heavenly Father with a sincere heart. This may require resolving certain personal and spiritual conflicts between yourself and God.

The Steps to Freedom in Christ found in appendix A are intended to help you resolve any conflicts that may exist between you and your heavenly Father, through repentance and faith in Him.

Essentially, the process helps you submit to God and resist the devil (see Jas. 4:7). This eliminates the influence of the devil in your life and connects you with God in a personal and powerful way. You will then be able to experience the peace of God that guards your heart and your mind (see Phil. 4:7), and you will sense the Holy Spirit bearing witness with your spirit that you are a child of God (see Rom. 8:16). Now, by the grace of God, you will be able to process the remaining issues in this chapter.

Many will be able to walk through these Steps to Freedom by themselves because Jesus Himself is the Wonderful Counselor. The likelihood of your gaining freedom will be greatly increased if you first read Neil's books *Victory over the Darkness* and *The Bondage Breaker*.

We encourage you to be alone with God, and give yourself three or four hours to go through these Steps. Find a quiet place where you will not be interrupted, and where you can verbally go through the Steps. You have nothing to lose by going through this process of submitting to God and resisting the devil, and you have a lot to gain.

The Steps to Freedom in Christ are nothing more than a fierce moral inventory intended to help you "clean house" and make room for Jesus to reign in His temple. There is one major caution, however. In our experience, severe cases will require the assistance of a godly encourager. If you really want to get well, you won't hesitate to ask a Christ-centered pastor or counselor for help.

COMMIT YOURSELF AS A CHILD OF GOD

How great is the love the Father has lavished on us, that we should be called children of God! And that is what we are! The reason the world does not know us is that it did not know him. Dear friends, now we are children of God, and what we will be has not yet been made known. But we know that when he appears, we shall be like him, for we shall see him as he is. Everyone who has this hope in him purifies himself, just as he is pure (1 John 3:1-3, *NIV*).

Knowing who God is and who we are in Christ are the two most essential beliefs that enable us to live a victorious life. God loves you because He is love. It is His nature to love you. He couldn't do anything other than that.

God is omnipotent; therefore you can do all things through Christ who strengthens you (see Phil. 4:13). God is omniscient; therefore He knows the thoughts and intentions of your heart (see Heb. 4:12,13). He knows what you need and He is able to meet every need.

God is omnipresent; therefore you are never alone, and He will never leave you nor forsake you. You have become a partaker of His divine nature (see 2 Pet. 1:4), because your soul is in union with Him. That is what it means to be spiritually alive *in* Christ. He has defeated the devil, forgiven your sins, given you eternal life, and you are now His child if you have received Him into your life. "To all who received him, to those who believed in his name, he gave the right to become children of God" (John 1:12, *NIV*). If the devil wanted to discourage you, all he would have to do is get you to believe a lie about who God is and who you are in Christ.

Recall from chapter 4 King David's depression, as expressed in Psalm 13:1,2: "How long, O Lord? Wilt Thou forget me forever? How long wilt Thou hide thy face from me? How long shall I take counsel in my soul, having sorrow in my heart all the day? How long will my enemy be exalted over me?"

David is depressed because what he believes about God is not true, and there goes his hope. An omniscient God couldn't forget him even for a moment, much less forever! And who is David taking counsel with? Himself! There are no answers there.

The *New International Version* translates "take counsel with my soul," as "wrestle with my thoughts." All depressed persons wrestle with their thoughts. Negative self-talk only fuels Satan's forces in the battle for the mind. We must take every thought captive to the obedience of Christ (see 2 Cor. 10:5), and then choose to think upon that which is true (see Phil. 4:8).

Notice how David overcomes his depression: "But I trust in your unfailing love; my heart rejoices in your salvation. I will sing to the Lord, for he has been good to me" (Ps. 13:5,6, *NIV*). David overcomes his depression by turning to God, who loves him; and by recalling to his mind the good that God has done for him.

Then David chooses to sing to the Lord. The immediate result of being filled with the Spirit is to give thanks, sing and make melody in our hearts to the Lord (see Eph. 5:18-20). That is an act of the will we can all freely exercise. Singing Christian hymns and choruses helps to refocus our minds.

May we strongly suggest that you flood your home and your mind with Christian songs and choruses. Martin Luther found great relief from his depression while singing. It must have prompted him to write "A Mighty Fortress Is Our God," which has been a great blessing to many for more than 500 years:

> Did we in our own strength confide,
> Our striving would be losing,
> Were not the right man on our side,
> The man of God's own choosing.
> Dost ask who that may be?
> Christ Jesus, it is He—
> Lord Sabaoth His name,
> From age to age the same,
> And He must win the battle.

At the end of this chapter is a tear-out page for you to use. On one side is a list of Scripture verses affirming who you are in Christ and showing how He meets our need for acceptance, security and significance. On the other side is an Overcomer's Covenant, based on our position in Christ. When you feel discouraged and depressed, this will help you refocus your mind to the truth of who you are in Christ and the position you have in Him.

Recall that this is what Jeremiah did in Lamentations 3:21-24:

Yet this I call to mind and therefore I have hope: Because of the Lord's great love we are not consumed, for his compassions never fail. They are new every morning; great is your faithfulness. I say to myself, "The Lord is my portion; therefore I will wait for Him" *(NIV)*.

COMMIT YOUR BODY TO GOD

Therefore, I urge you, brothers, in view of God's mercy, to offer your bodies as living sacrifices, holy and pleasing to God—this is your spiritual act of worship (Rom. 12:1, *NIV*).

Do you not know that your body is a temple of the Holy Spirit, who is in you, whom you have received from God? You are not your own; you were bought at a price. Therefore honor God with your body (1 Cor. 6:19,20, *NIV*).

Depression is a multifaceted problem that affects the body, soul and spirit. Consequently, a comprehensive cure for depression will require a whole answer. There are many forms of *biological* depression, and most can be detected by a comprehensive medical exam. However, a 10-minute checkup at an HMO will not be sufficient, nor will seeing a psychiatrist who only reads the symptoms to prescribe antidepressant medication. There is no precise way to measure brain chemistry.

If your depression is truly endogenous (originating within your body), you would want some collaborating evidence to validate any medical treatment. If finances or insurance will allow, find a medical doctor or psychiatrist who can administer the appropriate tests, and who understands the value of good nutrition. This is also the appropriate time to discuss antidepressant medication.

Many forms of biological depression can be diagnosed and easily treated. A disorder of the endocrine system can produce depressive symptoms. The endocrine system includes the thyroid, parathyroid, thymus, pancreas and adrenal glands. These glands produce hormones that are released directly into the blood system.

The thyroid gland controls metabolism. An underactive thyroid (hypothyroidism) will cause changes in mood, including depression. The treatment is to prescribe a thyroid hormone, not antidepressants.

The metabolism of sugar is especially important for maintaining physical and emotional stability. Hypoglycemia (low blood sugar) is known to produce emotional instability.

The pituitary gland in the brain produces a hormone known as ACTH, which stimulates the adrenal glands. The malfunctioning of either gland will produce lethargic behavior and depression. We discussed in chapter 2 the problem of adrenal exhaustion due to prolonged stress. The answer for that kind of depression is to get sufficient rest and supplement your diet with B-complex vitamins. For some people, vitamin B12 injections may be necessary. B12 deficiency can have several causes, but the most common cause is aging. As we advance in years, our stomachs produce less of the acid that is necessary to extract B12 from our food.

The fact that women suffer from depression more than men may be due to their biological makeup. Dr. Archibald Hart writes:

> The reproductive organs of the female are extremely prone to creating mood swings. The depression at the onset of menstruation, the premenstrual syndrome (PMS), the use of contraceptive pills, pregnancy, postpartum reactions, and menopause all revolve around the female's reproductive system. And as we currently understand it, the system is fraught with depression pitfalls.[3]

Medical tests for most of these conditions are fairly routine, and can be detected with a good medical examination. In addition, each of us should assume personal responsibility for finding the proper balance of rest, exercise and diet. To live a healthy life, we must be health oriented, not illness oriented.

We see the same dynamic in winning the battle for the mind. The answer is not to renounce all the lies. The answer is to choose the truth. But if you aren't aware that there are lies, and if you ignore what your body is telling you, then you will likely fall victim to the disease and the father of lies. If you start to sense that you are physically and mentally slipping back into a depression, don't just succumb to it; take charge of your life by praying as follows:

> *Dear heavenly Father, I submit myself to You as Your child, and I declare myself to be totally dependent upon You. I yield my body to You as a living sacrifice, and I ask You to fill me with Your Holy Spirit. I renounce the lies of the evil one and I choose to believe the truth as You have revealed it to us in Your holy Word. Give me the grace and the wisdom to resist the devil so that he will flee from me. I now commit myself to You, including my body as an instrument of righteousness. In Jesus' precious name I pray. Amen.*

COMMIT YOURSELF TO THE RENEWING OF YOUR MIND

Do not conform any longer to the pattern of this world, but be transformed by the renewing of your mind. Then you will be able to test and approve what God's will is—his good, pleasing and perfect will (Rom. 12:2, *NIV*).

Depression can be related to lifestyle, or precipitated by some crisis event. By lifestyle depression we mean a depressive state that began in early childhood or has existed for many years. It is possible that lifestyle depression could have hereditary connections. That possibility is more likely with bipolar rather than unipolar depression. In such cases, medication may be required for complete recovery, along with godly counsel.

It is far more common, however, for the cause of lifestyle

depression to be traceable to early childhood development, or living in an oppressive situation that created or communicated a sense of hopelessness and helplessness.

Learned helplessness can be unlearned by the renewing of our minds. Over time, our computerlike brains have been programmed to think negatively about ourselves, our circumstances and the future. These negative thoughts and lies have been deeply ingrained. Thousands and thousands of prior mental rehearsals have added to the feelings you are experiencing right now. The natural tendency is to ruminate on these negative thoughts.

It doesn't take long to establish your freedom in Christ, but it will take you the rest of your life to renew your mind and conform to the image of God.

Daniel Goldman, a *New York Times* columnist, explains in his book *Emotional Intelligence*, "One of the main determinants of whether a depressed mood will persist or lift is the degree to which people ruminate. Worrying about what's depressing us, it seems, makes the depression all the more intense and prolonged."[4]

How can we win the battle for our minds? Should we rebuke every negative thought? No! If you tried, that is all you would be doing the rest of your life. You would be like a person stuck in the middle of a lake with 12 corks floating around your head and a little hammer in your hand. All your energy would be expended trying to keep the corks submerged with the hammer while trying to tread water. You should ignore the corks and swim to shore.

Similarly, you overcome the father of lies by choosing the truth. You can do that if you have successfully submitted to God and resisted the devil. If you haven't, then you are bopping down corks and treading water.

There is a major difference between *winning* the spiritual battle for your mind and the long-term growth process of *renewing* your mind. It doesn't take long to establish your freedom in Christ, but it will take you the rest of your life to renew your mind and conform to the image of God. Although getting free in Christ can happen in a relatively short period of time, there is no such thing as instant maturity.

Once a person has established his or her identity and freedom in Christ, the process of renewing the mind is quite easy. That is why we encourage you to go through the Steps to Freedom in Christ first.

Changing false beliefs and attitudes is necessary to overcome depression. The world will put you down, and the devil will accuse you, but you don't have to believe either one. You must take every thought captive to the obedience of Christ. In other words, you have to believe the truth as revealed in God's Word. You don't overcome the father of lies by research or by reason, but by revelation. To this end, Jesus petitioned our heavenly Father in His High Priestly prayer on our behalf:

"I am coming to you [God] now, but I say these things while I am still in the world, so that they may have the full measure of my joy within them. I have given them your word and the world has hated them, for they are not of the world any more than I am of the world. My prayer is not that you take them out of the world but that you protect them from the evil one. They are not of the world, even as I am not of it. Sanctify them by the truth; your word is truth" (John 17:13-17, *NIV*).

God is not going to remove us from the negativity of this fallen world, but we are sanctified and protected by the truth of His Word. Jesus said, "These things I have spoken to you, that in Me you may have peace. In the world you have tribulation, but take courage; I have overcome the world" (John 16:33).

Renewing our minds with truth will not continue if we don't actively work to sustain it. David said in Psalm 119:15,16, "I will meditate on Thy precepts, and regard Thy ways. I shall delight in Thy statutes; I shall not forget Thy word."

Every mental stronghold that is torn down in Christ makes the next one easier. Every thought you take captive makes the next one more likely to surrender. Lifestyle depression is the result of repeated blows that come from living in a fallen world. Rehearsing the truth again and again is the key to renewing your mind.

COMMIT YOURSELF TO GOOD BEHAVIOR

> The things you have learned and received and heard and seen in me, practice these things; and the God of peace shall be with you (Phil. 4:9).

You cannot be instantly delivered from lifestyle depression; you have to grow out of it. It takes time to renew the mind, but it doesn't take time to change our behavior—which actually facilitates the process of renewing our minds, as well as positively affecting how we feel.

When Cain and Abel brought their offerings, the Lord was not pleased with Cain's.

> So Cain became very angry and his countenance fell. Then the Lord said to Cain, "Why are you angry? And why has your countenance fallen? If you do well, will not your countenance be lifted up? And if you do not do well, sin is crouching at the door; and its desire is for you, but you must master it" (Gen. 4:5-7).

In other words, you don't *feel* your way into good behavior, you *behave* your way into a good feeling. If you wait until you feel like doing what is right, you will likely never do it. Jesus said, "If you know these things, you are blessed *if you do them*" (John 13:17, emphasis added).

That is why much of the initial intervention for severe depression focuses on behavior. Schedule appointments and activities that pull you out of your negative mood. Force yourself to work, even though you may not feel like getting out of bed. Plan an activity and stick to it. Commit yourself to getting more exercise, and follow through. Start with a low-impact aerobic program, or take walks with friends and family members. Continue routine duties even though you feel as if you don't have the energy.

These behavioral interventions or activities are only a start in developing a lifestyle that is healthy. If these are too difficult or physically impossible, then seek the kind of medical help that will get you back on your feet.

Watch for certain negative behaviors that will only contribute to depression. Drowning out your sorrows with drugs and alcohol is at the top of this destructive list. Although using alcohol or drugs to cope with the difficulties of life or to medicate pain may bring temporary relief, it will only contribute to the depression.

To understand how living in an oppressive situation can result in depression and alcoholism see Neil's book *Freedom from Addiction*,[5] which he coauthored with Mike and Julia Quarles. Mike struggled with his identity, poor sense of worth and feelings of inadequacy. When he turned to alcohol to numb the pain, he became addicted. This behavior placed a great deal of stress on his relationship with his wife, Julia. They both struggled with defeat and depression until they found their freedom in Christ.

COMMIT YOURSELF TO MEANINGFUL RELATIONSHIPS

And let us consider how to stimulate one another to love and good deeds, not forsaking our own assembling together, as is the habit of some, but encouraging one another; and all the more, as you see the day drawing near (Heb. 10:24,25).

One of the major symptoms of depression is withdrawal from meaningful relationships, which would be number two on the list of destructive behaviors. Isolating yourself so you are alone with your negative thoughts will certainly contribute to a downward spiral.

You may feel that you need to be alone, but you need to stay in contact with the right people. Wrong associations will only pull you down. "Do not be deceived: 'Bad company corrupts good morals'" (1 Cor. 15:33). We suggest that you go see your pastor or find another godly pastor in your community. Tell him the struggle you are having with depression, and ask him what the church offers in terms of fellowship. A good church will have many meaningful activities, and small discipleship groups where you can get the prayer and care you need.

Anybody who has suffered from lifestyle depression for any length of time will have one or more people that need to be forgiven, and some that need reconciliation. We hope you resolved the need to forgive others as you went through the Steps to Freedom. Concerning the need to seek the forgiveness of others, Jesus said, "If therefore you are presenting your offering at the altar, and there remember that your brother has something against you, leave your offering there before the altar, and go your way; first be reconciled to your brother, and then come and present your offering" (Matt. 5:23,24). If you need to be forgiven of your sins, then go to God. But if you have offended or hurt someone else, don't go to God; go to that person and be reconciled. You will have little mental peace until you do both.

COMMIT YOURSELF TO OVERCOME EVERY LOSS

But whatever things were gain to me, those things I have counted as loss for the sake of Christ. More than that, I count all things to be loss in view of the surpassing value of knowing Christ Jesus my Lord, for whom I have suffered the loss all things, and count them but rubbish in order that I may gain Christ (Phil. 3:7,8).

Reactive depression is different from lifestyle depression in that it is triggered by some specific event or loss. This can be a real loss, an imagined one or simply a negative thought (lie) that is believed. Recall that Elijah's downward spiral began when he believed a lie and gave the wicked Jezebel more power in his life than God.

We all experience losses. How we handle any crisis will determine how fast we recover from the loss and how well we conform to the image of God. The following steps, adapted from Dr. Archibald Hart, will help you overcome your losses:[6]

1. IDENTIFY AND UNDERSTAND EACH LOSS

Most losses are easy to recognize, but some aren't. Changing jobs or moving to a new location can precipitate a depression. Even though both could be an improvement in social status and potential lifestyle, something was lost in the move. The move could break an attachment to old friends, familiar places or comfortable working conditions. The loss of a job could also include the loss of wages, social status, respect, etc.

People don't react the same to losses, because they have different values and different levels of maturity. To move out of denial and into the grieving process, you must understand what you are losing or have already lost. A person could be depressed because he didn't get the job he hoped for, or the promotion he wanted. Some have planned their lives to go a certain way, and now their dreams for the future have been dashed.

2. SEPARATE THE CONCRETE FROM THE ABSTRACT

Concrete losses can be seen, touched, measured and clearly defined. Abstract losses refer to personal goals, dreams and ideas. Overcoming concrete losses is usually easier because they are more definable.

They vary from losing a card game to losing a leg. Most wouldn't be very depressed about losing a card game, but if you were representing the United States in the world bridge championships and you lost the final game, it could be very depressing.

Abstract losses relate deeply to who we are and why we are here. Many concrete losses, such as the loss of a job, are contaminated with abstract losses. You could probably find a new job next week, but remain depressed because you feel the pain of rejection and think you are a failure. That is why it is so important to understand who we are in Christ, and to find our acceptance, security and significance in Him.

3. SEPARATE REAL, IMAGINED AND THREATENED LOSSES

You cannot process an imagined or threatened loss in the same way you can a real one. In a real loss you can face the truth, grieve the loss and make the necessary changes that make it possible to go on living in a meaningful way.

4. CONVERT IMAGINED AND THREATENED LOSSES TO REAL LOSSES

Imagined losses are distortions of reality. They are based on suspicions or lies we have believed, or on presumptions we have made. The mind wants to assume certain things when we don't know the facts and suspect that something may be in the works. Seldom does the mind assume the best.

We don't always act upon our assumptions, but if we do we shall be counted among the fools because "through presumption comes nothing but strife" (Prov. 13:10). It is more common to ruminate on various possibilities and consequences in our minds until we are depressed. The answer is to verify these assumptions, then follow Peter's advice: "Cast all your anxiety on Him because He cares for you. Be self-controlled and alert. Your enemy the devil prowls around like a roaring lion looking for someone to devour. Resist him, standing firm in the faith" (1 Pet. 5:7,8, *NIV*).

Threatened losses have the potential for being real losses. They include such things as the possibility of a layoff at work, or a spouse who threatens to leave you. Such threats can precipitate a depression, but because there is at the present no finality to the loss, it cannot be processed.

Sometimes it helps to imagine what the worst-case scenario may be, and then ask yourself the question, "Can I live with it?" This is part of preparing yourself for impermanence. We all face potential losses. No other person has the right to determine who you are, and cannot keep you from being the person God created you to be. So when someone threatens you, respond the way Peter advises:

> Who is going to harm you if you are eager to do good? But even if you should suffer for what is right, you are blessed. "Do not fear what they fear; do not be frightened." But in your hearts set apart Christ as Lord. Always be prepared to give an answer to everyone who asks you to give the reason for the hope that you have. But do this with gentleness and respect, keeping a clear conscience, so that those who speak maliciously against your good behavior in Christ may be ashamed of their slander. It is better, if it is God's will, to suffer for doing good than for doing evil (1 Pet. 3:13-17, *NIV*).

These are growth issues, not terminal ones, if you are viewing life from an eternal perspective. What is the worst thing that could happen to you? You could die. But is that intolerable? Paul said, "For to me, to live is Christ, and to die is gain" (Phil. 1:21). Put anything else in the formula, and the result is loss. If "For me to live is my health," then to die would be loss. If "For me to live is my family," then to die would be loss. This is not a license to commit suicide. It is a liberating truth that allows us to live responsible lives. The person who is free from the fear of death is free to live today.

5. FACILITATE THE GRIEVING PROCESS

The natural response to any crisis is first to deny that it is really happening, then to get angry that it did happen, then to try to alter the situation by bargaining with God or others, and when that doesn't work, to feel depressed.

You cannot successfully bypass the grieving process, but you can shorten it by allowing yourself to feel the full force of the loss. The fact that certain losses are depressing is reality. It hurts to lose something that has value to you. You cannot fully process your loss until you feel its full force. That must be what Jesus had in mind when He said, "Blessed are those who mourn, for they shall be comforted" (Matt. 5:4).

6. FACE THE REALITY OF THE LOSS

Only after you have faced its full force are you ready to deal with the reality of the loss. This is the critical juncture. Are we going to resign from life, succumb to the depression and drop out, or are we going to accept what we cannot change and let go of the loss? We can feel sorry for ourselves the rest of our lives, or we can decide to live with our losses and learn how to go on in a meaningful way.

7. DEVELOP A BIBLICAL PERSPECTIVE ON THE LOSS

The trials and tribulations of life are intended to produce proven character. Suffering is for the sake of righteousness (see chapter 9). We can potentially come through any crisis a better person than we were. Losses are inevitable. They are not intended to destroy you, but they will reveal who you are. Many people have discovered the truth of who they are in Christ as a direct result of losses. Each subsequent loss only deepens that reality, perfects our character and prepares us for an even greater ministry.

8. RENEW YOUR MIND TO THE TRUTH OF WHO YOU REALLY ARE

We are all going to be victimized by losses and abuses. We can drown in our own pity, blame others, claim that life isn't fair—and stay depressed the rest of our lives. Whether we remain victims is our choice. But we are not just products of our pasts. We are new creations in Christ, and nothing nor anybody on planet Earth can keep us from being the kind of people He created us to be.

Like the apostle Paul, we count everything but loss apart from the surpassing value of knowing Christ Jesus our Lord. "For we who live are constantly being delivered over to death for Jesus' sake, that the life of Jesus also may be manifested in our mortal flesh" (2 Cor. 4:11). Whenever this mortal life throws you a curve, remember these words of encouragement from your heavenly Father:

> You have forgotten that word of encouragement that addresses you as sons: "My son, do not make light of the Lord's discipline, and do not lose heart when he rebukes you, because the Lord disciplines those he loves, and he punishes everyone he accepts as a son." Endure hardship as discipline; God is treating you as sons. For what son is not disciplined by his father? If you are not disciplined (and everyone undergoes discipline), then you are illegitimate children and not true sons. Moreover, we have all had human fathers who disciplined us and we respected them for it. How much more should we submit to the Father of our spirits and live! Our fathers disciplined us for a little while as they thought best; but God disciplines us for our good, that we may share in his holiness. No discipline seems pleasant at the time, but painful. Later on, however, it produces a harvest of righteousness and peace for those who have been trained by it (Heb. 12:5-11, *NIV*).

COMMIT YOURSELF TO EXCHANGE YOUR ASHES FOR HIS BEAUTY

One woman shared with us that her best friend ran off with her husband 10 years earlier. She was deeply hurt by this incredible betrayal and disloyalty. She thought her life was ruined by those adulterers, and there was nothing she could do about it.

For 10 years she smoldered in depression. Feelings of resentment and plots of revenge ruminated in her mind. I told her, "I see you with one arm extended up to heaven where God has a firm grip on you. Your other arm is hanging on to your past and you aren't about to let go. You are not even hanging on to God, but your heavenly Father is hanging on to you, His beloved child. Isn't it time to let it go? You are only hurting yourself."

At the end of the conference the woman walked through the Steps to Freedom in Christ, and was able to let go of all that burden of resentment and anger. The next morning she was singing in the choir, exhibiting a countenance that portrayed a liberated child of God.

Let go of your past, and grab hold of God. It is your only hope. May these closing thoughts help you do just that:

Once I held in my tightly clenched fist...ashes. Ashes from a burn inflicted upon my ten-year-old body. Ashes I didn't ask for. The scar was forced on me. And for seventeen years the fire smoldered. I kept my fist closed in secret, hating those ashes, yet unwilling to release them. Not sure if I could. Not convinced it was worth it. Marring the things I touched and leaving black marks everywhere...or so it seemed. I tried to undo it all, but the marks were always there to remind me that I couldn't. I really couldn't. But God could! His sweet Holy Spirit spoke to my heart one night in tearful desperation. He whispered, "I want to give you beauty for your ashes, the oil of joy for your mourning and the garment of praise for your spirit of heaviness." I had never heard of such a trade as this: Beauty? Beauty for ashes? My sadly stained memory for the healing in His word? My soot-like dreams for His songs in the night? My helpless and hurting emotions for His ever constant peace?

How could I be so stubborn as to refuse an offer such as this? So willingly, yet in slow motion and yes, while sobbing, I opened my bent fingers and let the ashes drop to the ground. In silence, I heard the wind blow them away. Away from me...forever. I am now able to place my open hands gently around the fist of another hurting soul and say with confidence, "Let them go. There really is beauty beyond your comprehension. Go ahead—trust Him. His beauty for your ashes."[7]

Notes

1. Vincent van Gogh, *The Complete Letters*, Volume 3, p. 8, letter 521.
2. Sherwood Wirt and Kersten Beckstrom, *Living Quotations for Christians* (New York: HarperCollins, 1974), p. 35.
3. Archibald Hart, *Counseling the Depressed* (Dallas, Tex.: Word Books, 1987), p. 99.
4. Mitch and Susan Golant, *What to Do When Someone You Love Is Depressed* (New York: Villard, 1996), p. 23.
5. Neil T. Anderson, *Freedom from Addiction* (Ventura, Calif.: Regal Books, 1996). If you are struggling with sexual addiction, see Neil's book *A Way of Escape* (Eugene, Oreg.: Harvest House, 1994). Freedom in Christ Recovery Ministries is a branch of Freedom in Christ, which can be contacted at 491 East Lambert Rd., La Habra, CA, 90631, or by calling (562) 691-9128.
6. Archibald Hart, *Counseling the Depressed* (Dallas, Tex.: Word Books, 1987), pp. 133-143.
7. From a printout distributed by Honeycomb Publishing, Box 1434, Taylors, SC 29687. (n.d.)

IN CHRIST

I AM ACCEPTED

John 1:12	I am God's child.
John 15:15	I am Christ's friend.
Romans 5:1	I have been justified.
1 Corinthians 6:17	I am united with the Lord, and I am one spirit with Him.
1 Corinthians 6:20	I have been bought with a price. I belong to God.
1 Corinthians 12:27	I am a member of Christ's Body.
Ephesians 1:1	I am a saint.
Ephesians 1:5	I have been adopted as God's child.
Ephesians 2:18	I have direct access to God through the Holy Spirit.
Colossians 1:14	I have been redeemed and forgiven of all my sins.
Colossians 2:10	I am complete in Christ.

I AM SECURE

Romans 8:1,2	I am free from condemnation.
Romans 8:28	I am assured that all things work together for good.
Romans 8:31-34	I am free from any condemning charges against me.
Romans 8:35-39	I cannot be separated from the love of God.
2 Corinthians 1:21,22	I have been established, anointed and sealed by God.
Colossians 3:3	I am hidden with Christ in God.
Philippians 1:6	I am confident that the good work God has begun in me will be perfected.
Philippians 3:20	I am a citizen of heaven.
2 Timothy 1:7	I have not been given a spirit of fear, but of power, love and a sound mind.
Hebrews 4:16	I can find grace and mercy to help in time of need.
1 John 5:18	I am born of God and the evil one cannot touch me.

I AM SIGNIFICANT

Matthew 5:13,14	I am the salt and light of the earth.
John 15:1,5	I am a branch of the true vine, a channel of His life.
John 15:16	I have been chosen and appointed to bear fruit.
Acts 1:8	I am a personal witness of Christ.
1 Corinthians 3:16	I am God's temple.
2 Corinthians 5:17-21	I am a minister of reconciliation for God.
2 Corinthians 6:1	I am God's coworker (see 1 Corinthians 3:9).
Ephesians 2:6	I am seated with Christ in the heavenly realm.
Ephesians 2:10	I am God's workmanship.
Ephesians 3:12	I may approach God with freedom and confidence.
Philippians 4:13	I can do all things through Christ who strengthens me.

THE OVERCOMER'S COVENANT IN CHRIST

1. I place all my trust and confidence in the Lord, I put no confidence in the flesh and I declare myself to be dependent upon God.

2. I consciously and deliberately choose to submit to God and resist the devil by denying myself, picking up my cross daily and following Jesus.

3. I choose to humble myself before the mighty hand of God in order that He may exalt me at the proper time.

4. I declare the truth that I am dead to sin, freed from it and alive to God in Christ Jesus, since I have died with Christ and was raised with Him.

5. I gladly embrace the truth that I am now a child of God who is unconditionally loved and accepted. I reject the lie that I have to perform to be accepted, and I reject my fallen and natural identity which was derived from the world.

6. I declare that sin shall no longer be master over me because I am not under the law, but under grace, and there is no more guilt or condemnation because I am spiritually alive in Christ Jesus.

7. I renounce every unrighteous use of my body and I commit myself to no longer be conformed to this world, but rather to be transformed by the renewing of my mind. I choose to believe the truth and walk in it, regardless of my feelings or circumstances.

8. I commit myself to take every thought captive to the obedience of Christ, and choose to think upon that which is true, honorable, right, pure and lovely.

9. I commit myself to God's great goal for my life to conform to His image. I know that I will face many trials, but God has given me the victory and I am not a victim, but an overcomer in Christ.

10. I choose to adopt the attitude of Christ, which was to do nothing from selfishness or empty conceit, but with humility of mind. I will regard others as more important than myself; and not merely look out for my own personal interests but also the interests of others. I know that it is more blessed to give than to receive.

APPENDIX

STEPS TO FREEDOM
IN CHRIST

It is my deep conviction that the finished work of Jesus Christ and the presence of God in our lives are the only means by which we can resolve our personal and spiritual conflicts. Christ in us is our only hope (see Colossians 1:27), and He alone can meet our deepest needs of life: acceptance, identity, security and significance. The discipleship counseling process upon which these steps are based should not be understood as just another counseling technique that we learn. It is an encounter with God. He is the Wonderful Counselor. He is the One who grants repentance that leads to a knowledge of the truth which sets us free (see 2 Timothy 2:25,26).

The Steps to Freedom in Christ do not set you free. *Who* sets you free is Christ, and *what* sets you free is your response to Him in repentance and faith. These steps are just a tool to help you submit to God and resist the devil (see James 4:7). Then you can start living a fruitful life by abiding in Christ and becoming the person He created you to be. Many Christians will be able to work through these steps on their own and discover the wonderful freedom that Christ purchased for them on the cross. Then they will experience the peace of God which surpasses all comprehension, and it shall guard their hearts and their minds (see Philippians 4:7, *NASB*).

BEFORE YOU BEGIN

The chances of that happening and the possibility of maintaining that freedom will be greatly enhanced if you read *Victory over the Darkness* and *The Bondage Breaker* first. Many Christians in the Western world need to understand the reality of the spiritual world and our relationship to it. Some can't read these books or even the Bible with comprehension because of the battle that is going on for their minds. They will need the assistance of others who have been trained. The theology and practical process of discipleship counseling is given in my book, *Helping Others Find Freedom in Christ,* and the accompanying *Training Manual and Study Guide* and Video Training Program. The book attempts to biblically integrate the reality of the spiritual and the natural world so we can have a whole answer for a whole person.

In doing so, we cannot polarize into psychotherapeutic ministries that ignore the reality of the spiritual world or attempt some kind of deliverance ministry that ignores developmental issues and human responsibility.

YOU MAY NEED HELP

Ideally, it would be best if everyone had a trusted friend, pastor or counselor who would help them go through this process because it is just applying the wisdom of James 5:16: "Therefore confess your sins to each other and pray for each other so that you may be healed. The prayer of a righteous man is powerful and effective." Another person can prayerfully support you by providing objective counsel. I have had the privilege of helping many Christian leaders who could not process this on their own. Many Christian groups all over the world are using this approach in many languages with incredible results because the Lord desires for all to come to repentance (see 2 Peter 3:9), and to know the truth that sets us free in Christ (see John 8:32).

APPROPRIATING AND MAINTAINING FREEDOM

Christ has set us free through His victory over sin and death on the cross. However, appropriating our freedom in Christ through repentance and faith and maintaining our life of freedom in Christ are two different issues. It was for freedom that Christ set us free, but we have been warned not to return to a yoke of slavery which is legalism in this context (see Galatians 5:1) or to turn our freedom into an opportunity for the flesh (see Galatians 5:13). Establishing people free in Christ makes it possible for them to walk by faith according to what God says is true, to live by the power of the Holy Spirit and to not carry out the desires of the flesh (see Galatians 5:16). The true Christian life avoids both legalism and license.

If you are not experiencing freedom, it may be because you have not stood firm in the faith or actively taken your place in Christ. It is every Christian's responsibility to do whatever is necessary to maintain a right relationship with God and mankind. Your eternal destiny is not at stake. God will never leave you nor forsake you (see Hebrews 13:5), but your daily victory is at stake if you fail to claim and maintain your position in Christ.

YOUR POSITION IN CHRIST

You are not a helpless victim caught between two nearly equal but opposite heavenly superpowers. Satan is a deceiver. Only God is omnipotent, omnipresent and omniscient. Sometimes the reality of sin and the presence of evil may seem more real than the presence of God, but that's part of Satan's deception. Satan is a defeated foe and we are in Christ. A true knowledge of God and knowing our identity and position in Christ are the greatest determinants of our mental health. A false concept of God, a distorted understanding of who we are as children of God, and the misplaced deification of Satan are the greatest contributors to mental illness.

Many of our illnesses are psychosomatic. When these issues are resolved in Christ, our physical bodies will function better and we will experience greater health. Other problems are clearly physical and we need the services of the medical profession. Please consult your physician for medical advice and the prescribing of medication. We are both spiritual and physical beings who need the services of both the church and the medical profession.

WINNING THE BATTLE FOR YOUR MIND

The battle is for our minds, which is the control center of all that we think and do. The opposing thoughts you may experience as you go through these steps can control you only if you believe them. If you are working through these steps alone, don't be deceived by any lying, intimidating thoughts in your mind. If a trusted pastor or counselor is helping you find your freedom in Christ, he or she must have your cooperation. You must share any thoughts you are having in opposition to what you are attempting to do. As soon as you expose the lie, the power of Satan is broken.

The only way that you can lose control in this process is if you pay attention to a deceiving spirit and believe a lie.

YOU MUST CHOOSE

The following procedure is a means of resolving personal and spiritual conflicts which have kept you from experiencing the freedom and victory Christ purchased for you on the cross. Your freedom will be the result of what *you* choose to believe, confess, forgive, renounce and forsake. No one can do that for you. The battle for your mind can only be won as you personally choose truth. As you go through this process, understand that Satan is under no obligation to obey your thoughts. Only God has complete knowledge of your mind because He is omniscient—all-knowing. So we can submit to God inwardly, but we need to resist the devil by reading aloud each prayer and by verbally renouncing, forgiving, confessing, etc.

This process of reestablishing our freedom in Christ is nothing more than a fierce moral inventory and a rock-solid commitment to truth. It is the first step in the continuing process of discipleship. There is no such thing as instant maturity. It will take you the rest of your life to renew your mind and conform to the image of God. If your problems stem from a source other than those covered in these steps, you may need to seek professional help.

May the Lord grace you with His presence as you seek His face and help others experience the joy of their salvation.

Neil T. Anderson

PRAYER

Dear Heavenly Father,

We acknowledge Your presence in this room and in our lives. You are the only omniscient (all-knowing), omnipotent (all-power-ful), and omnipresent (always-present) God. We are dependent upon You, for apart from You we can do nothing. We stand in the truth that all authority in heaven and on earth has been given to the resurrected Christ, and because we are in Christ, we share that authority in order to make disciples and set captives free. We ask You to fill us with Your Holy Spirit and lead us into all truth. We pray for Your complete protection and ask for Your guidance. In Jesus' name, amen.

DECLARATION

In the name and authority of the Lord Jesus Christ, we command Satan and all evil spirits to release _____(name)_____ in order that _____(name)_____ can be free to know and choose to do the will of God. As children of God seated with Christ in the heavenlies, we agree that every enemy of the Lord Jesus Christ be bound to silence. We say to Satan and all your evil workers that you cannot inflict any pain or in any way prevent God's will from being accomplished in _____(name's)_____ life.

PREPARATION

Before going through the Steps to Freedom, review the events of your life to discern specific areas that might need to be addressed. For a more detailed review of your life, complete the Confidential Personal Inventory in the Appendix.

FAMILY HISTORY

- ❑ Religious history of parents and grandparents

- ❑ Home life from childhood through high school

- ❑ History of physical or emotional illness in the family

- ❑ Adoption, foster care, guardians

PERSONAL HISTORY

- ❑ Eating habits (bulimia, bingeing and purging, anorexia, compulsive eating)

- ❑ Addictions (drugs, alcohol)

- ❑ Prescription medications (what for?)

- ❑ Sleeping patterns and nightmares

- ❑ Rape or any other sexual, physical, emotional abuse

- ❑ Thought life (obsessive, blasphemous, condemning, distracting thoughts, poor concentration, fantasy)

- ❑ Mental interference during church, prayer or Bible study

- ❑ Emotional life (anger, anxiety, depression, bitterness, fears)

- ❑ Spiritual journey (salvation: when, how, and assurance)

Now you are ready to begin. The following are seven specific steps to process in order to experience freedom from your past. You will address the areas where Satan most commonly takes advantage of us and where strongholds have been built. Christ purchased your victory when He shed His blood for you on the cross. Realizing your freedom will be the result of what you choose to believe, confess, forgive, renounce and forsake. No one can do that for you. The battle for your mind can only be won as you personally choose truth.

As you go through these Steps to Freedom, remember that Satan will only be defeated if you confront him verbally. He cannot read your mind and is under no obligation to obey your thoughts. Only God has complete knowledge of your mind. As you process each step, it is important that you submit to God inwardly and resist the devil by reading aloud each prayer—verbally renouncing, forgiving, confessing, etc.

You are taking a fierce moral inventory and making a rock-solid commitment to truth. If your problems stem from a source other than those covered in these steps, you have nothing to lose by going through them. If you are sincere, the only thing that can happen is that you will get very right with God!

STEP 1
COUNTERFEIT VS. REAL

The first Step to Freedom in Christ is to renounce your previous or current involvement with satanically inspired occult practices and false religions. You need to renounce any activity or group that denies Jesus Christ, offers guidance through any source other than the absolute authority of the written Word of God or requires secret initiations, ceremonies or covenants.

In order to help you assess your spiritual experiences, begin this step by asking God to reveal false guidance and counterfeit religious experiences.

Dear Heavenly Father,

I ask You to guard my heart and my mind and reveal to me any and all involvement I have had either knowingly or unknowingly with cultic or occult practices, false religions or false teachers. In Jesus' name, I pray. Amen.

Using the Non-Christian Spiritual Experience Inventory on the following page, carefully check anything in which you were involved. This list is not exhaustive, but it will guide you in identifying non-Christian experiences. Add any additional involvement you have had. Even if you innocently participated in something or observed it, you should write it on your list to renounce, just in case you unknowingly gave Satan a foothold.

NON-CHRISTIAN SPIRITUAL EXPERIENCE INVENTORY

Please check all those that apply.

- ❏ Astral-projection
- ❏ Ouija board
- ❏ Table or body lifting
- ❏ Dungeons and Dragons
- ❏ Speaking in trance
- ❏ Automatic writing
- ❏ Magic Eight Ball
- ❏ Telepathy
- ❏ Using spells or curses
- ❏ Seance
- ❏ Materialization
- ❏ Clairvoyance
- ❏ Spirit guides
- ❏ Fortune-telling
- ❏ Tarot cards
- ❏ Palm reading
- ❏ Astrology/horoscopes
- ❏ Rod/pendulum (dowsing)
- ❏ Self-hypnosis
- ❏ Mental manipulations or attempts to swap minds
- ❏ New Age medicine

- ❏ Black and white magic
- ❏ Blood pacts or self-mutilation
- ❏ Fetishism (objects of worship, crystals, good-luck charms)
- ❏ Incubi and succubi (sexual spirits)
- ❏ Other

  _____

- ❏ Christian Science
- ❏ Unity
- ❏ The Way International
- ❏ Unification Church
- ❏ Mormonism
- ❏ Church of the Living Word
- ❏ Jehovah's Witnesses
- ❏ Children of God (Love)
- ❏ Swedenborgianism
- ❏ Unitarianism
- ❏ Masons

- ❏ New Age
- ❏ The Forum (EST)
- ❏ Spirit worship
- ❏ Other

  _____

- ❏ Buddhism
- ❏ Hare Krishna
- ❏ Bahaism
- ❏ Rosicrucianism
- ❏ Science of the Mind
- ❏ Science of Creative Intelligence
- ❏ Transcendental Meditation (TM)
- ❏ Hinduism
- ❏ Yoga
- ❏ Echkankar
- ❏ Roy Masters
- ❏ Silva Mind Control
- ❏ Father Divine
- ❏ Theosophical Society
- ❏ Islam
- ❏ Black Muslim
- ❏ Self-hypnosis
- ❏ Other

  _____

1. Have you ever been hypnotized, attended a New Age or parapsychology seminar, consulted a medium, spiritist or channeler? Explain.

2. Do you or have you ever had an imaginary friend or spirit guide offering you guidance or companionship? Explain.

3. Have you ever heard voices in your mind or had repeating and nagging thoughts condemning you or that were foreign to what you believe or feel, as if there were a dialogue going on in your head? Explain.

4. What other spiritual experiences have you had that would be considered out of the ordinary?

5. Have you ever made a vow, covenant or pact with any individual or group other than God?

6. Have you been involved in satanic ritual or satanic worship in any form? Explain.

When you are confident that your list is complete, confess and renounce each involvement whether active or passive by praying aloud the following prayer, repeating it separately for each item on your list:

Lord,

I confess that I have participated in _____*, and I renounce* _____*. Thank You that in Christ I am forgiven.*

If there has been any involvement in satanic ritual or heavy occult activity, you need to state aloud the following special renunciations which apply. Read across the page, renouncing the first item in the column of the Kingdom of Darkness and then affirming the first truth in the column of the Kingdom of Light. Continue down the page in this manner.

All satanic rituals, covenants and assignments must be specifically renounced as the Lord allows you to recall them. Some who have been subjected to satanic ritual abuse may have developed multiple personalities in order to survive. Nevertheless, continue through the Steps to Freedom in order to resolve all that you consciously can. It is important that you resolve the demonic strongholds first. Every personality must resolve his/her issues and agree to come together in Christ. You may need someone who understands spiritual conflict to help you maintain control and not be deceived into false memories. Only Jesus can bind up the brokenhearted, set captives free and make us whole.

KINGDOM OF DARKNESS	KINGDOM OF LIGHT
I renounce ever signing my name over to Satan or having had my name signed over to Satan.	I announce that my name is now written in the Lamb's Book of Life.
I renounce any ceremony where I might have been wed to Satan.	I announce that I am the bride of Christ.

I renounce any and all covenants that I made with Satan.	I announce that I am a partaker of the New Covenant with Christ.
I renounce all satanic assignments for my life, including duties, marriage and children.	I announce and commit myself to know and do only the will of God and accept only His guidance.
I renounce all spirit guides assigned to me.	I announce and accept only the leading of the Holy Spirit.
I renounce ever giving of my blood in the service of Satan.	I trust only in the shed blood of my Lord Jesus Christ.
I renounce ever eating of flesh or drinking of blood for satanic worship.	By faith I eat only the flesh and drink only the blood of Jesus in Holy Communion.
I renounce any and all guardians and satanist parents who were assigned to me.	I announce that God is my Father and the Holy Spirit is my Guardian by which I am sealed.
I renounce any baptism in blood or urine whereby I am identified with Satan.	I announce that I have been baptized into Christ Jesus and my identity is now in Christ.
I renounce any and all sacrifices that were made on my behalf by which Satan may claim ownership of me.	I announce that only the sacrifice of Christ has any hold on me. I belong to Him. I have been purchased by the blood of the Lamb.

STEP 2
DECEPTION VS. TRUTH

Truth is the revelation of God's Word, but we need to acknowledge the truth in the inner self (see Psalm 51:6). When David lived a lie, he suffered greatly. When he finally found freedom by acknowledging the truth, he wrote: "Blessed is the man...in whose spirit is no deceit" (Psalm 32:2). We are to lay aside falsehood and speak the truth in love (see Ephesians 4:15,25). A mentally healthy person is one who is in touch with reality and relatively free of anxiety. Both qualities should characterize the Christian who renounces deception and embraces the truth.

Begin this critical step by expressing aloud the following prayer. Don't let the enemy accuse you with thoughts such as: *This isn't going to work* or *I wish I could believe this, but I can't* or any other lies in opposition to what you are proclaiming. Even if you have difficulty doing so, you need to pray the prayer and read the Doctrinal Affirmation.

Dear Heavenly Father,

I know that You desire truth in the inner self and that facing this truth is the way of liberation (see John 8:32). I acknowledge that I have been deceived by the father of lies (see John 8:44) and that I have deceived myself (see 1 John 1:8). I pray in the name of the Lord Jesus Christ that You, Heavenly Father, will rebuke all deceiving spirits by virtue of the shed blood and resurrection of the Lord Jesus Christ. By faith I have received You into my life and I am now seated with Christ in the heavenlies (see Ephesians 2:6). I acknowledge that I have the responsibility and authority to resist the devil, and when I do, he will flee from me. I now ask the Holy Spirit to guide me into all truth (see John 16:13). I ask You to "search me, O God, and know my heart; try me and know my anxious thoughts; and see if there be any hurtful way in me, and lead me in the everlasting way" (Psalm 139:23,24, NASB). In Jesus' name, I pray. Amen.

You may want to pause at this point to consider some of Satan's deceptive schemes. In addition to false teachers, false prophets and deceiving spirits, you can deceive yourself. Now that you are alive in Christ and forgiven, you never have to live a lie or defend yourself. Christ is your defense. How have you deceived or attempted to defend yourself according to the following? Please check any of the following that apply to you:

SELF-DECEPTION
- ❏ Hearing God's Word but not doing it (see James 1:22; 4:17)
- ❏ Saying you have no sin (see 1 John 1:8)
- ❏ Thinking you are something when you aren't (see Galatians 6:3)
- ❏ Thinking you are wise in your own eyes (see 1 Corinthians 3:18,19)
- ❏ Thinking you will not reap what you sow (see Galatians 6:7)
- ❏ Thinking the unrighteous will inherit the kingdom (see 1 Corinthians 6:9)
- ❏ Thinking you can associate with bad company and not be corrupted (see 1 Corinthians 15:33)

SELF-DEFENSE
(Defending ourselves instead of trusting in Christ)
- ❏ Denial (conscious or subconscious refusal to face the truth)
- ❏ Fantasy (escaping from the real world)
- ❏ Emotional insulation (withdrawing to avoid rejection)
- ❏ Regression (reverting back to a less threatening time)
- ❏ Displacement (taking out frustrations on others)
- ❏ Projection (blaming others)
- ❏ Rationalization (making excuses for poor behavior)

For each of those things that you have checked, pray aloud:

Lord, I agree that I have been deceiving myself in the area of _____. Thank You for forgiving me. I commit myself to know and follow Your truth. Amen.

Choosing the truth may be difficult if you have been living a lie (being deceived) for many years. You may need to seek professional help to weed out the defense mechanisms you have depended upon to survive. The Christian needs only one defense—Jesus. Knowing that you are forgiven and accepted as God's child is what sets you free to face reality and declare your dependence on Him.

Faith is the biblical response to the truth and believing the truth is a choice. When someone says, "I want to believe God, but I just can't," they are being deceived. Of course you can believe God. Faith is something you decide to do, not something you feel like doing. Believing the truth doesn't make it true. It's true; therefore, we believe it. The New Age movement is distorting the truth by saying we create reality through what we believe. We can't create reality with our minds; we face reality. It is what or who you believe in that counts. Everybody believes in something, and everybody walks by faith according to what he or she believes. But if what you believe isn't true, then how you live (walk by faith) won't be right.

Historically, the Church has found great value in publicly declaring its beliefs. The Apostles' Creed and the Nicene Creed have been recited for centuries. Read aloud the following affirmation of faith, and do so again as often as necessary to renew your mind. Experiencing difficulty in reading this affirmation may indicate where you are being deceived and under attack. Boldly affirm your commitment to biblical truth.

DOCTRINAL AFFIRMATION

I recognize that there is only one true and living God (see Exodus 20:2,3) who exists as the Father, Son and Holy Spirit and that He is worthy of all honor, praise and glory as the Creator, Sustainer and Beginning and End of all things (see Revelation 4:11; 5:9,10; 22:13; Isaiah 43:1,7,21).

I recognize Jesus Christ as the Messiah, the Word who became flesh and dwelt among us (see John 1:1,14). I believe that He came to destroy the works of Satan (see 1 John 3:8), that He disarmed the rulers and authorities and made a public display of them, having triumphed over them (see Colossians 2:15).

I believe that God has proven His love for me because when I was still a sinner, Christ died for me (see Romans 5:8). I believe that He delivered me from the domain of darkness and transferred me to His kingdom, and in Him I have redemption—the forgiveness of sins (see Colossians 1:13,14).

I believe that I am now a child of God (see 1 John 3:1-3) and that I am seated with Christ in the heavenlies (see Ephesians 2:6). I believe that I was saved by the grace of God through faith, that it was a gift, and not the result of any works on my part (see Ephesians 2:8,9).

I choose to be strong in the Lord and in the strength of His might (see Ephesians 6:10). I put no confidence in the flesh (see Philippians 3:3) for the weapons of warfare are not of the flesh (see 2 Corinthians 10:4). I put on the whole armor of God (see Ephesians 6:10-20), and I resolve to stand firm in my faith and resist the evil one.

I believe that apart from Christ I can do nothing (see John 15:5), so I declare myself dependent on Him. I choose to abide in Christ in order to bear much fruit and glorify the Lord (see John 15:8). I announce to Satan that Jesus is my Lord (see 1 Corinthians 12:3), and I reject any counterfeit gifts or works of Satan in my life.

I believe that the truth will set me free (see John 8:32) and that walking in the light is the only path of fellowship (see 1 John 1:7). Therefore, I stand against Satan's deception by taking every thought captive in obedience to Christ (see 2 Corinthians 10:5). I declare that the Bible is the only authoritative standard (see

2 Timothy 3:15,16). I choose to speak the truth in love (see Ephesians 4:15).

I choose to present my body as an instrument of righteousness, a living and holy sacrifice, and I renew my mind by the living Word of God in order that I may prove that the will of God is good, acceptable and perfect (see Romans 6:13; 12:1,2). I put off the old self with its evil practices and put on the new self (see Colossians 3:9,10), and I declare myself to be a new creature in Christ (see 2 Corinthians 5:17).

I trust my heavenly Father to fill me with His Holy Spirit (see Ephesians 5:18), to lead me into all truth (see John 16:13), and to empower my life that I may live above sin and not carry out the desires of the flesh (see Galatians 5:16). I crucify the flesh (see Galatians 5:24) and choose to walk by the Spirit.

I renounce all selfish goals and choose the ultimate goal of love (see 1 Timothy 1:5). I choose to obey the two greatest commandments: to love the Lord my God with all my heart, soul and mind, and to love my neighbor as myself (see Matthew 22:37-39).

I believe that Jesus has all authority in heaven and on earth (see Matthew 28:18) and that He is the Head over all rule and authority (see Colossians 2:10). I believe that Satan and his demons are subject to me in Christ since I am a member of Christ's Body (see Ephesians 1:19-23). Therefore, I obey the command to submit to God and to resist the devil (see James 4:7), and I command Satan in the name of Christ to leave my presence.

Step 3
Bitterness vs. Forgiveness

We need to forgive others in order to be free from our pasts and to prevent Satan from taking advantage of us (see 2 Corinthians 2:10,11). We are to be merciful just as our heavenly Father is merciful (see Luke 6:36). We are to forgive as we have been forgiven (see Ephesians 4:31,32). Ask God to bring to mind the names of those people you need to forgive by expressing the following prayer aloud:

Dear Heavenly Father,

I thank You for the riches of Your kindness, forbearance and patience, knowing that Your kindness has led me to repentance (see Romans 2:4). I confess that I have not extended that same patience and kindness toward others who have offended me, but instead I have harbored bitterness and resentment. I pray that during this time of self-examination You would bring to my mind those people that I need to forgive in order that I may do so (see Matthew 18:35). I ask this in the precious name of Jesus. Amen.

As names come to mind, list them on a separate sheet of paper. At the end of your list, write "myself." Forgiving yourself is accepting God's cleansing and forgiveness. Also, write "thoughts against God." Thoughts raised up against the knowledge of God will usually result in angry feelings toward Him. Technically, we don't forgive God because He cannot commit any sin of commission or omission. But we do need to specifically renounce false expectations and thoughts about God and agree to release any anger we have toward Him.

Before you pray to forgive these people, stop and consider what forgiveness is, what it is not, what decision you will be making and what the consequences will be. In the following explanation, the main points are in bold print:

Forgiveness is not forgetting. People who try to forget find they cannot. God says He will remember our sins no more (see Hebrews 10:17), but God, being omniscient, cannot forget. Remember our sins no more means that God will never use the past against us (see Psalm 103:12). Forgetting may be the result of forgiveness, but it is never the means of forgiveness. When we bring up the past against others, we are saying we haven't forgiven them.

Forgiveness is a choice, a crisis of the will. Since God requires us to forgive, it is something we can do. However, forgiveness is difficult for us because it pulls against our concept of justice. We want revenge for offenses suffered. However, we are told never to take our own revenge (see Romans 12:19). You say, "Why should I let them off the hook?" That is precisely the problem. You are still hooked to them, still bound by your past. **You will let them off your hook, but they are never off God's.** He will deal with them fairly—something we cannot do.

You say, "You don't understand how much this person hurt me!" But don't you see, they are still hurting you! How do you stop the pain? **You don't forgive someone for their sake; you do it for your own sake so you can be free. Your need to forgive isn't an issue between you and the offender; it's between you and God.**

Forgiveness is agreeing to live with the consequences of another person's sin. Forgiveness is costly. You pay the price of the evil you forgive. You're going to live with those consequences whether you want to or not; your only choice is whether you will do so in the bitterness of unforgiveness or the freedom of forgiveness. Jesus took the consequences of your sin upon Himself. All true forgiveness is substitutionary because no one really forgives without bearing the consequences of the other person's sin. God the Father "made Him who knew no sin to be sin on our behalf, that we might become the righteousness of God in Him" (2 Corinthians 5:21, *NASB*). Where is the justice? It's the cross that makes forgiveness legally and morally right: "For the death that He died, He died to sin, once for all" (Romans 6:10, *NASB*).

Decide that you will bear the burdens of their offenses by not using that information against them in the future. This doesn't mean that you tolerate sin. You must set up scriptural boundaries to prevent future abuse. Some may be required to testify for the sake of justice but not for the purpose of seeking revenge from a bitter heart.

How do you forgive from your heart? You acknowledge the hurt and the hate. If your forgiveness doesn't visit the emotional core of your life, it will be incomplete. Many feel the pain of interpersonal offenses, but they won't or don't know how to acknowledge it. Let God bring the pain to the surface so He can deal with it. This is where the healing takes place.

Don't wait to forgive until you feel like forgiving; you will never get there. Feelings take time to heal after the choice to forgive is made and Satan has lost his place (see Ephesians 4:26,27). **Freedom is what will be gained, not a feeling.**

As you pray, God may bring to mind offending people and experiences you have totally forgotten. Let Him do it even if it is painful. Remember, you are doing this for your sake. God wants you to be free. Don't rationalize or explain the offender's behavior. Forgiveness is dealing with your pain and leaving the other person to God. Positive feelings will follow in time; freeing you from the past is the critical issue right now.

Don't say, "Lord, please help me to forgive" because He is already helping you. Don't say, "Lord, I want to forgive," because you are bypassing the hard-core choice to forgive which is your responsibility. Focus on each individual until you are sure you have dealt with all the remembered pain—what they did, how they hurt you, how they made you feel: rejected, unloved, unworthy, dirty, etc.

You are now ready to forgive the people on your list so you can be free in Christ, with those people no longer having any control over you. For each person on your list, pray aloud:

> *Lord, I forgive* _____ *(name the person)* _____
> *for* _____ *(verbally share every hurt and pain the Lord brings to*
> *your mind and how it made you feel)* _____.

After you have forgiven every person for every painful memory, then finish this step by praying:

> *Lord, I release all these people to You, and I release my right to*
> *seek revenge. I choose not to hold on to my bitterness and anger,*
> *and I ask You to heal my damaged emotions. In Jesus' name, I*
> *pray. Amen.*

STEP 4
REBELLION VS. SUBMISSION

We live in rebellious times. Many believe it is their right to sit in judgment of those in authority over them. Rebelling against God and His authority gives Satan an opportunity to attack. As our commanding General, the Lord tells us to get into ranks and follow Him; He will not lead us into temptation, but will deliver us from evil (see Matthew 6:13).

We have two biblical responsibilities regarding authority figures: Pray for them and submit to them. The only time God permits us to disobey earthly leaders is when they require us to do something morally wrong before God or attempt to rule outside the realm of their authority. Pray the following prayer:

Dear Heavenly Father,

You have said that rebellion is like the sin of witchcraft and insubordination is like iniquity and idolatry (see 1 Samuel 15:23). I know that in action and attitude I have sinned against You with a rebellious heart. Thank You for forgiving my rebellion, and I pray that by the shed blood of the Lord Jesus Christ all ground gained by evil spirits because of my rebelliousness will be canceled. I pray that You will shed light on all my ways that I may know the full extent of my rebelliousness. I now choose to adopt a submissive spirit and a servant's heart. In the name of Christ Jesus, my Lord, amen.

Being under authority is an act of faith. You are trusting God to work through His established lines of authority. There are times when employers, parents and husbands are violating the laws of civil government which are ordained by God to protect innocent people against abuse. In these cases, you need to appeal to the state for your protection. In many states, the law requires such abuse to be reported.

In difficult cases, such as continuing abuse at home, further counseling help may be needed. And, in some cases, when earthly authorities have abused their position and are requiring disobedience to God or a compromise in your commitment to Him, you need to obey God, not man.

We are all admonished to submit to one another as equals in Christ (see Ephesians 5:21). However, there are specific lines of authority in Scripture for the purpose of accomplishing common goals:

Civil government (see Romans 13:1-7; 1 Timothy 2:1-4;
    1 Peter 2:13-17)

Parents (see Ephesians 6:1-3)

Husbands (see 1 Peter 3:1-4) or wives (see Ephesians 5:21;
    1 Peter 3:7)

Employers (see 1 Peter 2:18-23)

Church leaders (see Hebrews 13:17)

God (see Daniel 9:5,9)

Examine each area and confess those times you have not been submissive by praying:

> *Lord, I agree I have been rebellious toward*_____
> _____. *I choose to be submissive and obedient to your Word. In Jesus' name, amen.*

STEP 5
PRIDE VS. HUMILITY

Pride is a killer. Pride says, "I can do it! I can get myself out of this mess without God or anyone else's help." Oh no, we can't! We absolutely need God, and we desperately need each other. Paul wrote: "For it is...we who worship by the Spirit of God, who glory in Christ Jesus, and who put no confidence in the flesh" (Philippians 3:3). Humility is confidence properly placed. We are to be "strong in the Lord and in his mighty power" (Ephesians 6:10). James 4:6-10 and 1 Peter 5:1-10 reveal that spiritual conflict follows pride. Use the following prayer to express your commitment to live humbly before God:

> *Dear Heavenly Father,*
>
> *You have said that pride goes before destruction and an arrogant spirit before stumbling (see Proverbs 16:18). I confess that I have lived independently and have not denied myself, picked up my cross daily and followed You (see Matthew 16:24). In so doing, I have given ground to the enemy in my life. I have believed that I could be successful and live victoriously by my own strength and resources. I now confess that I have sinned against You by placing my will before Yours and by centering my life around myself instead of You. I now renounce the self-life and by so doing cancel all the ground that has been gained in my members by the enemies of the Lord Jesus Christ. I pray that You will guide me so that I will do nothing from selfishness*

*or empty conceit, but with humility of mind I will regard others
as more important than myself (see Philippians 2:3). Enable me
through love to serve others and in honor prefer others (see
Romans 12:10). I ask this in the name of Christ Jesus, my Lord.
Amen.*

Having made that commitment, now allow God to show you any
specific areas of your life where you have been prideful, such as:

❑ Having a stronger desire to do my will than God's will;
❑ Being more dependent upon my strengths and resources than
God's;
❑ Too often believing that my ideas and opinions are better than
others';
❑ Being more concerned about controlling others than developing
self-control;
❑ Sometimes considering myself more important than others';
❑ Having a tendency to think that I have no needs;
❑ Finding it difficult to admit that I was wrong;
❑ Having a tendency to be more of a people-pleaser than a God-
pleaser;
❑ Being overly concerned about getting the credit I deserve;
❑ Being driven to obtain the recognition that comes from
degrees, titles and positions;
❑ Often thinking I am more humble than others;
❑ These other ways:

_____

For each of these that has been true in your life, pray aloud:

*Lord, I agree I have been prideful by*_____
_____ . *I choose to
humble myself and place all my confidence in You. Amen.*

STEP 6
BONDAGE VS. FREEDOM

The next step to freedom deals with habitual sin. People who have been caught in the trap of sin-confess-sin-confess may need to follow the instructions of James 5:16, "Confess your sins to each other and pray for each other so that you may be healed. The prayer of a righteous man is powerful and effective." Seek out a righteous person who will hold you up in prayer and to whom you can be accountable. Others may only need the assurance of 1 John 1:9: "If we confess our sins, He is faithful and righteous to forgive us our sins and to cleanse us from all unrighteousness" (*NASB*). Confession is not saying "I'm sorry"; it's saying "I did it." Whether you need the help of others or just the accountability to God, pray the following prayer:

Dear Heavenly Father,
You have told us to put on the Lord Jesus Christ and make no provision for the flesh in regard to its lust (see Romans 13:14, NASB). I acknowledge that I have given in to fleshly lusts which wage war against my soul (see 1 Peter 2:11). I thank You that in Christ my sins are forgiven, but I have transgressed Your holy law and given the enemy an opportunity to wage war in my physical body (see Romans 6:12,13; Ephesians 4:27; James 4:1; 1 Peter 5:8). I come before Your presence to acknowledge these sins and to seek Your cleansing (see 1 John 1:9), that I may be freed from the bondage of sin. I now ask You to reveal to my mind the ways that I have transgressed Your moral law and grieved the Holy Spirit. In Jesus' precious name, I pray. Amen.

The deeds of the flesh are numerous. Many of the following issues are from Galatians 5:19-21. Check those that apply to you and any others you have struggled with that the Lord has brought to your mind. Then confess each one with the concluding prayer.

Note: Sexual sins, eating disorders, substance abuse, abortion, suicidal tendencies, perfectionism and fear will be dealt with later in this Step, beginning on page 321.

- ☐ Stealing
- ☐ Lying
- ☐ Fighting
- ☐ Jealousy
- ☐ Envying
- ☐ Outbursts of anger

- ☐ Complaining
- ☐ Criticizing
- ☐ Lusting
- ☐ Cheating
- ☐ Gossiping
- ☐ Controlling
- ☐ Procrastinating

- ☐ Swearing
- ☐ Greediness
- ☐ Laziness
- ☐ Divisiveness
- ☐ Gambling
- ☐ Other_____
  _____

Dear Heavenly Father,
I thank You that my sins are forgiven in Christ, but I have walked by the flesh and therefore sinned by_____
_____. Thank You for cleansing me of all unrighteousness. I ask that You would enable me to walk by the Spirit and not carry out the desires of the flesh. In Jesus' name, I pray. Amen.

It is our responsibility not to allow sin to reign in our mortal bodies by not using our bodies as instruments of unrighteousness (see Romans 6:12,13). If you are struggling or have struggled with sexual sins (pornography, masturbation, sexual promiscuity, etc.) or are experiencing sexual difficulty in your marriage, pray as follows:

Lord,
I ask You to reveal to my mind every sexual use of my body as an instrument of unrighteousness. In Jesus' precious name, I pray. Amen.

As the Lord brings to your mind every sexual misuse of your body, whether it was done to you—rape, incest or other sexual abuse—or willingly by you, renounce every occasion:

Lord,

I renounce ____(name the specific misuse of your body)____
with ____(name the person)____ and ask You to break that
bond.

Now commit your body to the Lord by praying:

Lord,

I renounce all these uses of my body as an instrument of
unrighteousness and by so doing ask You to break all bondages
Satan has brought into my life through that involvement. I confess
my participation. I now present my body to You as a living sacrifice,
holy and acceptable unto You, and I reserve the sexual use of my
body only for marriage. I renounce the lie of Satan that my body
is not clean, that it is dirty or in any way unacceptable as a result
of my past sexual experiences. Lord, I thank You that You have
totally cleansed and forgiven me, that You love and accept me
unconditionally. Therefore, I can accept myself. And I choose to do
so, to accept myself and my body as cleansed. In Jesus' name,
amen.

SPECIAL PRAYERS FOR SPECIFIC PROBLEMS

HOMOSEXUALITY

Lord,

I renounce the lie that You have created me or anyone else to
be homosexual, and I affirm that You clearly forbid homosexual
behavior. I accept myself as a child of God and declare that You
created me a man (woman). I renounce any bondages of Satan
that have perverted my relationships with others. I announce that
I am free to relate to the opposite sex in the way that You intended.
In Jesus' name, amen.

ABORTION

Lord,

> *I confess that I did not assume stewardship of the life You entrusted to me. I choose to accept your forgiveness, and I now commit that child to You for Your care in eternity. In Jesus' name, amen.*

SUICIDAL TENDENCIES

Lord,
> *I renounce suicidal thoughts and any attempts I have made to take my own life or in any way injure myself. I renounce the lie that life is hopeless and that I can find peace and freedom by taking my own life. Satan is a thief and he comes to steal, kill and destroy. I choose to be a good steward of the physical life that You have entrusted to me. In Jesus' name, I pray. Amen.*

EATING DISORDERS OR SELF-MUTILATION

Lord,

> *I renounce the lie that my value as a person is dependent upon my physical beauty, my weight or size. I renounce cutting myself, vomiting, using laxatives or starving myself as a means of cleansing myself of evil or altering my appearance. I announce that only the blood of the Lord Jesus Christ cleanses me from sin. I accept the reality that there may be sin present in me due to the lies I have believed and the wrongful use of my body, but I renounce the lie that I am evil or that any part of my body is evil. My body is the temple of the Holy Spirit and I belong to You, Lord. I receive Your love and acceptance of me. In Jesus' name, amen.*

SUBSTANCE ABUSE

Lord,

I confess that I have misused substances (alcohol, tobacco, food, prescription or street drugs) for the purpose of pleasure, to escape reality or to cope with difficult situations—resulting in the abuse of my body, the harmful programming of my mind and the quenching of the Holy Spirit. I ask Your forgiveness. I renounce any satanic connection or influence in my life through my misuse of chemicals or food. I cast my anxiety onto Christ Who loves me, and I commit myself to no longer yield to substance abuse, but to the Holy Spirit. I ask You, Heavenly Father, to fill me with Your Holy Spirit. In Jesus' name, amen.

DRIVENNESS AND PERFECTIONISM

Lord,

I renounce the lie that my self-worth is dependent upon my ability to perform. I announce the truth that my identity and sense of worth are found in who I am as Your child. I renounce seeking the approval and acceptance of other people, and I choose to believe that I am already approved and accepted in Christ because of His death and resurrection for me. I choose to believe the truth that I have been saved, not by deeds done in righteousness, but according to Your mercy. I choose to believe that I am no longer under the curse of the law because Christ became a curse for me. I receive the free gift of life in Christ and choose to abide in Him. I renounce striving for perfection by living under the law. By Your grace, Heavenly Father, I choose from this day forward to walk by faith according to what You have said is true by the power of Your Holy Spirit. In Jesus' name, amen.

PLAGUING FEARS

Dear Heavenly Father,

I acknowledge You as the only legitimate fear object in my life. You are the only omnipresent (always present) and omniscient (all-knowing) God and the only means by which all other fears can be expelled. You are my sanctuary. You have not given me a spirit of timidity, but of power and love and discipline. I confess that I have allowed the fear of man and the fear of death to exercise control over my life instead of trusting in You. I now renounce all other fear objects and worship You only. I pray that You would fill me with Your Holy Spirit that I may live my life and speak your Word with boldness. In Jesus' name, I pray. Amen.

After you have confessed all known sin, pray:

Dear Heavenly Father,

I now confess these sins to You and claim my forgiveness and cleansing through the blood of the Lord Jesus Christ. I cancel all ground that evil spirits have gained through my willful involvement in sin. I ask this in the wonderful name of my Lord and Savior, Jesus Christ. Amen.

STEP 7
ACQUIESCENCE VS. RENUNCIATION

Acquiescence is passively giving in or agreeing without consent. The last step to freedom is to renounce the sins of your ancestors and any curses which may have been placed on you. In giving the Ten Commandments, God said: "You shall not make for yourself an idol, or any likeness of what is in heaven above or on the earth beneath or in the water under the earth. You shall not worship them or serve them; for I, the LORD your God, am a jealous God, visiting the iniquity of the fathers on the children, on the third and the fourth generations of those who hate Me" (Exodus 20:4,5, *NASB*).

Familiar spirits can be passed on from one generation to the next if not renounced and if your new spiritual heritage in Christ is not proclaimed. You are not guilty for the sin of any ancestor, but because of their sin, Satan may have gained access to your family. This is not to deny that many problems are transmitted genetically or acquired from an immoral atmosphere. All three conditions can predispose an individual to a particular sin. In addition, deceived people may try to curse you, or satanic groups may try to target you. You have all the authority and protection you need in Christ to stand against such curses and assignments.

Ask the Lord to reveal to your mind the sins and iniquities of your ancestors by praying the following prayer:

> *Dear Heavenly Father,*
> *I thank You that I am a new creation in Christ. I desire to obey Your command to honor my mother and my father, but I also acknowledge that my physical heritage has not been perfect. I ask you to reveal to my mind the sins and iniquities of my ancestors in order to confess, renounce and forsake them. In Jesus' name, I pray. Amen.*

Now claim your position and protection in Christ by making the following declaration verbally, and then by humbling yourself before God in prayer.

DECLARATION

> I here and now reject and disown all the sins and iniquities of my ancestors, including _____(name them)_____. As one who has been delivered from the power of darkness and translated into the kingdom of God's dear Son, I cancel out all demonic working that has been passed on to me from my ancestors.

As one who has been crucified and raised with Jesus Christ and who sits with Him in heavenly places, I renounce all satanic assignments that are directed toward me and my ministry, and I cancel every curse that Satan and his workers have put on me. I announce to Satan and all his forces that Christ became a curse for me (see Galatians 3:13) when He died for my sins on the cross. I reject any and every way in which Satan may claim ownership of me. I belong to the Lord Jesus Christ who purchased me with His own blood. I reject all other blood sacrifices whereby Satan may claim ownership of me. I declare myself to be eternally and completely signed over and committed to the Lord Jesus Christ. By the authority I have in Jesus Christ, I now command every spiritual enemy of the Lord Jesus Christ to leave my presence. I commit myself to my heavenly Father to do His will from this day forward.

PRAYER

Dear Heavenly Father,

I come to You as Your child purchased by the blood of the Lord Jesus Christ. You are the Lord of the universe and the Lord of my life. I submit my body to You as an instrument of righteousness, a living sacrifice, that I may glorify You in my body. I now ask You to fill me with Your Holy Spirit. I commit myself to the renewing of my mind in order to prove that Your will is good, perfect and acceptable for me. All this I do in the name and authority of the Lord Jesus Christ. Amen.

Once you have secured your freedom by going through these seven steps, you may find demonic influences attempting reentry, days or even months later. One person shared that she heard a spirit say to her mind, "I'm back," two days after she had been set free. "No, you're not!" she proclaimed aloud. The attack ceased immediately. One victory does not constitute winning the war. Freedom must be maintained. After completing these steps, one jubilant lady asked, "Will I always be like this?" I told her that she would stay free as long as she remained in right relationship with God. "Even if you slip and fall," I encouraged, "you know how to get right with God again."

One victim of incredible atrocities shared this illustration: "It's like being forced to play a game with an ugly stranger in my own home. I kept losing and wanted to quit, but the ugly stranger wouldn't let me. Finally I called the police (a higher authority), and they came and escorted the stranger out. He knocked on the door trying to regain entry, but this time I recognized his voice and didn't let him in."

What a beautiful illustration of gaining freedom in Christ. We call upon Jesus, the ultimate authority, and He escorts the enemy out of our lives. Know the truth, stand firm and resist the evil one. Seek out good Christian fellowship, and commit yourself to regular times of Bible study and prayer. God loves you and will never leave or forsake you.

AFTERCARE

Freedom must be maintained. You have won a very important battle in an ongoing war. Freedom is yours as long as you keep choosing truth and standing firm in the strength of the Lord. If new memories should surface or if you become aware of lies that you have believed or other non-Christian experiences you have had, renounce them and choose the truth. Some have found it helpful to go through the steps again. As you do, read the instructions carefully.

For your encouragement and further study, read *Victory over the Darkness* (or the youth version *Stomping Out the Darkness*), *The Bondage Breaker* (adult or youth version) and *Released from Bondage*. If you are a parent, read *Spiritual Protection for Your Children*. *Walking in the Light* was written to help people understand God's guidance and discern counterfeit guidance. Also, to maintain your freedom, we suggest the following:

1. Seek legitimate Christian fellowship where you can walk in the light and speak the truth in love.

2. Study your Bible daily. Memorize key verses.

3. Take every thought captive to the obedience of Christ. Assume responsibility for your thought life, reject the lie, choose the truth and stand firm in your position in Christ.

4. Don't drift away! It is very easy to get lazy in your thoughts and revert back to old habits or patterns of thinking. Share your struggles openly with a trusted friend. You need at least one friend who will stand with you.

5. Don't expect another person to fight your battle for you. Others can help, but they can't think, pray, read the Bible or choose the truth for you.

6. Continue to seek your identity and sense of worth in Christ. Read *Living Free in Christ* and the devotional, *Daily in Christ*. Renew your mind with the truth that your acceptance, security and significance is in Christ by saturating your mind with the following truths. Read the entire list of who you are "In Christ" (p. 291) and the Doctrinal Affirmation (in Step 2) aloud morning and evening over the next several weeks (and look up the verses referenced).

7. Commit yourself to daily prayer. You can pray these suggested prayers often and with confidence:

DAILY PRAYER

> *Dear Heavenly Father,*
>
> *I honor You as my sovereign Lord. I acknowledge that You are always present with me. You are the only all-powerful and wise God. You are kind and loving in all Your ways. I love You and thank You that I am united with Christ and spiritually alive in Him. I choose not to love the world, and I crucify the flesh and all its passions.*
>
> *I thank You for the life that I now have in Christ, and I ask You to fill me with Your Holy Spirit, that I may live my life free from sin.*

I declare my dependence upon You, and I take my stand against Satan and all his lying ways. I choose to believe the truth and I refuse to be discouraged. You are the God of all hope, and I am confident that You will meet my needs as I seek to live according to Your Word. I express with confidence that I can live a responsible life through Christ who strengthens me.

I now take my stand against Satan and command him and all his evil spirits to depart from me. I put on the whole armor of God. I submit my body as a living sacrifice and renew my mind by the living Word of God in order that I may prove that the will of God is good, acceptable and perfect. I pray these things in the precious name of my Lord and Savior, Jesus Christ. Amen.

BEDTIME PRAYER

Thank You, Lord, that You have brought me into Your family and have blessed me with every spiritual blessing in the heavenly realms in Christ. Thank You for providing this time of renewal through sleep. I accept it as part of Your perfect plan for Your children, and I trust You to guard my mind and my body during my sleep. As I have meditated on You and Your truth during this day, I choose to let these thoughts continue in my mind while I am asleep. I commit myself to You for Your protection from every attempt of Satan or his emissaries to attack me during sleep. I commit myself to You as my Rock, my Fortress and my Resting Place. I pray in the strong name of the Lord Jesus Christ. Amen.

CLEANSING HOME/APARTMENT

After removing all articles of false worship from home/apartment, pray aloud in every room if necessary:

Heavenly Father,
We/I acknowledge that You are Lord of heaven and earth. In Your sovereign power and love, You have given us/me all

things richly to enjoy. Thank You for this place to live. We/I claim this home for our/my family as a place of spiritual safety and protection from all the attacks of the enemy. As children of God seated with Christ in the heavenly realm, we/I command every evil spirit claiming ground in the structures and furnishings of this place, based on the activities of previous occupants, to leave and never return. We/I renounce all curses and spells utilized against this place. We/I ask You, Heavenly Father, to post guardian angels around this home (apartment, condo, room, etc.) to guard it from attempts of the enemy to enter and disturb Your purposes for us/me. We/I thank You, Lord, for doing this, and pray in the name of the Lord Jesus Christ. Amen.

LIVING IN A NON-CHRISTIAN ENVIRONMENT

After removing all articles of false worship from your room, pray aloud in the space allotted to you:

Thank You, Heavenly Father, for my place to live and be renewed by sleep. I ask You to set aside my room (portion of my room) as a place of spiritual safety for me. I renounce any allegiance given to false gods or spirits by other occupants, and I renounce any claim to this room (space) by Satan based on activities of past occupants or me. On the basis of my position as a child of God and a joint-heir with Christ who has all authority in heaven and on earth, I command all evil spirits to leave this place and never to return. I ask You, Heavenly Father, to appoint guardian angels to protect me while I live here. I pray this in the name of the Lord Jesus Christ. Amen.

Freedom in Christ Resources

Part One: *Resolving Personal Conflicts*

Part Two: *Resolving Spiritual Conflicts*

Victory over the Darkness
by Neil Anderson

Start here! This best-seller combined with *The Bondage Breaker* will show you how to find your freedom in Christ. Realize the power of your identity in Christ!

Paper $10 • 245 pp. B001
Study Guide • Paper $9 • 139 pp. G001

The Bondage Breaker
by Neil Anderson

This best-seller shares the definitive process of breaking bondages and the *Steps to Freedom in Christ*. Read this with *Victory over the Darkness* and you will be able to resolve your personal and spiritual conflicts.

Paper $10 • 247 pp. B002
Study Guide • Paper $6 • 121 pp. G002

Living Free in Christ
by Neil Anderson

Based on the inspirational "Who Am I?" list from *Victory over the Darkness*, here are 36 powerful chapters and prayers that will transform your life and dramatically show how Christ meets all of your deepest needs!

Paper $14 • 310 pp. B008
Free in Christ Audio $10 • A030

The Steps to Freedom in Christ
by Neil Anderson

This is a handy version of *The Steps to Freedom in Christ*, the discipleship counseling process from *The Bondage Breaker*. It is ideal for personal use or for helping another person who wants to find his or her freedom.

Paper $2 • 20 pp. G004

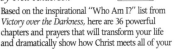

Daily in Christ
by Neil and Joanne Anderson

This uplifting 365-day devotional will encourage, motivate and challenge you to live *Daily in Christ*. There's a one-page devotional and brief heartfelt prayer for each day. Celebrate and experience your freedom all year.

Hard $17 • 365 pp. B010

The Steps to Freedom in Christ Video
with Neil Anderson

In this special video experience, Dr. Neil Anderson personally leads you or a loved one through the bondage-breaking Steps to Freedom in Christ in the privacy of your living room. Includes *The Steps to Freedom in Christ* booklet.

Video $20 • 70 minutes • V010

Breaking Through to Spiritual Maturity
by Neil Anderson

This is a dynamic Group Study of *Victory over the Darkness* and *The Bondage Breaker*. Complete with teaching notes for a 13-week (or 26-week) Bible study, with reproducible handouts. Ideal for Sunday School classes, Bible studies and discipleship groups.

Paper $17 • 151 pp. G003

Spiritual Warfare
by Dr. Timothy Warner

This concise book offers balanced, biblical insights on spiritual warfare with practical information and ammunition for winning the spiritual battle. Every reader will benefit by learning from the author's extensive experience.

Paper $9 • 160 pp. B007

Resolving Personal Conflicts
by Neil Anderson

This series covers the first half of Dr. Anderson's exciting conference. Learn the truth about who you are in Christ, how to renew your mind, heal damaged emotions and truly forgive others (Part 1 of a 2-part series).

Videotape Set $95 • 8 lessons V001
Audiotape Set $40 • 8 lessons A001
Additional workbooks $5 • Paper 32 pp. W001

Resolving Spiritual Conflicts
by Neil Anderson

This series offers the second half of Dr. Anderson's exciting conference. Every believer needs to fully understand his or her position, authority and protection in Christ, and the enemy's tactics (Part 2 of a 2-part series).

Videotape Set $95 • 8 lessons V002
Audiotape Set $40 • 8 lessons A002
Additional workbooks $6 • Paper 49 pp. W002

Resolving Spiritual Conflicts & Cross-Cultural Ministry
by Dr. Timothy Warner

This series has powerful lessons on missions, world-view and warfare relationships that are extremely helpful for every Christian. It provides key insights for spiritual growth and ministry.

Videotape Set $85 • 8 lessons V005
Audiotape Set $35 • 8 lessons A005
Additional workbooks $6 • paper 47 pp. W005

Available at your local Christian bookstore or from
Freedom in Christ
491 E. Lambert Road
La Habra, CA 90631-6136

Phone: (562) 691-9128 Fax (562) 691-4035
Internet: www.ficm.org
E-mail: mail@ficm.org

reedom in Christ Resources

Helping Others Find Freedom in Christ
by Neil Anderson

This book provides comprehensive, hands-on biblical discipleship counseling training for lay leaders, counselors and pastors, equipping them to help others. This resource is Part 3, continuing from the message of Parts 1 and 2.

Paper $13 • 297 pp. B015

Training Manual and Study Guide

Helping Others Find Freedom in Christ Video Training Program

This Video Training Program is a complete training kit for churches and groups who want to establish a free-dom ministry using *The Steps to Freedom in Christ*. Includes four 45-minute video lessons, a *Helping Others Find Freedom in Christ* book, a *Training Manual/Study Guide* and six *The Steps to Freedom in Christ* guidebooks.

Video Training Program $90 • V015

Released from Bondage
by Neil Anderson

This book shares true stories of freedom from obsessive thoughts, compulsive behaviors, guilt, satanic ritual abuse, childhood abuse and demonic strongholds, combined with helpful commentary from Dr. Anderson.

Paper $13 • 258 pp. B006

Freedom from Addiction
by Neil Anderson and Mike and Julia Quarles

A book like no other on true recovery! This unique Christ-centered model has helped thousands break free from alcoholism, drug addiction and other addictive behaviors. The Quarles' amazing story will encourage every reader!

Hard $19 • 356 pp. B018   Paper $13 • 356 pp. B019
Video Study $90 • V019

Freedom from Addiction Video Study
by Neil Anderson and Mike and Julia Quarles

A dynamic resource for recovery group leading pastors and Christian counselors. A step-by-step study that changes lives.

Video Study $90 • V019 - Workbook • Paper $15 • 206 pp. G019

Spiritual Conflicts and Counseling
by Neil Anderson

This series presents advanced counseling insights and practical, biblical answers to help others find their freedom in Christ. It is the full content from Dr. Anderson's advanced seminar of the same name.

Videotape Set $95 • 8 lessons V003
Audiotape Set $40 • 8 lessons A003
Additional Workbooks $8 • Paper 53 pp. W003

Setting Your Church Free
by Neil Anderson and Charles Mylander

This powerful book reveals how pastors and church leaders can lead their entire churches to freedom by discovering the key issues of both corporate bondage and corporate freedom. A must-read for every church leader.

Paper $13 • 352 pp. B012

Setting Your Church Free Video Conference
by Neil Anderson and Charles Mylander

This leadership series presents the powerful principles taught in *Setting Your Church Free*. Ideal for church staffs and boards to study and discuss together. The series ends with the *Steps to Setting Your Church Free*.

Videotape Set $95 • 8 lessons V006
Audiotape Set $40 • 8 lessons A006
Additional workbooks $6 • paper 42 pp. W006
Corporate Steps $2 • G006

Topical Resources

The Common Made Holy
by Neil Anderson and Robert Saucy

An extraordinary book on how Christ transforms the life of a believer. Dr. Anderson and Dr. Saucy provide answers to help resolve the confusion about our "perfect" identity in Christ in our "imperfect" world.

Hard $19 • 375 pp. B017
Study Guide $8 • 200 pp. G017

Rivers of Revival
by Neil Anderson and Elmer Towns

Answers what many Christians are asking today: "What will it take to see revival?" Examines the fascinating subject of personal revival, and past and current evangelistic streams that could help usher in global revival.

Hard $19 • 288 pp. B023

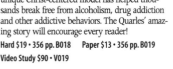

Walking in the Light
by Neil Anderson

Everyone wants to know God's will for his life. Dr. Anderson explains the fascinating spiritual dimensions of divine guidance and how to avoid spiritual counterfeits. Includes a personal application guide for each chapter.

Paper $13 • 234 pp. B011

A Way of Escape
by Neil Anderson

Talking about sex is never easy. This vital book provides real answers for sexual struggles, unwanted thoughts, compulsive habits or a painful past. Don't learn to just cope; learn how to resolve your sexual issues in Christ.

Paper $10 • 238 pp. B014

Freedom in Christ Resources

Topical Resources Continued

The Christ-Centered Marriage
by Neil Anderson and Charles Mylander

Husbands and wives, discover and enjoy your freedom in Christ together! Break free from old habit patterns and enjoy greater intimacy, joy and fulfillment.

Paper $13 • 300 pp. B025

The Christ-Centered Marriage Video Seminar
by Neil Anderson and Charles Mylander

Everything you need in one package for setting marriages free in Christ. Thirteen short video discussion/starter segments enhance using the book and study guide. A great resource for pastors, Christian marriage counselors and Sunday School teachers.

Video Seminar $90 • V020

Paper $6   Marriage Steps • Paper $6 • 3 Versions

Parenting Resources

Spiritual Protection for Your Children
by Neil Anderson and Peter and Sue VanderHook

The fascinating true story of an average middle-class American family's spiritual battle on the home front and the lessons we can all learn about protecting our families from the enemy's attacks. Includes helpful prayers for children of various ages.

Hardcover $19 • 300 pp. B021

The Seduction of Our Children
by Neil Anderson

This parenting book and series will change the way you view the spiritual development of your children. Helpful insights are offered on many parenting issues, such as discipline, communication and spiritual oversight of children. A panel of experts share their advice.

Paper $9 • 245 pp. B004
Videotape Set $85 • 6 lessons V004
Audiotape Set $35 • 6 lessons A004
Additional workbooks $4 • 49 pp. W004

Youth Resources

Stomping Out the Darkness
by Neil Anderson and Dave Park

This youth version of *Victory over the Darkness* shows youth how to break free and discover the joy of their identity in Christ (Part 1 of 2).

Paper $9 • 210 pp. B101

Study Guide Paper $8 • 137 pp. G101

The Bondage Breaker Youth Edition
by Neil Anderson and Dave Park

This best-seller shares the process of breaking bondages and the *Youth Steps to Freedom in Christ*. Read this with *Stomping Out the Darkness* (Part 2 of 2).

Paper $8 • 227 pp. B102

Study Guide Paper $6 • 128 pp. G102

Youth Resources Continued

Busting Free!
by Neil Anderson   and Dave Park

This is a dynamic Group Study of *Stomping Out the Darkness* and *The Bondage Breaker Youth Edition*. It has complete teaching notes for a 13-week (or 26-week) Bible study, with reproducible handouts. Ideal for Sunday School classes, Bible studies and youth discipleship groups of all kinds.

Paper $17 • 163 pp. G103

Youth Topics

Leading Teens to Freedom in Christ
by Neil Anderson and Rich Miller

This youth version provides comprehensive, hands-on biblical discipleship counseling training for parents, youth workers and youth pastors, equipping them to help young people. This resource is Part 3 continuing from the message of Parts 1 and 2.

Paper $13 • 300 pp. B112

Know Light, No Fear
by Neil Anderson and Rich Miller

In this youth version of *Walking in the Light* young people learn how to know God's will for their lives. They will discover key truths about divine guidance and helpful warnings for avoiding spiritual counterfeits.

Paper $10 • 250 pp. B111

Purity Under Pressure
by Neil Anderson and Dave Park

Real answers for real world pressures! Youth will find out the difference between being friends, dating and having a relationship. No hype, no big lectures; just straightforward talk about living free in Christ.

Paper $9 • 200 pp. B104

To My Dear Slimeball
by Rich Miller

In the spirit of C. S. Lewis's *Screwtape Letters*, this humorous story, filled with biblical truth, is an allegory of the spiritual battle every believer faces. Discover how 15-year-old David's life is amazingly similar to your own.

Paper $9 • 250 pp. B103

Youth Devotionals

These four 40-day devotionals help young people understand God's love and their identity in Christ. Teens will learn to establish a positive spiritual habit of getting into God's Word on a daily basis.

Extreme Faith
Paper $8
200 pp. B108

Reality Check
Paper $8
200 pp. B107

Awesome God
Paper $8
200 pp. B108

Ultimate Love
Paper $8
209 pp. B109

How Freedom in Christ Resources Work Together

This chart shows "at a glance" how Freedom in Christ's resources AND conferences interrelate and their correct order of progression from basic to advanced.

Part One

THIS IS FREEDOM IN CHRIST'S CORE MESSAGE OF RESOLVING PERSONAL AND SPIRITUAL CONFLICTS

- Victory Over the Darkness
- Victory Over the Darkness Study Guide
- Living Free in Christ
- Daily in Christ

"If you hold to My teaching, you are really My disciples. Then you will know the truth, and the truth will set you free."

See separate list for youth or young adult resources!

Part Two

- The Bondage Breaker
- The Bondage Breaker Study Guide
- Steps to Freedom in Christ
- Spiritual Warfare

- Breaking Through to Spiritual Maturity Teaching Guide *(Covers parts 1 and 2)*

"Resolving Personal Conflicts" and "Resolving Spiritual Conflicts" Conference and Audios/Videos *(Covers Parts 1 and 2)*

"Free in Christ" Audio and "Steps to Freedom in Christ" Video

"Resolving Spiritual Conflicts and Cross-cultural Ministry" Conference and Audios/Videos *(Covers Parts 1 and 2)*

"Living Free In Christ" Conference *(Covers Parts 1 and 2)*

Part Three

PRACTICAL BIBLICAL ANSWERS FOR DISCIPLESHIP COUNSELING

- Helping Others Find Freedom in Christ
- Helping Others Find Freedom in Christ Training Manual and Study Guide
- Released From Bondage
- Freedom From Addiction
- Ministering The Steps To Freedom in Christ

"Spiritual Conflicts and Counseling" Audios/Videos

"Helping Others Find Freedom in Christ" Video Training Program

"Helping Others Find Freedom in Christ" Counseling Demonstration Video

"Church Leadership and Discipleship Counseling" Conference

"Freedom From Addiction" Conference and Video Study

Part Four

CHURCH LEADERSHIP

- Setting Your Church Free
- Steps to Setting Your Church Free

"Setting Your Church Free" Conference and Audios/Videos

Topical

- The Common Made Holy
- The Common Made Holy Study Guide
- Rivers of Revival
- Walking in the Light
- A Way of Escape
- The Christ-Centered Marriage
- Steps To Setting Your Marriage Free (3 Versions)
- Spiritual Protection for Your Children
- The Seduction of Our Children

"The Christ-Centered Marriage" Conference and Video Seminar

"The Seduction of Our Children"

Contact Freedom in Christ at:

491 E. Lambert Road
La Habra, CA 90631-6136
Phone: (562) 691-9128
Fax: (562) 691-4035

World Wide Web:
www.ficm.org
Email:
mail@ficm.org